First published in 2015 by
I.B.Tauris & Co Ltd
London • New York
www.ibtauris.com

ISBN: 978 1 78076 634 8
eISBN: 978 0 85773 713 7

A full CIP record for this book is available from the British Library
A full CIP record is available from the Library of Congress

Library of Congress Catalog Card Number: available

Typeset in Newgen Knowledge Works, Chennai
Printed and bound by TJ International Ltd, Padstow, Cornwall

Barry Anthony

# MURDER, MAYHEM

# And

# MUSIC HALL

## The Dark Side of Victorian London

**I.B. TAURIS**

LONDON · NEW YORK

**Barry Anthony** is an historian with a particular interest in the Victorian and Edwardian period who has written extensively about popular culture and entertainment. He is the author of *Chaplin's Music Hall* and *The King's Jester: The Life of Dan Leno, Victorian Comic Genius* (both I.B.Tauris) and co-author, with Richard Brown, of a groundbreaking study of the early British cinema, *A Victorian Film Enterprise*.

# Contents

# List of Illustrations

# TIMELINE

**1829**

29 September: creation of the Metropolitan Police Force.

**1837**

20 June: accession of Queen Victoria.

**1839**

September: first photograph of London taken at Charing Cross. 28 October: first performance of *Jack Sheppard* at Adelphi Theatre, Strand.

**1841**

6 March: first sitting of The Judge and Jury Society at the Garrick's Head, Covent Garden.

**1849**

W. G. Ross performs the ballad 'Sam Hall' at the Cyder Cellars, Maiden Lane.

**1851**

1 May: opening of the Great Exhibition.

**1854–56**

Crimean War.

**1856**

1 January: creation of the Metropolitan Board of Works.

**1857–8**

Indian Mutiny.

**1857**

September: passing of the Obscene Publications Act.

**1859**

May: Lord Chamberlain bans any Jack Sheppard play on the London stage.

**1860**

18 November: issue one of *Charley Wag; the New Jack Sheppard*.

**1861**

1 April: first portrayal of Widow Twankey, Strand Theatre.

18 May: death of Renton Nicholson.

11 November: Offences Against the Person Act sets the age of sexual consent at 12 years and removes death penalty for anal sexual intercourse.

**1862**

April: Middlesex magistrates refuse entertainment licences for The Coal Hole and the Cyder Cellars.

**1864**

11 January 1864: opening of Charing Cross railway station.

17 October: opening of the Strand Music Hall.

**1868**

11 November: death of pornographer William Dugdale in Clerkenwell Prison.

21 December: opening of the Gaiety Theatre.

**1870**

28 April: arrest of transvestites Ernest Boulton and Frederick Park at the Strand Theatre.

**1871**

28 January: fall of Paris to German forces.

**1872**

10 August: Licensing Act restricts public house opening times.

**1874**

June: Lord Chamberlain bans the cancan on London stage.

**1875**

January: demolition of Northumberland House, last of the Strand's seventeenth-century palaces.

13 August: Offences Against the Persons Act raises the age of sexual consent to 13 years.

**1878**

January: demolition of Temple Bar.

**1879**

4 April: opening of *Madame Favart* at Strand Theatre.

**1881**

28 December: Savoy Theatre becomes the first public building in the world to be illuminated entirely by electricity.

**1882**

4 December: official opening of Royal Courts of Justice, Strand.

**1884**

30 May: explosion of Fenian bomb at Scotland Yard.

**1885**

14 August: Criminal Law Amendment Act raises age of sexual consent from 13 to 16. All sexual acts between men made illegal.

26 December: opening of *Little Jack Sheppard* at Gaiety Theatre.

**1888**

31 August: murder of Mary Ann Nichols, possibly the first victim of 'Jack the Ripper'.

17 September: opening of the Parnell Commission at the Royal Courts of Justice, Strand.

30 October: opening of *Faust Up to Date* at Gaiety Theatre, Strand.

**1889**

16 March: disappearance of Mabel Love.

21 March: creation of London County Council.

26 August: Cruelty to Children Act.

**1890**

24 May: opening of Tivoli Music Hall.

**1891**

25 September: suicide of Alexander Woodburn Heron.

7 November: first London performance of 'Ta-ra-ra-boom-de-ay'.

16 November: Charles Le Grand sentenced to 20 years for extortion.

5 December: start of the Florence St John divorce case.

**1893**

6 June: murder of Maud Merton at Wormwood Scrubs.

25 July: execution of Police Constable George Samuel Cook at Newgate Prison.

**1894**

17 October: first public exhibition of motion pictures in United Kingdom.

**1895**

14 February: first performance of Oscar Wilde's *The Importance of Being Earnest*.

**1896**

25 January: death of actor Claude Marius Duplany.

**1897**

16 December: murder of actor William Terriss outside Adelphi Theatre.

**1901**

22 January: death of Queen Victoria.

**1903**

4 July: closure of Gaiety Theatre.

# 1

# WHERE'S TROY?

'I always think,' said the fair man, as the train moved slowly across Blackfriars Bridge, 'that yonder crescent of lamps and their reflections in the river are the prettiest sight in London.'
'I never see them,' said the dark man, 'without remembering that behind them lies the Strand.'
'And above the Strand, thank God,' said the fair man's wife, 'is Heaven.'
'And below it?' asked the dark man.
'There's nothing below it', said the old man in spectacles; 'you can't get any lower down than the Strand.'[1]

The railway passengers depicted in Robert Blatchford's Dismal England were travelling towards the Strand at the close of the nineteenth century. Had they chosen to visit the street of which they shared such a poor opinion they would have found a three-quarters of a mile district of central London dedicated to all forms of leisure, pleasure and entertainment. The ornately decorated façades of recently constructed theatres, restaurants, hotels and public houses jostled with earlier buildings whose irregular dimensions housed a multitude of shops, clubs, newspaper offices and dingy back rooms that were often put to disreputable uses. 'To Let' notices abounded in the area, joining an eye-bruising gallery of posters pasted wherever an empty space occurred. Not confined to walls and hoardings, advertising found a mobile expression in the sad-faced army of sandwich board men who trudged with their placards along the street gutters. Pavements in the Strand were crowded until late at night, while the narrow roadway was often blocked by a hopeless tangle of horse-drawn buses, Hansom cabs and private and commercial vehicles.

A walk or drive along the Strand during the Victorian era was to endure an assault on all the senses. The hubbub of general conversation, street music and newsboys' cries was underscored by the heavy, muffled sound of iron-rimmed wheels on the roadway's wooden paving blocks. Even when the choking fog associated with the nearby Thames was not present, the Strand offered an overpowering blend of smells: horse-dung, cigar smoke, beer, cooked food, perfumes both brash and sophisticated, and the inevitable odour of a tightly packed mass of people. And the touch of others was impossible to avoid: involuntary collisions, impatient pushes, the passing caress of a fallen woman and, perhaps, the faintest sensation of alien fingers delving into one's purse or inner pocket.

Back in Tudor times there were palaces in the Strand, a fairy-tale vision of turrets, towers and crested gatehouses. Having already existing for at least 500 years, the thoroughfare followed the gentle curve of the river between the City of London and Westminster, providing a necessary land route between the capital's financial and political centres. At some time during the Middle Ages the upper bend of the road had became shadowed by Maiden Lane, a parallel track that marked the boundary of extensive vegetable plots and orchards belonging to the Abbey of Westminster. By the start of the seventeenth century, both sides of the Strand were lined with the mansions of noble families – Cecil House, Exeter House, Bedford House and Wimbledon House to the north, and Arundel House, Somerset House, Salisbury House, Durham House, York House and Northumberland House extending southward to the river. With the passage of time an expanding urban population began to encroach on the grand residences. The pleasant riverside gardens, terraces and landing steps lost their attraction as the Thames grew increasingly congested and polluted. Gradually the Strand's aristocratic residents relocated to rural areas outside London. Property developers moved in to demolish the palaces, retaining only their names to distinguish the streets running off the Strand. Of the original palaces, Northumberland House alone survived into the nineteenth century, its long façade marking the western end of the Strand until 1874. Closer to the city, Holywell Street, a narrow lane that left and rejoined the Strand, preserved a number of overhanging houses from before the Great Fire of 1666. The very eastern boundary of the street was defined by Temple Bar, an ornate gateway to the city erected in 1672.

**ILLUSTRATION 1.** Western end of the Strand, showing the façade of Northumberland House, early 1860s.

Having bid farewell to their upmarket neighbours, the remaining residents of the Strand carried on with their workaday lives. More taverns, shops, playhouses and brothels were opened and, to minister to the occasional spiritual needs of the increasing population, the decayed church of St Clement Danes was reconstructed in 1682. From its position in the centre of the road St Clements dominated the area, providing a joyful 'oranges and lemons' peel of bells that became enshrined in the children's nursery rhyme. Thirty years later a second island church, St Mary le Strand, was built, following an act of parliament which decreed the creation of 50 new London churches. To make the most of limited space, houses grew taller and narrower, providing shops on street level with several floors of storage and accommodation above. Such perpendicular elevation and the narrowness of the road combined to create an overshadowed and overcrowded architectural ravine. From about 1680, the public footpath actually passed though a building – the covered arcade of shops known as the Exeter Change which had been built on the site of Exeter House. Commerce of every kind thrived in the locality, with Hungerford Market opening alongside Northumberland House in the late seventeenth century. To the north of the Strand, the elegant dwellings and piazzas built on the site of the Convent or Covent gardens in the 1630s soon lost their upper-class appeal when a vegetable market was established nearby. A century later a more successful experiment in fashionable living was initiated on the other side of the Strand by the brothers John and Robert Adam, their Adelphi development consisting of streets of classically inspired houses and a stately terrace overlooking the Thames.

The expansion of London rapidly eliminated all traces of the countryside that once lay close to the Strand. But, amid the smoke of countless chimneys and the endless clatter of town life, its inhabitants still paid lip service to a rustic past. A steady stream of employment-seeking migrants came from the country, but many others who had lived in the city for generations still indulged in pastoral pursuits. To mark the onset of summer, crowds gathered to decorate and dance around a Maypole, not the modestly sized structure of the typical village green, but a 100-foot metro-pole which was situated on the site of the medieval Strand Cross and the future location of St Mary le Strand. Such an overtly pagan display was disapproved of by the Puritans who destroyed the landmark at the time of the Civil War, only for a bigger and better Maypole to arise at the restoration of King Charles II. On the decay of the 'Merry Monarch's' pole, a replacement was set up near Somerset House in 1713. Its existence was short lived, prompting the Reverend James Bramston to elegise in 1729:

> Kings and Comedians are mortal found,
> Caesar and Pinkethman are under Ground.
> What's not destroy'd by Time's Devouring hand?
> Where's Troy, and where's the Maypole in the Strand?

Another Mayday celebration – the procession of milkmaids carrying pails garlanded with spring flowers – was witnessed close to the

Strand by Samuel Pepys in 1667. The famous diarist was interested to note that among the spectators watching the event in Drury Lane was the demurely dressed Nell Gwynn, then London's most famous actress and courtesan. In apparent imitation of the milkmaids, chimney sweeps also began to parade on Mayday. Blackened, but bedecked with the fresh leaves of 'Jack in the Green', their aim was to collect money to help compensate for lack of work during the summer months. Mayday continued to be celebrated into the Victorian era, although with cows kept in the dark, polluted vaults beneath the Adelphi, and sweeps exposing their boy 'apprentices' to the carcinogenic interiors of soot-encrusted chimneys, the countryside seemed very far away.

Despite the harsh conditions suffered by workers, the Strand was at the forefront of technical innovation in many areas. With the manufacturing revolution of the eighteenth and nineteenth centuries producing a vast choice of consumer products its shops attracted hordes of shoppers and sightseers. From the mid-nineteenth century, window displays became more flamboyant as large sheets of plate glass replaced small panes set in heavy frames. In West Strand an early shopping mall in the form of the glass-roofed Lowther Arcade provided sheltered accommodation for an enticing collection of fancy goods and toy shops. At intervals along the Strand carved wooden 'Red Indian Chiefs' advertised the presence of specialist tobacconists and cigar stores. Newsagents and bookshops offered the cheap outpourings of steam printing presses – ephemeral part-issue penny fiction, satirical journals, erotic paperbacks, comic songsters and guides to the town and its entertainments. Prominently exhibited prints of general and more specific interests were eventually replaced with photographs of royalty, political leaders and attractive actresses. Many publishers set up offices in the Strand, some fly-by-night and others who occupied the same premises for prolonged periods.

Potential customers were attracted to the Strand by the increasing ease of access. They travelled on cheap steamboats (from around 1820), omnibuses (1829 onwards) and railway trains. From 1848 it was possible to travel to Waterloo Station and make the short journey across Waterloo Bridge, paying a halfpenny toll for the privilege, a scenario that continued until 1878 when the toll was stopped. By

1864 European visitors could take a boat-train to Charing Cross, exiting directly onto the Strand via the station hotel's elaborate French Renaissance-style frontage. In 1870 an underground railway station opened at the bottom of Villiers Street alongside the arches of the mainline terminus. Also known as Charing Cross, the station was part of a major town-planning development that changed the nature of central London. The construction of a grand Thames Embankment from Westminster to Blackfriars replaced the chaotic collection of wharves, storage sheds and landing stages that had proliferated along the old foreshore and introduced not only the District Railway line, but a much needed modern drainage system. Such facilities were urgently required for the large number of hotels that were opening in and around the Strand, not least the luxurious Savoy Hotel (1889) that was equipped with so many bathrooms that the builder asked whether it had been designed for amphibious guests. Catering facilities also expanded, with the opening of restaurants such as Gow's, Simpson's and Romano's, and there was a proliferation of coffee houses, oyster shops, wine lodges and cigar divans offering food and drink.

During the first half of the nineteenth century the Strand's reputation as a place of recreation was reinforced by new and expanded forms of entertainment. Where amateurs had previously 'obliged' at 'Free and Easy' concerts, professional performers started to appear in the singing rooms of taverns. Venues such as the Coal Hole, Strand, and the Cyder Cellars,[2] Maiden Lane, offered food and drink and rowdy, male-dominated entertainment. Nearby in Covent Garden, Evans's Hotel set its standards substantially higher with choral singing and operatic excerpts offsetting the red-nose comedians. A couple of streets away at the Garrick's Head, self-styled 'Lord Chief Baron' Renton Nicholson presided over mock trials that amused audiences by their irreverence and indecency. In the mid 1860s the purpose-built Strand Music Hall presented considerably more refined entertainment in a tobacco- and alcohol-free environment, and, as a result, proved to be a miserable failure. Opening as the Strand Music Hall closed, Gatti's Music Hall (situated beneath the arches of Charing Cross Station in Villiers Street) was more successful than its upmarket predecessor, but it was not until

ILLUSTRATION 2. The Strand, photographed during the early 1860s.

1890 that the Tivoli provided the Strand with a fully fledged and flourishing variety theatre.

The entertainments offered at some locations changed in nature over the years. Astley's Middlesex Amphitheatre, an arena for equestrian exhibition, opened in Wych Street in 1806 close to St Clement Danes, but was replaced by the Olympic Theatre in 1813. Nearby, at 169 Strand the ancient Talbot Inn gave way to Barker's Panorama in 1803, which in turn became Royal Strand Theatre, a long-term home for musical burlesque. And the pavement-straddling Exeter Change – which at times housed a magic lantern show, a puppet theatre and a first floor menagerie – was demolished in 1829 to rise again as Exeter Hall, a 4,000-seat auditorium used for public meetings and orchestral concerts. After a long period as the only theatres operating in the area, Drury Lane (1663) and Covent Garden (1732) found themselves in competition with the Lyceum (1809), the Adelphi (1819), the Gaiety (1868), the Vaudeville (1870), the Opera Comique (1871),[3] the Savoy (1881) and Terry's (1887) in the Strand; and, in adjoining streets, the new Lyceum (1834), the Globe (1868) and the Avenue (1881).

Pleasure-seeking crowds and well-stocked shops provided a rich picking ground for criminals of all types. In his 1860 autobiography, Renton Nicholson described how honest, respectable citizens nicknamed 'flats' were preyed upon by a 'circumscribed and degenerate race' known as 'sharps'.[4] Confidence tricksters, passers of counterfeit coins, blackmailers, illegal bookmakers, burglars, muggers, pickpockets, pornographers and shoplifters swarmed to the Strand like bedbugs to a cheap hotel. Bogus and real beggars were supplemented by professional cadgers who sometimes worked in organised gangs. One of the largest industries, prostitution, was not illegal, but was at the centre of criminal activities such as bribery, extortion, theft, procurement of underage girls and violent behaviour by pimps. A parasitical, alternative society existed in the Strand and in the nearby slums of Clare Market, Covent Garden and Drury Lane. In an attempt to combat the indigenous lawlessness of the area, London's first formally organised police force, the Bow Street Runners, was set up in 1750. The Metropolitan Police Force replaced the older organisation in 1829, and, like its predecessor, operated out of a central station situated in Bow Street. At the eastern end of the Strand the mock Gothic Royal Courts of Justice, opened by Queen Victoria in 1882, displaced an area previously notorious for a high concentration of bawds and bagnios. The courts, during their construction, overlooked Temple Bar where the decapitated heads of lawbreakers were once exhibited. Scattered in a dismal corona around the area were the offices of solicitors and private detectives.

The police were directed to enforce order as well as law, their duties to deal with spontaneous and unpredictable conduct by groups and individuals, along with the carefully planned, covert activities of the criminal underworld. With virtually no restrictions on public house opening times prior to the 1872 Licensing Act, the consequences of drunkenness were such a problem that

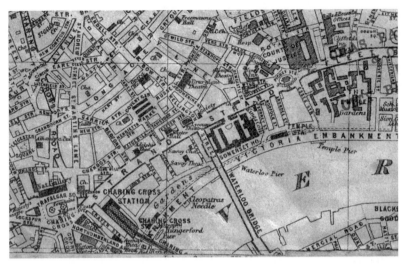

ILLUSTRATION 3. The Strand, c.1890. House numbering ran consecutively: starting at Charing Cross at the south side, extending to the mid 200s at Temple Bar and then returning to the mid 400s at the Western end.

they were only acted upon when they became extreme. A major public nuisance was that of 'Jolly Dogs', parties of men from well-off backgrounds who drank to excess in the various taverns and night houses, then rampaged through the London streets perpetrating violent acts and destructive practical jokes. Although not as ingenious in their mischief-making, working-class drinkers provided a similarly intransigent problem. Even after the 1872 Act, French journalist Max O'Rell was shocked by the situation:

> The drunkenness in the streets is indescribable. On Saturday nights it is a general witches Sabbath. The women drink to almost as great an extent as the men [...] The Englishman is only noisy when he is drunk; then he becomes combative and wicked. One half of the murders one hears of are committed under the influence of drink.[5]

Lone drunks were usually left to the mercy of pickpockets or less gentle robbers and were only taken into custody when their actions became a threat to others. Police spent more of their time attempting to control the groups of intoxicated roughs and prostitutes who molested and insulted passers-by. There were increasing calls for the police to take greater measures to clear the unruly groups from the Strand area and to prevent the culture of the slums causing offence to the rest of society. Highly visible displays of mass drunkenness were not only abhorrent to members of the general public – many local councillors, magistrates and members of parliament were involved in the brewing industry, while large numbers of middle-class investors and the Inland Revenue also benefited from the sales of alcohol. Understandably, such interested parties preferred not to have the effects of 'The Demon Drink' demonstrated quite so publicly in the heart of London.

Although, in the words of the music-hall song, the Strand remained 'the place for fun and noise, all amongst the girls and boys',[6] by the dawn of the twentieth century the increased powers of central and local government had largely tamed the wilder nature of the street. Public house opening hours were limited and licences withdrawn from those that did not comply with regulations. Since the early days of Queen Victoria's reign there had been plans to expand what the Gaiety Theatre's first manager described as an 'overgorged alley'.[7] With the increased impetus to engage in town planning, stimulated by the creation of the Metropolitan Board of Works (1856) and the London County Council (1889), many of the slum areas were demolished and their potentially criminal inhabitants dispersed. The widening of the Strand and the construction of the Aldwych in 1902 also resulted in the destruction of Wych Street and Holywell Street, both ancient homes of prostitutes and pornographers. Having often been vilified in their seventy-year history, the police began to earn the respect of the general public. Popular fiction, which once celebrated the anti-establishment exploits of highwaymen, pirates and youthful burglars, began to chronicle the cases of cerebral and analytical detectives. Songs, dances and other material performed on the variety stage became less risqué as music halls were transformed into limited companies with middle-class shareholders to safeguard and placate. The proliferation of suburban theatres, music halls and the earliest cinemas meant that there were fewer reasons for those seeking entertainment to make the journey into central London.

When the Gaiety Theatre was demolished in 1903 a swarm of rats was said to have scuttled from the ruins, searching for new hiding places in the darker recesses of the immediate area. It was an obvious metaphor for a process in which the irregular, chaotically overcrowded tenements of the Strand were being replaced by well-planned and easily managed buildings. A sign of things to come was provided by

Effingham House, a six-storey block of offices built on the corner of Arundel Street and the Strand in 1891. In place of the steep, creaking stairs familiar to visitors doing business in the area, a fast and efficient lift was available to all floors. In 1896 the Hotel Cecil opened on the site of Cecil Street and Salisbury Street, with 800 bedrooms, bars, a restaurant and lounges offering the very latest in comfort and elegance. A new Gaiety was created on an imposing corner site, its deep alcoves and ostentatious cupola suggesting an edifice of more august usage than mere entertainment. Even a palace of sorts returned to lord over the street, the Strand Palace Hotel, which completely dwarfed its homely neighbour, Haxell's Hotel, when it opened in 1909.

As a centre for frivolous entertainment and uninhibited pleasure-seeking, the Strand became a 'land of lost content' for those who remembered the street from their youth. The glaring signs, slow-moving traffic, blaring music, sex shows, gambling joints and parading prostitutes that might be considered undesirable in a modern city became transformed into colourful aspects of a romantic past. Those who had not succumbed to syphilis or cirrhosis of the liver penned affectionate accounts of their enjoyably misspent youth. 'One of the Old Brigade', writing in 1906, regretted 'night houses and comfortable taverns demolished and transformed into plate-glass abominations run by foreigners and Jews, while hulking louts in uniform, electro-plate and the shabby-genteel masher have taken the place of solid silver spoons and a higher type of humanity'.[8] As those dyspeptic and racist veterans who remembered the Strand in the nineteenth century passed away, new generations dismayed by the stark realities of world wars, economic depression and social upheaval invested the area with even greater Elysian qualities. The reality of the Victorian Strand became buried, not – like Troy – by time's accumulating detritus, but by the softly falling fairy dust of nostalgia. Glamorous Gaiety girls in Hansom cabs and gas-lit stage doors with their attendant Johnnies came to represent this mythic past, while layers of false memory and wishful thinking concealed the remains of a society that struggled to contain its subversive, criminal and unruly elements.

The following investigations into the darker social history of nineteenth-century London are based largely on contemporary newspaper reports. Although such accounts inevitably reflect the prejudices and concerns of their publishers and readers, they also provide countless intimate details of everyday life in and around the

Strand. The picture that emerges is of ordinary and not so ordinary individuals interacting within an environment saturated with history, but susceptible to rapid and unpredictable change. Among the people who appear are a few outright villains, such as Charles Le Grand, the psychotic blackmailer thought by some to be 'Jack the Ripper'; Paul Baron, an extortionate and menacing barber; and Helen Schmidt and William Schneider who stole from men distracted by their prostitute accomplice. There are others who were inadvertently thrown into situations which placed them on the wrong side of the law – suicidal teenage actress, Mabel Love; deranged Major Frank Foster who disrupted a performance at the Gaiety Theatre; PC Sam Cooke whose relationship with a 'fallen woman' ended in a double tragedy; and George Edwin Bishop, a theatrical agent who proved incapable of keeping or arranging engagements. And then there are those who refused to abide by the prevailing moral consensus – transvestites Ernest Boulton and Frederick Park; the irrepressible pornographer, William Dugdale; the Rabelaisian host of many late night entertainments, Renton Nicholson; burlesque star, Florence St John, who became a regular visitor to the divorce courts; and the music-hall artist, Lottie Collins, the performer of a song and dance which permanently linked the 1890s with naughtiness. Each of the characters whose follies and foibles are described was, to a greater or lesser extent, influenced by the physical nature of the Strand – as a hideaway, a place of work, a base for nefarious activities, a pleasure resort or a source of literary inspiration.

In answer to the Reverend Bramston's rhetorical queries, the once-lofty Maypole in the Strand was moved in the early 1700s to Wantage, in Essex, having shrunk to a 20-foot stump by the time Sir Isaac Newton decided that it would make an ideal support for a large telescope. Further afield, the site of Troy was unearthed at Hissarlik in Turkey by Heinrich Schliemann in a series of excavations during the 1870s and 1880s. The protagonists of Murder, Mayhem and Music Hall, are, like Caesar, long 'under ground'. But together with William Pinkethman, the ad-libbing comedian of Drury Lane and Bartholomew Fair, their lives are worthy of re-examination as extreme representatives of a disruptive counterculture that history has largely seen fit to overlook.

# 2

# THE DISAPPEARANCE OF LOVE

Mabel Love stepped delicately out of the Gaiety Theatre into the noise and bustle of the Strand. It was midday on Saturday, 16 March 1889 and as usual, the pavements were teeming with men and women of all descriptions. There were pinched-faced cockneys from the slums of Drury Lane; foreign tourists just arrived at Charing Cross railway station; bemused folk up from the country; curates attending religious meetings at Exeter Hall; prim lady shoppers and their maids; a few early prostitutes; a drove of well-healed club members waddling off to long lunches; and the usual collection of shabby-genteel types hoping to scrounge the price of their next drink or meal. It was a procession that had run continuously for many years, with vice and virtue jostling for the most advantageous positions. But Mabel would have stood out from the crowd at any time in the Strand's long and varied history. In keeping with her position as an up-and-coming actress, she was chicly dressed in a black and white striped skirt and terracotta-coloured cape with white fur trim and glittering gilt buttons. A feathered slouch hat sat precariously upon a mop of golden curls. Her rosebud lips, fresh complexion, wide eyes and pretty dimples were already the subject of photographs offered for sale around the town. Had she been a little closer to the toyshops of Lowther Arcade passers-by might have mistaken her for some masterly example of the doll-maker's art. Mabel, however, was no beautiful automaton. She was a wilful teenager who had decided to teach her parents a severe lesson. Within a few hours newspapers would be running sensational reports of her disappearance, some hinting at the lurid possibilities of forced abduction and sexual intrigue.

The Love family had lived close to the Strand for many years. Mabel's grandfather, William Edward Love (1806–67), had started

Miss MABEL LOVE.

W. & D. DOWNEY          57 & 61, EBURY STREET
PHOTOGRAPHERS          LONDON, S.W.
COPYRIGHT

**ILLUSTRATION 4.** Mabel Love in *Faust Up to Date*.

his working life as a journalist, but soon utilised a natural vocal dexterity by becoming a 'polyphonist', otherwise known as a ventriloquist. For many years he toured Britain and Europe with a highly successful one-man show which often involved rapid costume changes as he portrayed both male and female characters. In 1859, a series of strokes put an end to his career and plunged him and his family into financial crisis. Rescue came from an unexpected quarter when the newly appointed Rector of St Clement Danes, the Revd Richard Henry Killick, alerted the press to his impoverished state. The theatrical profession rallied round and a special benefit evening was held at Sadler's Wells Theatre on 29 March 1862. Enough money was raised to provide William, his wife Eliza and daughter Kate with a home at 33 Arundel Street, a road which ran south from the Strand, down to the banks of the Thames. The Loves had not been established in their new residence for long when the end of Arundel Street became transformed into a gigantic building site with hundreds of navvies labouring to rebuild the untidy, stinking foreshore as a broad and stately embankment. William Love died in 1867 after which Eliza busied herself with running number 33 as a boarding house. The Revd Killick continued to promote the causes of the poorer population of the area until 1869 when he moved to Chadwell St Mary, a less challenging parish, near Tilbury in Essex.

Almost 20 years before Mabel appeared at the Gaiety, her mother Kate Love had been a regular performer at the same theatre. Like her daughter, she made her debut at an early age, appearing in straight drama, musical burlesque, comic opera and in at least one pantomime at the Theatre Royal, Covent Garden. Her brief career started at the St James's Theatre in 1867 when she played in the same production as the young Henry Irving, later to become the most famous actor in Victorian England. Kate's time on the stage coincided with a series of reforms which resulted in theatre-going becoming a fashionable, middle-class recreation rather than a vulgar pastime of the dissolute and lower classes. John Hollingshead, the manager of the Gaiety Theatre recalled:

> The old theatres of the sixties were nearly all badly built, badly lighted, badly seated, with inconvenient entrances, narrow winding passages, and the most defective sanitary arrangements. They smelled of escaped gas, orange peel, tom-cats, and mephitic vapours.[1]

The movement towards improving the status of the theatre was led by the actor-manager Marie Wilton, who not only improved the physical comfort of the theatre, but provided performers with better pay and conditions. With her husband Squire Bancroft, she was instrumental in introducing a new form of drama, typified by the thoughtful, domestic comedies of their friend, T. W. Robertson. In 1890 she recalled that in the earlier part of the century, for a member of the middle classes to become an actor 'meant exile from home, family, friends, and general respectability'.[2] Although early in her career Marie Wilton had sung, danced and exposed her legs in musical burlesque, by the end of the 1890s her husband, like Irving, had been knighted and she had become Lady Bancroft.

Despite the general brevity of her roles, Kate Love's appearance made a major impression. The singer Emily Soldene remembered her appearing in Chilperic, at the Lyceum Theatre in 1870:

> There was a particularly beautiful girl there – a Miss Love. She was a great swimmer, and she had a particularly beautiful mother, who used to be behind the scenes very frequently. I don't know whether she was a swimmer, too, but if she were, judging from her elegant appearance, she kept above water all the time.[3]

Emily also recollected that female performers appearing in tights added extra volume to their trunks by padding them with newspaper: 'and so every girl regarded her Daily Telegraph, not only as a source of information, but as a necessary and not-to-be-done-without adjunct to her nightly and personal charms.'[4] Whether or not she resorted to crumpling The Daily Telegraph, Kate's looks gave every indication that she might enjoy a successful career if she chose to pursue it. But immediately after appearing in the first English version of Offenbach's La Belle Helene at the Gaiety she elected to take another course of action.

Her marriage to Lewis Grant Watson at St Clement Danes on 22 November 1871 bumped Kate several places up the social scale. He was a middle-class merchant who had been presented at court, while his brother, Robert Grant Watson, was a writer and diplomat, serving at one time as first Secretary of the British Embassy in Washington. It was considerably less embarrassing to be introduced as the sister-in-law of the author of *A History of Persia from the Beginning of the Nineteenth Century to the Year 1858* than as the daughter of the multi-voiced, cross-dressing presenter of *Love's Lucubrations*. The difficulties inherent in moving from one class to another had already been explored by T.W. Robertson in an 1867 drama written for Marie Wilton and Squire Bancroft. In *Caste* an aristocratic army officer, the Hon George Eustace Fairfax Algernon D'Alroy, confounds his friend, Captain Hawtree, and alienates his mother, the Marquise de St Maur, by marrying Esther Eccles, a pretty young ballet dancer. 'I was in the front rank', declares Esther, 'now I'm of high rank.' Reflecting popular opinion, Captain Hawtree, himself a parvenu, is pessimistic about the union:

> All these marriages of people with common people are very well in novels, and plays on the stage, because the real people don't exist, and have no relatives who exist, and no connections and so no harm's done, and it's rather interesting to look at; but in real life, with real relations, and real mothers, and so forth, it's absolute bosh – it's worse; it's utter social and personal annihilation and individual damnation.

*Caste* was provided with a conveniently happy ending, but the offstage reality was that such inter-class marriages were still largely frowned upon during the latter part of the century.

After a time in Folkestone on the Kent coast, the Watsons moved to Chelsea where they resided in the fashionable Fulham Road. Their oldest child Kate was born in 1873, followed by Mabel in 1874, Blanche in 1880 and Victor in 1882. Having made a good marriage despite her theatrical background, Kate had an inclination that her children might follow the same route. It was a hazardous strategy for there was extreme prejudice against girls becoming actresses or dancers. As late as 1889 the Liberal Member of Parliament Samuel Smith claimed 'that only a small proportion of the children employed early in theatres came to any good, and that to the great bulk of little girls it meant hopeless ruin'.[5] Mabel, aged 12, entered the profession at a later age and higher level than the hundreds of working-class children given temporary employment as elves and fairies in Christmas pantomimes, but she had been trained as a dancer and that generated a considerable degree of disapprobation. Ballet girls were particularly frowned upon, as commented upon by another MP: 'by far the majority of the ballet girls who have passed their prime went on to the streets.'[6]

Appropriately for an actress whose later fortune relied so heavily on her physical appearance, Mabel was cast as a flower in her earliest role. She played the Rose in the first stage adaptation of Lewis Carroll's *Alice in Wonderland* which was produced at the Prince of Wales Theatre at Christmas 1886. A year later she was engaged for the pantomime *Jack and the Beanstalk* at the Theatre Royal, Covent Garden, where she was described as 'a remarkably dainty and neat transformation dancer, Sunbeamy Mabel Love' (she used her mother's maiden name, Love, rather than the family name, Watson).[7] On 30 October 1888 she appeared at the Gaiety Theatre for the first time. As with theatres run by the Bancrofts, the Gaiety set high standards for customer comfort, incorporating an elegant restaurant under the same roof and a lobby perfumed by scented fountains. The theatre had opened in 1868, joining the nearby Strand Theatre as a home of burlesque for the next 20 years. Although the Bancrofts' realistically observed 'cup and saucer' dramas may have replaced the banal farces and overblown melodramas that predominated during the first half of the century, the upside-down world of musical burlesque with its cross-dressing, elaborate word play and whimsical plots still retained a firm hold on the public's favour. In fact, the improvements in theatre design and facilities inspired by Marie and Squire Bancroft meant that the often risqué burlesque became more acceptable to middle-class audiences.

*Faust Up to Date* was a typical example of the genre. Like most burlesques, the production was a loose parody of a well-known original, in this case Gounod's 1864 grand opera *Faust*. The Faust legend, in which an elderly German doctor sells his soul to Mephistopheles for a chance to enjoy the sexual pleasures of youth, had recently been presented to the theatre-going public by Henry Irving. His production of *Faust* at the Lyceum Theatre, a few yards from the Gaiety, was packed with grandiose special effects and was just the sort of self-indulgent spectacle that burlesque aimed to deflate. A secondary layer of humour was added to the pastiche by the satirising of contemporary events and culture. In the play, two popular London entertainments – the Italian Exhibition at Earl's Court and the Irish Exhibition at Olympia – were relocated to Nuremberg, while much of the dialogue poked fun at current news stories. Particular fun was derived from the Parnell Commission, an official enquiry that had just commenced at the newly built

Royal Courts of Justice, nearby in the Strand. While the unfolding horrors of the 'Jack the Ripper' killings in London's East End were apparently considered unsuitable material for facetious comment, the Irish Nationalist leader Charles Stewart Parnell and his possible involvement in a series of crimes, involving murder, was considered fair game. A comic song 'Ballyhooly' performed by the Gaiety's principle comedian E. J. Lonnen (as Mephistopheles) included a number of references to the commission and its deliberations.

Sexual titillation was also a common element in burlesque. The innocent Marguerite (played by a very worldly Florence St John), whom Faust sought to seduce, was renamed Meg and presented as a bejewelled barmaid who sang:

A simple little maid,
Of the swells I am afraid,
I tell them when they're forward they must mind what they're about.
I never go to balls,
Or to plays or music halls,
And my venerated mother always knows when I am out.

As young Faust, Fanny Robina appeared in the traditional tights of a male impersonator, while a troupe of attractive female dancers wore similarly abbreviated costumes. Fourteen-year-old Mabel seems to have featured in a show-stopping *Pas de Quatre*, danced at the commencement of the second act.[8] Wearing narrow-waisted, low-cut bodices and knee-length skirts with lace petticoats, the four vivandieres, or camp followers, performed a graceful dance to a captivating melody composed by the Gaiety's conductor Meyer Lutz. A feature of this elegantly erotic *Pas de Quatre* was the sequence in which the dancers stood directly behind each other, extending their black silk-stockinged legs in a series of provocative kicks. A few critics grumbled that such amusement should not be derived from literary and operatic masterpieces, but no concerns were raised about youthful Mabel's participation in the show.

On 16 March 1889, Mabel walked to the Gaiety from the Love's house in Arundel Street where her family, the Watsons, had taken up residence. She had been appearing in *Faust Up to Date* for almost five months and had made the short journey many times before. Today she was making a regular Saturday morning excursion to collect her pay of £3 2s 4d. On the way she brooded over events that had occurred the previous evening, angry words having been exchanged with her mother over some trifling matter. After collecting the money, Mabel decided not to go home directly but to turn right toward the Adelphi Theatre. As always a stirring melodrama was on offer, with 'Breezy Bill' Terriss appearing as the hero and an ill-omened actor Richard Archer Prince playing a minor role. Stopping off at the Great Northern Railway booking office she asked to see the *ABC*, a periodical listing train timetables. Having obtained the information she required, she set off once more, walking towards Piccadilly Circus before catching a King's Cross omnibus. Alighting at Euston Station, she purchased a ticket and then sat like a well-behaved doll for four hours before taking the 6.30 p.m. train to Holyhead.

Panic broke out at 33 Arundel Street while Mabel was still waiting for her train. As she was due to appear in the Saturday afternoon matinee she was missed almost immediately. The police were notified and the Gaiety's manager, George Edwardes, engaged the services of private detective Maurice Moser, a celebrated police inspector who had just resigned from the Criminal Investigations Department. Thoughts turned to what fate might have befallen Mabel. Had she been subjected to some dastardly criminal assault, either of a sexual nature or to rob her of expensive jewellery? Was an older woman she had been seen talking to in the Strand a procuress luring her into an illicit venture? Fear of 'Jack the Ripper' extended across the whole of London, even though his murders had been confined to the East End. The Love family had already been the victim of a minor crime perpetrated in the Strand; in 1867 a boy pickpocket had snatched Grandma Eliza's purse containing three guineas, only to be apprehended in a traditional 'stop thief' chase. Perhaps no offence had been committed against Mabel. She may have suffered sudden illness or an accident that robbed her of her memory. While investigations proceeded, an embargo on newspaper coverage was successfully maintained. But on Tuesday the story broke with bold headlines proclaiming 'Disappearance of Young Actress!'

Mabel was neither in captivity nor in a coma. From Holyhead she had caught the overnight ferry to Ireland, arriving in Dublin on Sunday morning. After booking into one of the city's best hotels, the Clarence, she unsuccessfully tried to obtain an engagement at the Theatre Royal. On the Monday she left the Clarence and moved to a lodging house at 44 Lower Gardiner Street where she prepared to wait for a number of touring theatrical companies who were due to arrive in Dublin. With no change of clothes and a limited amount of money, Mabel must have been relieved when Superintendent Reddy of the Dublin Police paid her a visit. In a roundabout series of communications it appears that the manager of the Theatre Royal, having recognised a description of the fugitive actress, had contacted George Edwardes who, in turn, alerted Maurice Moser who then telegraphed the Irish police. Reddy soon persuaded Mabel to return home. After a stormy crossing she arrived back in London on Thursday evening. The crowd who had gathered at Euston Station to witness her return were disappointed. Always resourceful, Moser had met her at Holyhead and escorted her off the train at Willesden, finishing the journey home by London underground.

After several days of public speculation about Mabel's fate, her family and their representatives were at pains to dispel any suggestions of a sexual motive for the escapade. A liaison at such an early age would not have been propitious for her career. There would also have been serious consequences for any man involved in her disappearance. The Criminal Law Amendment Act of 1885 had made it an offence to abduct a girl under the age of 18 for the purpose of carnal knowledge, while the same legislation had raised the age of consent from 13 to 16. Maurice Moser reported that she had been 'staying in one of the most respectable houses in Dublin [...] that she arrived in Dublin entirely alone, and had been staying alone ever since'. He added reassuringly that 'no harm of any kind had come to her'.[9] Young Mabel was confirmed to be unsullied. She had apparently encountered no one of Faustian intent and her reputation and, by association, that of the Gaiety Theatre, was intact.

The happy restoration of normality was not to last. In less than four months Mabel was once again the subject of sensational headlines which involved not only the Gaiety, but the whole theatre world in a heated controversy. After six weeks she was re-engaged to play her old role in Faust Up to Date. Despite appearing onstage for only ten minutes in each performance, she was rapidly becoming a widely recognised actress. She had already started a long love affair with the camera that was to lead to her becoming one of the most photographed of Victorian and Edwardian theatrical celebrities. Before the advent of the picture postcard in about 1900,

Mabel's beautiful, enigmatic features had often been reproduced as magazine illustrations and in commercial 'cabinet' photographs. Even Mabel seemed fascinated by her appearance, if one believes a reporter from The Entr'acte who, in May 1889, claimed to have seen her gazing at photographs of herself in a shop window.[10]

When not contemplating her own loveliness, Mabel might have become aware of proposed legislation that was to have a major impact on the employment of young people in the theatre. Fiercely debated throughout the summer of 1889, the Cruelty to Children Bill contained a provision to prevent the employment of juveniles aged 10 or under in the theatre. One of the bill's principal supporters, the women's suffrage campaigner Millicent Garrett Fawcett, took every opportunity to describe the adverse effects, both moral and physical, that the theatre exerted on young performers. Fawcett's impassioned but sometimes ill-informed attacks precipitated a tragedy in June 1889 when, after reading her account of the supposed ill-treatment of his daughter, Nathaniel Currah murdered the head of the Letine acrobatic troupe. Mabel was indirectly referred to in parliament when John Gilbert Talbot, MP for Oxford University and a member of the Royal Commission on Education, declared that 'he knew from private, well-informed sources that the children who took part in the representation of Alice in Wonderland the other year evinced the greatest interest and delight in their performances'.[11] Although the so-called 'Children's Charter' had no direct bearing on Mabel, her next impulsive action was to lead to her name becoming widely discussed in connection with the bill and the subsequent act which became law in August 1889.

In the early hours of 16 July 1889, Mabel slipped out of 33 Arundel Street and wandered down to the Victoria Embankment. At 4.30 a.m. she threw herself from Whitehall Steps into the Thames. A police constable who heard the splash blew his whistle, alerting a sub-inspector on a floating fire station. A small boat was launched and Mabel was dragged, apparently barely conscious, from the water. After a few hours recovering in St Giles Infirmary, she was taken to Bow Street Police Court where she was charged with attempted suicide. For someone who had recently attempted to take her own life, she struck observers as being remarkably calm. Her water-damaged clothes had been discarded and she now appeared in a fetching outfit calculated to soften the heart of the hardest magistrate:

> Her hat, a dainty white straw, was adorned with a sea-white ribbon. She wore a deep-blue frock, short enough to display a pretty pair of ankles and a pair of tiny feet encased in a very dainty little pair of shoes. A blue and white blouse trimmed with a neat blue collar completed the charming toilet of this interesting young lady.[12]

Mr Vaughan, the magistrate, questioned Mabel:

> 'How old are you, child?'
> 'Fifteen next birthday.'
> 'Now, my child, how came you to jump into the river? Why should you, so young, seek to destroy yourself?'
> 'I was so miserable. I can't understand why I did it. I did not know what I was doing.'

Mabel's mother was next to be interrogated:

> 'Can you account for this conduct?'
> 'Yes, I think I can. She has been studying very hard lately, and has had some very sleepless nights. She is studying for the stage. I wish to send her away into the country.'
> 'This was at four o'clock in the morning. How did she get out?'
> 'I don't know. We all came home from the theatre as usual last night and she went to her room. She is now acting at the Gaiety.'
> 'It seems to me you ought to communicate at once with the manager of the theatre and tell him it is utterly impossible for her to resume engagement at present. She must cease study altogether, and unless such arrangement is made I cannot let her go.'

Kate Watson assured Mr Vaughan that an arrangement would be made to send her away immediately. Satisfied that convalescence in the bracing surroundings of the Scottish countryside would help dispel the polluting influence of the Gaiety, the magistrate dismissed Mabel with a few words of advice:

> 'I am very sorry for you. It is a very great pity you should excite yourself in the way you have done. I think that you should be taken away from the stage at once, and think no more about your work. Go and live in the fresh, pure, air and try to forget your misery. And on no account look at a book again for some time to come.'

Like her Dublin adventure, Mabel's preferred mode of self-destruction could be linked to a sexual motive. Suicide by drowning, though not entirely the prerogative of the harlot, was widely seen as the final, despairing act of a 'fallen' or 'ruined' woman. Although statistics do not appear to substantiate the popular perception, the downward plunge from bridge or bank into the redemptive waters of the heavily polluted Thames was enshrined in popular art and literature. When such deaths did occur they were probably motivated by desperation rather than remorse, but, for those who expected repentance from women guilty of sexual misdemeanours, the image of the drowned sinner was far too attractive to relinquish.

The anti-theatre lobby was quick to seize on Mabel's case. Millicent Garrett Fawcett attacked *Faust Up to Date* for its debased and debasing moral tone. 'I am told by one who has been to see the play', she wrote, 'it is a *pot-pouri* of allusions to the latest nastiness of the Divorce Case and breach of promise cases.'[13] In response to her criticism, George Edwardes invited her to see the show. She was not impressed, sending him a long report that concluded: 'it was a depressing performance with hardly any real fun or humour in it; leaving an impression (as Mr Ruskin said of the pantomime of *The Forty Thieves*) of "an ugly and disturbing dream."'[14] The recent marriage of a music-hall performer, Belle Bilton, to the young Lord Dunlo caused the *Birmingham Daily Post* to express itself on caste and on Mabel's recent unhappiness:

> Following close upon the announcement of this new prize for the footlights, comes the story of a blank which seems to provide the needful wholesome antidote and corrective. We refer to the attempted suicide of the young burlesque actress MABEL LOVE, of the Gaiety Theatre, who was fished out of the Thames in an almost lifeless condition at an early hour yesterday morning. The unhappy girl, who resided not far from the Thames Embankment, said her life was so miserable that she had determined to end it, and with this object she rose at the early hour of three o'clock and threw herself into the river at Whitehall Steps.[15]

Such comments probably did not worry Mabel and her family. Within a short time she was back on the stage, boosted by a huge amount of free publicity and with even more photographic portraits pouring onto the market. Perhaps Dublin was not such a long and unexpected journey to take; Mabel's mother, Kate Watson, was born there, after all. And Mr Vaughan failed to ask her whether she was as

ILLUSTRATION 5. Mabel Love performs the Skirt dance, a cabinet photo from the 1890s.

strong a swimmer as her athletic mother. Mabel's disappearance and suicide attempt may have been genuine manifestations of teenage angst, but they did nothing to harm her future career.

Mabel grew into a strikingly beautiful woman with her face and form reproduced on countless 'cabinet' photographs, cigarette cards and picture postcards. There were pictures of Mabel looking sultry; Mabel looking coy; Mabel soulful; Mabel radiant; Mabel in black and white; Mabel tinted or tinselled; and for some fortunate fans, there were portraits of Mabel inscribed with a languid, flowing signature. Likenesses of Mabel stood on mantelpieces, were secreted under pillows and filled albums. Her theatrical appearances were just as important for generating two-dimensional images as they were for providing theatregoers with live entertainment.

Although Mabel never became another Marie Wilton, she proved herself to be a popular performer who adapted readily to changing fashions. In 1890 she appeared with the matinee idol William Terriss in a revival of his famous nautical melodrama *The Harbour Lights*. After a long-running engagement at the Lyric Theatre in the comic opera *La Cigale* (1890–91), she became a solo dancer in operatic ballets at the Theatre Royal, Covent Garden. At Christmas 1891 she joined Dan Leno, Marie Lloyd and a host of other music-hall comedians in *Humpty Dumpty* at the Theatre Royal, Drury Lane, the first of many pantomime appearances in London and the provinces. During the early 1890s her most significant contribution to the theatre was as an exponent of the skirt dance, a graceful performance that involved manipulating loose dresses and petticoats, often under atmospheric stage lighting. By the end of the decade, straight acting had largely replaced musical comedy as she played opposite such notable actors as Lewis Waller and Herbert Beerbohm Tree. As with many other stage stars, Mabel was attracted to the increasingly respectable variety theatre in the Edwardian period, which presented potted dramas sandwiched between animal acts and trick cyclists. There were also critically acclaimed appearances in plays by Somerset Maugham and George Bernard Shaw late in her career and an appearance in at least one silent film. Mabel retired in 1918, but never left the theatre. She opened a stage school in 1926 and made a brief comeback in May 1938 when she appeared in *Profit and Loss* at the Embassy Theatre.

If Mabel's features were open to all, her heart and its secrets were securely closed. There were, of course, many admirers. In 1894 20-year-old Winston Churchill wrote requesting an autograph and it was rumoured that the aging Prince of Wales had asked her for something more intimate. Having been the centre of fevered gossip twice in her first 15 years, she avoided any further discussion of her personal life. Mabel seems not to have married, but had a daughter named Mary, born in about 1914. History repeated itself for a third time when 13-year-old Mary Love made her stage debut at the Gaiety watched by a proud mother. As with Mabel, Mary first appeared in a famous children's story, playing Tootles in J. M. Barrie's *Peter Pan*. She went on to live a dramatic and ultimately tragic life, dying in poverty unaware that she had inherited a small fortune from her late mother's estate.

# 3

# THE DARK ARCHES

Had Mabel Love been held for ransom, attacked by a maniac or lured into a life of sinfulness, nobody would have been particularly surprised. The Strand had a reputation for wickedness and hardly a week went by without newspapers reporting a serious felony committed in its neighbourhood, or well-meaning social reformers railing against the immorality to be found there. Outbreaks of public disorder were common as police struggled to control the pleasure-seekers who flooded into the area attracted by taverns, theatres, music halls and brothels. Violence, vice and criminal behaviour were commonly encountered, their repugnant or attractive qualities constantly embellished in songs, dramas and works of fact and fiction.

The ceaseless battle that the Victorians fought against crime was the price they paid for a ready supply of cheap labour. During the mid-nineteenth century the streets adjoining the north side of the Strand represented the boundary of an intricate network of slums, with the courts and tenements of Seven Dials, Covent Garden, Drury Lane and Clare Market harbouring many thousands of poorly paid workers and hardened lawbreakers. The Strand itself might have been designed for the benefit of criminals. Every few yards, a side-street or alley offered a means of escape for a fleeing miscreant after which a maze of streets made pursuit virtually impossible. Just off the main thoroughfare were many dark passages and secluded corners where illicit activities might be perpetrated without fear of disturbance. And day and night the Strand provided a constantly replenished supply of distracted, gullible, often incapacitated victims.

The Strand had its own patron sinner in the form of Jack Sheppard, a youthful burglar who became enshrined as a major character in eighteenth- and nineteenth-century popular literature.

After an early childhood spent in poverty, Jack was fortunate to be employed as a shop boy by a wool draper with premises in the Strand. William Kneebone taught him to read and arranged for him to be apprenticed to a carpenter in nearby Wych Street, generous acts which Jack later repaid by robbing his old employer. Had he completed his apprenticeship, Jack might have provided an excellent, but uninspiring, example to similarly underprivileged young men. As it was, after almost serving the full term of his seven years' indenture, he embarked on a life of criminality which quickly led to his public execution. Despite the paltriness of his crimes – stealing spoons, tankards, bales of cloth – he captured the public imagination with his swagger, audacity and irrepressible spirit. His reckless villainy, relationships with women of the town, four daring escapes from captivity and, not least, his adoption of gentleman's clothing, combined to make him a London legend long before his body was cut down from the Tyburn gallows. Quickly taking his place in urban folklore, he was the original 'Jack the lad'. He did not become a dull 'chippie' stained with sawdust and smelling of wood-glue, rather an escapist fantasy to thousands of boys and young men. Jack not only encouraged his followers to think out of the box, he also showed them how to break out of it.

By the time 22-year-old Jack was executed in 1724, he had already become the subject of popular street ballads and a widely circulated print based on a portrait by the king's painter, James Thornhill. Four years later John Rich's *The Beggar's Opera* employed aspects of Sheppard's character and career in a revolutionary musical play which satirised greed and corruption among all classes. Jack's potential for fictional embellishment and interpretation became even greater and, perhaps, more troubling during the early Victorian period. With an increasingly literate population possessing a voracious appetite for recreational reading, an industry providing low cost and formulaically written literature soon immerged. The success of Harrison Ainsworth's three-volume romance *Jack Sheppard* in 1839 generated a flood of cheap imitations depicting their hero as a freedom-spirited individual at war with repressive society. With no great love or respect for authority, the urban poor readily identified with Jack and his modern disciples such as *Charley Wag, or the New Jack Sheppard*. In the late 1850s Henry Mayhew considered that

**ILLUSTRATION 6.** A romanticised Jack Sheppard portrayed by Mrs Keeley, Adelphi Theatre, 1839.

'of all books, perhaps, none has ever had so baleful effect upon the young mind, taste, and principles as Jack Sheppard'.[1]

Immediately following the publication of Ainsworth's novel, Jack's fictional form was given flesh and blood at several theatres. The most famous early production took place at the Adelphi Theatre in the Strand. Opening in October 1839, J. B. Buckstone's *Jack Sheppard* featured Mary Anne Keeley in the title role. Jack, although idle and quick-tempered, was portrayed as a victim of a complex conspiracy, led astray by a conniving master criminal, Jonathan Wild, who was in the pay of the Prime Minister, Sir Robert Walpole. In a series of 'epochs' or time frames Jack's criminality was shown as an almost inevitable rebellion against control and incarceration in both material and social terms. When produced in poorer areas, dramas featuring Jack Sheppard usually played to partisan audiences who hurled abuse at those that sought to imprison their hero and, by implication, themselves. Although little could be done to cut off the supply of popular literature, it was possible to curtail theatrical representation. In May 1859 the Lord Chamberlain – responsible for the licensing of plays in the United Kingdom, a situation that lasted up to 1967 – banned the production of any play with 'Jack Sheppard' in the title. It was an injunction that gratified Lloyd's Weekly Newspaper:

> Years ago we pointed out the debasing, the brutalising influence Mr Ainsworth's hero exerted over the minds of thousands of poor children. But still the burglar trod the boards, and still the gallery applauded him. Managers reaped golden harvests, and the police courts were full of juvenile criminals. Little Jack Sheppards and Blueskins stalked proudly about London alleys, and as they daringly robbed, believed themselves to be the hero. It is to the credit of the present lord chamberlain that he has said, this stage burglar should strut his hour no longer. With much pleasure, in concluding, do we announce that Mr Jack Sheppard has taken his final leave of the English stage.[2]

Jack Sheppard had a more saturnine companion in the criminal pantheon of the Strand. The thief Jack Hall, who also enjoyed a period of notoriety during the early eighteenth century, was vividly resurrected in a popular song of the late 1840s. Hall was born in Bishop's Head Court, Gray's Inn Lane, Holborn, in about 1676, and at the age of seven was sold by his parents to a chimney sweep. After some time serving as a 'climbing boy', he realised that it would be more profitable and less dangerous to go down people's pockets than up their chimneys. He became skilled at 'filing a cly', i.e., pick-pocketing and also developing expertise with the 'drag', a hook fastened onto a stick used to fish items out of open windows. Like all pickpockets, he gravitated towards crowded areas, stealing watches, cash and handkerchiefs from victims attending churches, fairs, markets and playhouses. Punishments were inflicted on him with fluctuating severity. Early in his criminal career he was committed to Bridewell Prison, where he was ordered to 'milly dolly', i.e., to beat hemp. In 1698 he was whipped for stealing a pair of shoes and in 1700 was sentenced to

THE CYDER CELLARS.—"SAM HALL."

**ILLUSTRATION 7.** W. G. Ross performing 'Sam Hall' at the Cyder Cellars, 1849.

death only to be reprieved on the condition that he left the country. Defying banishment, he returned to rob a stagecoach, a crime that resulted in him being branded on the cheek and imprisoned for two years. Finally, a violent housebreaking in which he threatened to kill a child resulted in another capital sentence. Shortly before his execution at Tyburn on 17 December 1707, he denied that 'he had made a Contract with the Prince of Darkness, for a set time to act his Villainies in'.[3]

Based on earlier Jack Hall ballads, 'Sam Hall' emerged from music hall's earliest period when singing rooms attached to taverns started to provide formal programmes of entertainment. The song, in which W. G. Ross portrayed the final moments of a malevolent chimney sweep, was closely linked with one of London's longest surviving entertainment venues, the Cyder Cellars. Often referred to in the same breath as the Coal Hole (another tavern singing room in Fountain Court, Strand), the Cyder Cellars, at 20/21 Maiden Lane, was far older than its neighbour, having its origins in the early 1700s. As might be imagined, the establishment was located underground, continuously serving up late night entertainments while the area above it changed with the passing years. On its upper levels the building was sub-divided in the middle of the eighteenth century, one part forming the house in which the painter Turner was born and another section functioning as a spacious auction room and art gallery. In 1844 the exhibition area became the Maiden Lane Synagogue, supplying a spiritual dimension to a building long associated with drunken revelry. At the time that the well-known comic singer Ross began to perform 'Sam Hall', audiences were directed to the Cellars by an illuminated lantern hanging above an alley running off the Strand. Alongside the Cyder Cellars, the Adelphi Theatre was a relative newcomer to the street scene.

Shortly before 11 p.m. when Ross was due to perform, many patrons left the tables where they were eating and drinking to crowd before a small, scaffold-like platform. As the singer appeared from behind a screen, he was greeted by a torrent of applause which soon subsided into a deathly silence. Biting on a bone-white clay pipe and wearing a costume as black as the infamous knocker on the gates of Newgate Prison, he portrayed Sam Hall immediately before his public execution. Shuddering in fear and fury, he contemplated his imminent death. The music was dirge-like, Ross's acting horrifically realistic. His voice faltered and broke, an 'intense whisper',[4] giving way at the end of each verse to an explosive curse:

Oh, my name it is Sam Hall,
Chimney sweep! Chimney sweep!
Oh, my name it is Sam Hall,
Chimney sweep!
My name it is Sam Hall,
I have robb'd both great and small.
And now I pay for all,
Damn my eyes.

My master taught me flam,[5]
Taught me flam,
My master taught me flam,
Though he know'd it all for bam[6]
And now I must go hang –
Damn my eyes.

I goes up Holborn Hill in a cart,
In a cart.
I goes up Holborn Hill in a cart,
At St Giles takes my gill,

And at Tyburn makes my will,
Damn my eyes.

Then the sheriff he will come,
He will come,
Then the sheriff he will come,
And he'll look so gallows glum,
And he'll talk of kingdom come,
Blast his eyes.

Then the hangman will come too,
Will come too,
Then the hangman will come too,
With all his bloody crew,
And he'll tell me what to do,
Blast his eyes.

And now I go upstairs,
Goes upstairs,
And now I goes upstairs,
Here's an end to all my cares,
So tip up all your prayers,
Blast your eyes.

Unlike most hit songs which enjoy only a limited period of popularity or become occasionally resurrected reminders of past times,
'Sam Hall' transmuted from its original form, engendering a string
of alternative versions that conveyed a similarly unrepentant message.
In the same way that the 1890s success 'Ta-ra-ra-boom-de-ay' and its
subsequent parodies became identified with unbridled sexuality, 'Sam
Hall' perpetuated the image of a doomed renegade at war with society. As such, the song was absorbed into Irish and American folksong,
in more recent times being performed and recorded by The Dubliners
and Johnny Cash. Although the song quoted here appears to be that
presented by Ross, the vehemence of the performance and the constantly repeated oaths inspired several coarse and obscene variants, not
least Nobby Hall who 'only had one ball'.[7]

In its own day Ross's song was also seen as powerful propaganda
against capital punishment. *Reynolds's Newspaper* commented:

In pointing, therefore, to the remarkable exhibition given by Mr Ross,
in his song of 'Sam Hall' at the Cider Cellars, in Maiden Lane, we

must contend, that in point of practical effect upon society and upon mankind his wonderfully true and terrible picture of the last reflections of a condemned felon, before his execution, is more calculated to give the coup de grace to that frightful system of death-punishment for crime committed between man and man than all the homilies and all the eloquence that has ever been expended on the topic.[8]

The very audiences who were thrilled by the fictional exploits of Jack Sheppard and Sam Hall were at risk from their real life counterparts when they left the various places of entertainment in and around the Strand. 'One of the Old Brigade' recalled:

> The approaches to Evans's after dark were by no means free of danger in the long-ago sixties. The market porters, who for the main part were cut-purses and pugilists, were apt to waylay solitary foot passengers whilst awaiting the arrival of the vegetable vans […] The old Olympic, hard by, was another nasty place to leave after the performance, except in a cab. Within fifty yards the alleys bristled with footpads, and any foolhardy pedestrian traversing the dimly-lighted Drury Lane or Newcastle Street was pretty sure not to reach civilization without a very rough experience from the denizens of Vinegar Yard and Betterton Street.[9]

ILLUSTRATION 8. The Dark Arches, Adelphi Terrace, 1850.

Just off the Strand was a place darker than the Coal Hole and more subterranean than the Cyder Cellars. During the first half of the century the network of large tunnels, storage vaults and underground stables, known as the Adelphi Arches, were generally regarded with fear and loathing. Stretching back from the river for 265 feet, the multi-levelled structures fulfilled the practical function of raising Adelphi Terrace up to the level of the Strand. Viewed from the Thames, the effect was spectacular. A series of immense arches rose solidly from the foreshore, surmounted by the cast-iron railings and tall Georgian houses of the Terrace. But, in pre-Embankment times, river water frequently flooded the arches, depositing large amounts of raw sewerage beneath the elegant accommodation above. Rats abounded, frequently sharing the damp alcoves and passages with horses, cows and human occupants.

The Arches provided a refuge for the homeless and a hideout for criminals. Many of the poorest prostitutes used the gloomy surroundings to mask their ragged clothing and unhealthy appearance. In September 1852 the police discovered 15-year-old Mary Ann Palmer lying helpless and covered with syphilitic ulcers. After leaving her home in Paddington the previous year she had met another girl, Sara Cunningham, at the Victoria Theatre ('The Old Vic'), Waterloo. They both started to work as prostitutes within the Arches, Sara taking up her place at 8.30 a.m. and returning to lodgings in Charles Street, Drury Lane, at 9 p.m. Mary Ann had no home to go to and when discovered, it transpired that she had not left the Arches for five months. Her subsequent death in St Martin's Workhouse was attributed to 'dropsy of the chest, occasioned by starvation and neglect'.[10]

Those occupying the Arches often preyed on each other. At 4 o'clock on the morning of 23 August 1842 Thomas Murray, a pot boy who lived in Drury Lane, decided to sleep in the Arches. It was not a wise decision for when he awoke his boots, worth 2s, had been stolen from his feet. His miseries were compounded when, without the respectability of footwear, he was charged with vagrancy. Surprisingly, the case was solved after John Wilson was arrested in Covent Garden wearing the very same boots. Despite claiming he had purchased them, Wilson was found guilty and sentenced to ten years' transportation. In November 1865 three homeless boys who were discovered totally naked in the Arches explained that their ragged clothing had been stolen by a gang of adults.[11] Although common, such incidents were eclipsed by the rowdiness that occurred when hundreds of men, women and children congregated in and around the Arches to indulge in what was widely condemned as anti-social behaviour. Many of the revellers arrived on the paddle-wheel steamboats which charged only a halfpenny for the voyage between London Bridge and Adelphi Pier. In 1858 the *Daily News* castigated the police for a half-hearted effort to control the situation:

> The present state of the Adelphi and its black arches on a Sunday is as great an abomination as can possibly exist in London. It may safely be affirmed that for open violation of the decencies of life it is not equalled by the most depraved part of the eastern end of the metropolis [...] A very slight addition to the strength of the police force, and a little patience, would serve effectively to arrest this frightful and most serious evil.[12]

Although few respectable people cared or dared to visit the Arches, many would have been made aware of their baleful appearance and reputation by a painting exhibited at the Royal Academy in 1858. Augustus Leopold Egg's triptych, later titled *Past and Present*, depicted the destructive consequences of a wife's adultery on a middle-class family. Scene one, hung in the central position, was a flashback which depicted the woman prostrated before her husband who was grinding her lover's image underfoot. The second scene, hung to the left, was set five years later and showed two teenage sisters grieving the loss of their outcast mother and recently deceased father. On the right, scene three showed the mother and her bastard child sheltering at the mouth of one of the Adelphi Arches. A tattered poster advertised Tom Taylor's drama *Victims* and the fallen woman looked towards the inviting waters of the Thames. Originally untitled, the paintings were accompanied by a diary entry:

> August the 4th – Have just heard that B – has been dead for more than a fortnight, so his poor children have now lost both parents. I hear that she was seen on Friday near the Strand, evidently without a place to lay her head. What a fall hers has been.

In the course of time a degree of order was imposed on the Adelphi Arches. The feeble illumination provided by a few gas lamps and by portholes set into the vaulted ceilings was greatly enhanced, while the construction of the Victoria Embankment in the late 1860s made it easier to maintain control over those entering the area.

Light of a different kind was shed by the aspiring educationalist Quintin Hogg who persuaded two young crossing sweepers to attend an ad hoc reading lesson. Using bibles as textbooks and a tallow candle stuck in a beer bottle for lighting, Hogg started to instruct his pupils. The first and only lesson was short lived for a suspicious policeman caused the class to rapidly dismiss itself. Undaunted, Hogg established a ragged school in nearby York Place in 1864, eventually founding the Regents Street Polytechnic for adult education. Despite improvements, the Arches were still spoken of in dramatically classical terms: their gloom was 'stygian', their layout 'labyrinthine' and their moral character 'Augean'. By the late nineteenth century, their continued existence acted as a tangible reminder of an age of epic iniquity and a convenient point from which modern reforms might be measured.

Public behaviour might have improved, but it was still likely to cause offence. In 1883 *Reynolds's Newspaper* reported;

> The Bow-street case yesterday, in which the nightly condition of Charing-cross was spoken of in very plain words, deserves public attention. Nowhere else in Europe, probably with the single exception of the Haymarket and its purlieus, could such a scene of riotous disorder be found as that which only too often prevails at the west end of the Strand. Respectable women going to take trains from Charing-cross are insulted by language which is worse than obscene, and gestures which are even worse. We pay enough for the police in London to demand much stronger surveillance of the streets than is at present the case.[13]

Five years later, in 1887, the same newspaper revealed that there had been little change in the situation:

> Several women were charged at Bow-street on Wednesday with disorderly conduct in the Strand. In support of the charges Mr Glenny, of 290, Strand, appeared and made a statement as to the dreadful condition of the thoroughfare. He said that scarcely any respectable person could pass along between ten and half-past

twelve without being hustled and robbed. The women worked in couples, one taking hold of each arm of the victim, or else in gangs. Countrymen staying at the various hotels and elderly gentlemen are their especial prey. Sometimes they met in gangs to fight and indulge in the most revolting language.[14]

The interface between the public perception of good and evil was seldom more clearly revealed as in the area around Exeter Hall. In 1884 a French journalist Max O'Rell wrote:

> If you would be thoroughly edified, take a walk along the Strand in the month of May. There stands in this thoroughfare an immense hall belonging to the Young Men's Christian Association. This building, which ought to be called Salvation Hall, is simply named Exeter Hall. It is in this place that, from the first to the thirty-first of May, the various angelical, evangelical, and archangelical societies successively hold their annual conferences, called May Meetings. It is Salvation Fair. To Exeter Hall throng *la gent trotte-menu* from all parts of the United Kingdom to their souls' spring-cleaning. For a whole month, the air of the Strand is impregnated with an odour of sanctity [...] of which it stands sadly in need, to speak the truth; it is a spectacle thoroughly English, to see on one side of a street – the north side of the Strand – edifying groups, unctuous specimens of the most austere virtue; on the other side, a few yards off, groups of unfortunate, shameless women, dirty, intoxicated, daring specimens of the lowest debauch: on the right, hymns; on the left, obscene songs; on the right, the Bible and the Gospel; on the left, beer, gin [...] and the rest.[15]

Bad behaviour was not confined to hooligans and harlots. Prior to the 1872 Licensing Act a chaotic confederacy of drunken military officers, legal and medical students, aristocratic ne'er-do-wells, sportsmen and journalists ran amok throughout the night, their 'larks', 'frolics' and 'sprees' involving fighting, criminal damage and the perpetration of 'pranks' whose humour was assessed by the degree of inconvenience that they caused to the wider community. One of the less malicious manifestations of the Jolly Dogs' sense of fun occurred early one May morning at the start of the 1860s when a party of young officers stole into Haxell's Hotel, 369–75 Strand. A large number of clergymen staying at the hotel for an annual conference awoke to find that the shoes they had left outside their bedrooms for cleaning had mysteriously been swapped for those of a smaller or larger colleague. Usually the

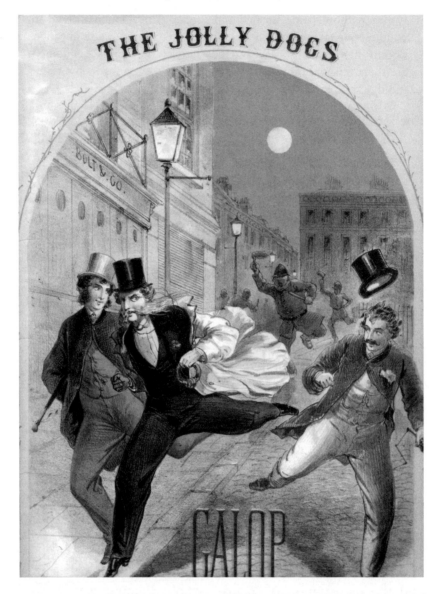

**ILLUSTRATION 9.** Upper class hooligans depicted on a sheet music cover of 1865.

upper-class yobs contented themselves with nefarious activities: smashing windows and street lights, wrenching knockers and bells from front doors, sweeping glasses and bottles from bar counters, and provoking 'rows' in which hats were bashed and watches snatched. Major sporting events such as the Derby or University Boat Race provided the excuse for disturbances which the police stood little chance of controlling. On the music-hall stage Lions Comiques, George Leybourne and 'The Great Vance' presented such acts of violence and vandalism as jovial high-spirits. The sheet music of Vance's 'Slap Bang, Here We Are Again! Or, The School of Jolly Dogs' (1865) depicted three fashionably dressed revellers setting out on an evening's hell-raising:

> At eight o'clock they sally forth
> Because you know it's dark.
> 'Follow my leader' cries the chief,
> Tonight we'll have a lark'
>
> Spring-heeled Jack and all his pals
> With their nocturnal larks
> I'm sure were not a patch upon
> This school of modern sparks.[16]

Although the 1872 Act resulted in a large-scale decrease in public disorder, a hard core of bohemians continued the roistering tradition until the end of the century. Often frequenting Romano's restaurant and bar at 399–400 Strand, a group which included the comedian Arthur Roberts and several journalists from The Sporting Times did its utmost to maintain a low moral tone and ignoble spirit. Of its number the talented cartoonist, Phil May was the most creative and persistent mischief maker. He was a graduate of a hard school having slept rough when he first came to London from his native Leeds. A naturally wild and bohemian temperament led to him failing at various jobs – clerk, trainee jockey and bit-part actor – before he achieved national success with his witty and economically drawn cartoons of everyday life. His output was prolific, as was his consumption of whiskey. One episode is sufficient to indicate his idea of practical joking. He and a group of friends had come across an unfinished roadwork where the labourers had left their picks and shovels. The barriers were removed to a quiet street off the Strand, either Surrey Street or Norfolk Street, and the group amused themselves by excavating a large hole: 'When the exercise had produced a useful sweat, and a good section of the road was 'up,' Time was called, they downed tools, and went back to Romano's.'[17]

The general public in the Strand was also at risk from violent or unpredictable acts performed by individuals, usually precipitated by alcohol, mental health problems or, in some cases, sheer poor judgement. Any of these categories might explain the commotion caused by a member of the audience at the Strand Theatre on Saturday, 18 November 1865. As usual, the majority of the stalls were occupied by ladies and gentlemen customarily attired in evening dress. One female patron, however, caused a major breech in the uniformity. A 'tall and remarkably pretty woman' took her seat and attracted immediate attention by the 'extraordinary lowness' of her dress. The audience were scandalised, particularly the female element in whom 'a painful sensation was clearly perceptible'. The embarrassing situation came to a head during an interval when a voice from the gallery made a comment relating either to the extreme nature of the costume or to the physical attributes of its wearer. She drew her cape over her shoulders and left the theatre amid hisses from the gallery and a 'stern silence, not less eloquent, in the stalls and boxes'. At the time the unholy alliance between the bourgeois orthodoxy of lower house and the libertarian impertinence of the upper was considered to be a triumph of 'censorship of manners in a quarter where, according to conventional estimate, refinement is least to be expected'.[18]

An interruption of a more threatening nature occurred during the run of Faust Up to Date at the Gaiety Theatre. Shortly before 10 p.m. on 29 September 1889 an occupant of the stalls, unusually costumed in gaiters and leggings, threw a bouquet onto the stage, accompanying the gesture with an exhibition of 'indecent' behaviour. Having been quickly hustled out of the auditorium, the man made his way to the Gaiety's bar where he quickly became embroiled in another scene. He indignantly declared himself to be an officer in the English army, whereupon he was challenged by another theatre-goer: 'I am also an officer in the English army, and I demand your name and address.' Although threatened with being reported to the Commander-in-Chief of the British Army, the Duke of Cambridge, the bouquet thrower still refused to give his name. He pleaded tearfully: 'I am not drunk, but irritated. I behaved in a blackguardly manner. I am a major, but I have a promotion to a colonelcy and I go out to India tomorrow morning.' Observing his distress, a number of bystanders intervened on his behalf and the confrontation was brought to a close. He later repeated his story and claimed that if he was reported for such disgraceful conduct his long-awaited promotion would be cancelled. Any sympathy he might have elicited evaporated when he 'made use of a vile remark' in front of the barmaids who had refused to serve him whiskey.[19]

The staff and audience at the Gaiety may have had a lucky escape, for the troublesome officer, Major Frank Foster of the 34th Foot, possessed a revolver and claimed to be 'the finest shot in the army'. Later in the evening he was ejected from the St James's Restaurant where he had accused other customers of having robbed him. A quick thinking commissionaire confiscated the pistol still in its case before firmly grasping Foster's collar and arm and delivering him into the custody a policeman. At Marlborough Street Police Court the next day the major was charged with being drunk and disorderly, refusing to leave the restaurant and having a firearm in his possession. Still wearing his gaiters, but with the addition of a leather cricket cap, he continued to behave in such an eccentric manner that it was clear that drink was not the sole cause of his problems. Two doctors found him not to be responsible for his actions, a diagnosis that he partially agreed with. His madness, he stated, was caused by dealing in stocks and shares: 'It is the Stock Exchange. It sends all the brokers off their heads. I will be all right as long as you keep me away from the Stock Exchange.' It seems that Major Foster might not have been kept away from the Stock Exchange, as two weeks later he was charged with obtaining a diamond ring on false pretences. It was reported that he had been insane for six weeks, the result of sunstroke contracted in Burma and excessive drinking.[20]

Perhaps the most unusual incidence of public disorder in the Strand occurred on the evening of 26 June 1889 when the police fought a pitched battle with members of an evangelical religious organisation. Founded in London's East End in 1865, the Christian Mission was renamed the Salvation Army in 1878. A concentration on tackling the social issues of poverty, prostitution and drunkenness, combined with a disregard for the edicts of self-serving local authorities, frequently caused the movement to come into conflict with the law. When pimps and publicans organised gangs to attack Salvation Army public rallies and mission halls, the police often intervened to arrest the victims rather than the aggressors. In return, the leadership of the Salvation Army instructed its members, many of whom were reformed alcohol and drug abusers and prostitutes, not to pay fines, a course of action that usually resulted in terms of imprisonment. With the announced attendance of over 100 ex-prisoners, the June meeting in Exeter Hall was always likely to be of a highly charged nature. The procession from the Salvation Army's headquarters in Queen Victoria Street to the Strand had been set on a collision course some days before when the organisers of the event decided to ignore the Metropolitan Police's instructions to travel along the Thames Embankment and then to approach the hall in small groups. Although the suggested route was more direct, the army decided that it would march defiantly through enemy country – past the taverns of Fleet Street, past the prostitutes of the Strand and up to the very doors of Exeter Hall.

Coming down Ludgate Hill with the dome of St Paul's in the background, the procession made an impressive sight. Banners from local branches were proudly flourished and two brass bands played joyful anthems. Most of the 1,000 men and women wore blue and red uniforms, with about 100 men dressed in white convict clothes bearing broad, black arrows. The City of London had no objection to the march and its police officers provided an escort to the limit of their jurisdiction, the Royal Courts of Justice in the Strand. There, a line of Metropolitan Police officers had assembled to prevent any further progress. The procession surged on regardless and a police inspector ordered his men into action. With no love and very little respect for each other, the police and Salvationists clashed violently. Like the hooligans who were paid to disrupt their activities, the police attempted to snatch banners and to smash expensive musical instruments. The marchers fought back with unexpected force, pushing the police before them. A bizarre twist to the conflict occurred when a number of 'roughs' who had been watching events unfold took exception to the police tactics and joined the battle on the side of the Salvation Army. Some of the fiercest fighting took place around the banner of the Torquay branch. The Devonians had good reason to defend their flag for in the years 1886 to 1888, 20 of their congregation had received prison sentences for marching on Sundays with musical instruments. Eventually, the police halted and dispersed the demonstration at Wellington Street, within a short distance of Exeter Hall. The battered and bloodied Salvationists made their way gradually into the meeting, leaving the Strand littered with the debris of a major riot.

# 4

# THE LORD CHIEF BARON OF THE COAL HOLE

Regency rakes and dandies did not pack up their pantaloons and playing cards when Queen Victoria came to the throne. If anything, after 1837 the carousing existence of the late Georgian gentleman was democratised and extended to a wider social class, reduced in grandeur of costume and levels of expenditure, but enhanced by new and more organised forms of recreation. Renton Nicholson was one of the leading entrepreneurs seeking to capitalise on the new pleasure-seeking public, promoting his various ventures in writings that extolled the 'flash' life. His natural habitat was the Strand tavern where he introduced entertainments that both mocked and shocked early Victorian society. Widely celebrated and condemned during his own time, he was described after his death as a symptom of national decadence and personal moral degeneracy. But to others he was a reminder of less repressive times, before hypocrisy and dogma began to impinge on the individual's cherished freedom to behave badly.

Born in the Hackney Road, East London, on 4 April 1809, Nicholson lost both parents at an early age. He was brought up by his brother, a clerk in a City banking house, and his two sisters who contributed to the family budget by running a small school. They had moved to Islington, a semi-rural suburb, whose close proximity to the centre of London made it 'a colony of bankers' and merchants' clerks'.[1] Despite such clerical predominance, young Renton was soon exposed to a strongly subversive influence – he became friendly with England's greatest clown, Joseph Grimaldi. Situated locally on the banks of the New River, Sadler's Wells Theatre, with its explosive, authority-bashing, anarchistic pantomimes proved a powerful magnet to the schoolboy. In later years Nicholson cherished a memory of the lecherous 'Joey' on a ladder peeping through a window at a young woman and singing:

> Oh, see that pretty creature there!
> Oh, how handsome – oh, how fair!

More prosaically, Grimaldi employed him to spy on the street vendors outside the 'Wells' to report on the sale of any 'spurious' tickets.[2]

At the age of 12 Nicholson gained experience of a population far different from that of Islington. As a pawnbroker's assistant in Shadwell, close to the docks in East London, he rapidly gained experience of the predatory side of human nature. It was, he remembered, a community of 'land-sharks, who, as a body, embraced publicans, pawnbrokers, lodging house-keepers, slop-sellers, crimps, pimps, and *prostrates* – fallen one'.[3] Flourishing side whiskers and a rapidly expanding waistline combined to give the teenage pawnbroker's assistant the appearance of a man of more advanced years. With his mature looks and a natural aptitude for having a good time, 'Nick' slotted easily into the raffish company of prize-fighters, comic singers, 'gay' women and gambling men.

Moving from Shadwell after three years to a pawnbroker's business in Kensington and subsequently the West End, Nicholson began to receive revealing insights into the circulation of money, at least in the more transient areas of society. When it came to pledging their personal possessions for cash advances, gamblers were frequent customers, but he found that a more reliable income was that derived from 'soiled doves' and 'fallen angels':

> It will be seen that my vicinity was peopled by gay life, and I daily came in contact with the sisterhood in the way of trade. It was the custom of my employer, 'for a consideration,' to lend per night valuable articles of jewellery; also to accommodate those customers, the frail and the fair, well known to us, by allowing them to have their bracelets, necklaces, diamond ear-rings, &c., out for a night's use, without paying the redemptive money. This sort of irregular business induced much association with that peculiar class of society; and here I may pause to pay a tribute to their good faith and integrity. Although we frequently lent goods in that manner, to the extent of three or four thousands in intrinsic value, we never lost an article: all were safely returned, and the hire of them paid for to the scruple.[4]

**ILLUSTRATION 10.** Renton Nicholson portrayed on the cover of his 1860 autobiography.

A role-call of Nicholson's 'gay'[5] acquaintances and customers in the late 1820s included Louisa Devenish, Amy Hope, Polly Edwards, Charlotte Lloyd, the Goddess Diana, Fair Glover, Fat Glover, Fanny Golby, Polly Hague, Betsy Johnson and Jew Bella.

With nine years of experience behind him, Nicholson decided to become his own master, opening a jeweller's shop at 99 Quadrant, Regent Street, in 1830. It was a short-lived venture for he became insolvent in December 1831. At the age of 21 he spent a month in the King's Bench Prison, the first of many periods of incarceration resulting from financial embarrassments. At the time, there were five privately run prisons in London to which creditors might consign debtors who were unable to repay even trifling amounts. The Fleet and the Marshalsea (famously evoked by Dickens in *Little Dorrit*) were closed by an act of parliament in 1842, leaving Horsemonger Lane, Whitecross Street and the King's (later Queen's) Bench to operate until the passing of the Bankruptcy Act of 1869. Inmates were deprived of their liberty, but, depending on what funds they could muster, were able to secure room upgrades, visit the prison's coffee house or tavern and purchase items from many shops and stalls situated within the walls. A convivial and gregarious prisoner, Nicholson regarded the gaol almost as an educational establishment. 'My knowledge of refined life', he wrote, 'has been mostly gleaned, and materially improved by associations therein.'[6]

Ejection from prison was sometimes worse than imprisonment. On one of the occasions that the penniless Nicholson was released from 'Barrett's Hotel', i.e., Whitecross Street Prison, he was compelled to sleep rough in St James's Square, Piccadilly, until he was noticed by an emaciated, but once beautiful prostitute. It would be good to have a name by which to remember his frail rescuer – a simple Mary, Rose or Polly on which to hang his description of the woman who leant over him with the sympathetic words: 'Have you gone to sleep, old fellow? You are not accustomed to these buffetings. Come with me; I can give you a resting place, at least for to-night.' As it is, her namelessness reinforces the transience of her short life. Provided with a sofa in her poorly furnished attic, Nicholson was sufficiently restored in spirits to borrow a guinea from an acquaintance and to improve his appearance sufficiently to find employment. But it was too late to help 'Anonyma'. She succumbed rapidly to tuberculosis and, as she had predicted, did not outlive her potted geranium. For Nicholson, she and the other prostitutes who rallied round to help her in her final illness came to symbolise not only the inequality, but the social unfairness of the times in which he lived:

> They were all kind, generous-hearted creatures, not selfish, and cold, and dead to feeling, as ye are, ye men of the world, who have made their condition what it is, and by whose report the world only knows of them.[7]

At Christmas 1842 Nicolson painted a sympathetic picture of a prostitute in his poem 'A Sigh for the Sorrowful' published in *The Era*:

> Her fallen spirit mingles with scenes of saffron guile,
> But, Oh! Her heart remembers when guiltless she could smile:
> And blazing fires roaring through parlour windows seem,
> But lamps to recollections of childhood's happy dreams;
> She walks the streets in penance, in sorrow, and in blight –
> No hope revives her wasted form on merry Christmas night.[8]

The rotund 'Nick' continued to bounce between shady occupations and questionable money-making schemes throughout the 1830s. Often associated with London gaming establishments, he also ran a gambling marquee at racecourses during the summer months. At various times he worked as an attorney's 'fag', a wine merchant and a partner in a billiard saloon. His marriage in 1836 to 17-year-old Eliza, whom he characteristically described as 'as handsome as a peacock and as well bred as Eclipse',[9] hardly generated a more responsible approach. Their cigar shop in Warwick Street, Regent Street, also served as an unlicensed tavern and gambling den. Although trade was good, previous debts soon caught up with him and he was 'bowled out, sued, bummed, and placed once more in Barrett's Hotel'.[10]

On release from Whitecross Street Prison, Nicholson again found himself in a dire situation. Only now he had a young wife to starve alongside him. After several dispiriting attempts to interest publishers in a series of studies of London life titled *Tales of the Town, or Cockney Adventures*, he persuaded the newspaper proprietor, Joseph Last, to listen while he read the manuscript. Last was sufficiently impressed to propose that he issue a new weekly periodical to which Nicholson would contribute 12 columns for a salary of £3. With a

£1 advance, the now successful author raced home to his hungry wife, stopping off at the local butcher's to pay off his account and to purchase two pounds of chuck steak.

The following day, Nicholson and Last prepared a prospectus:

NEW WEEKLY PUBLICATION
SIZE OF THE SATIRIST NEWSPAPER
PRICE 2d. ONLY!
On SATURDAY, June 3rd, 1837, will be published.
THE FIRST NUMBER OF
THE TOWN;
COMPRISING OF ORIGINAL SKETCHES OF THE

Metropolitan Gaming Houses–Free and Easies–The Prisons–The Swell Mob–Flats and Sharps–Parish Worthies–Licensed Victuallers–Pawnbrokers and their Assistants–Cigar Shops and Pretty Women–Now-street Officers-The Doings of Courtesans and Demireps of Quality, &c. &c.; with Criticism on Actors and the Theatres and all places of Public Amusement.

Published close to the west end of Holywell Street at 310 Strand, the paper consisted of four large pages with woodcut illustrations. Although there were some attempts to criticise social evils and malpractice, most of The Town's content consisted of knowingly worded descriptions of taverns, brothels, gambling dens and free and easy concerts, with particular attention paid to actresses, prostitutes and pretty waitresses. Nicholson and his co-writers were all intimately acquainted with the 'flash' world. Among those involved with the frequently criticised periodical were Henry Pellett, an ex-clerk and solicitor; John Dalrymple, a writer of burlesques and a Mr Somerville (an ex-soldier). Illustrations were the work of Archibald Henning who went on to supply cartoons for the humorous magazine Punch when it was launched in 1841. Theatrical expertise was supplied by the 'English Improvisatore' Charles Sloman, already celebrated as a singer, songwriter and, above all, master of the impromptu rhyme.

The process by which The Town gave way to Nicholson's next venture was explained in a brief-lived revival of the publication, edited and largely written by the comedian Henry G. Brooks:

almost from the commencement of The TOWN, the Garrick's Head Hotel, in Bow Street, the property of Simpson of the Albion, had been peculiarly favoured by its editor; independent of frequent long articles praising the establishment and small puff paragraphs scattered about the publication, he gave to the house his personal patronage and also that of his friends. Every speculation of 'Tommy Simpson' such as *Bal Masques*, etc., were – as it is technically termed – 'written up.' This line of conduct procured for him the friendship of Mr Simpson [...] who having for some months vainly struggled to make a business of the tap department of the Garrick's Hotel, cordially and with 'outstretched arms' received the proposition that Nicholson should become the managing director of the hotel department of the house. From this period we may date the gradual decline of the TOWN as a publication, and the rise of the Garrick's Head.[11]

After 156 provocative numbers, The Town was brought to a close on Saturday, 23 May 1840. In what appears to have been a seamless transition, Nicholson became manager of the Garrick's Head and Town Hotel, opposite the Theatre Royal, Covent Garden, later entering into partnership with its owner, Thomas Bartlett Simpson. Among several contributors to The Town who joined him in the new venture was Charles Sloman acting as chairman of the nightly concerts. It was at Sloman's suggestion that the first convocation of the Judge and Jury Society took place on 6 March 1841. The 'Society' mimicked legal proceedings, treating subjects such as seduction, adultery and divorce with a course and salacious humour. Adverts inserted in the theatrical press suggested the content of the entertainments:

A serious, momentous and stoddling case of Crim. Con., being the affair lately so much whispered about in the circles of the Ton, 'Viscount Limpus v. the Hon. Powderham Pelter Plantagenet Priapus Pulverton.

A case of Seduction and Breach of Promise of Marriage, 'Meekmaid v. Rushington'. The details of this case will forcibly illustrate the stratagems and contrivances of the art of seduction, and exhibit the perils of the tower of virtue under fire of the monster mortar, Vice.[12]

Witnesses, legal councils and sometimes eminent figures were represented by actors and comedians, while female characters were played by men in drag, the chief representative of flighty prostitutes and querulous old women being 'The Protean Witness', Henry G. Brooks. Promoting himself to the rank of 'Lord Chief Baron', Nicholson occupied the judge's bench with aplomb. A

# NICHOLSON'S
# JUDGE & JURY
## SOCIETY,
## CYDER CELLARS,
### Maiden Lane, Covent Garden,
Strand Entrance, 2 doors West of Adelphi Theatre,

### Friends, Lovers & COUNTRYMEN!
## COME AND BEHOLD
# LUNACY MADE EASY
### UNDER
## "THE WIND'EM UP ACT!"
# THE POSES PLASTIQUES!
### BEFORE AND AFTER THE TRIAL.
#### IN THE
# CONCERT,
### All the available Talent.
### Commencing at half-past Seven precisely.

### Shrove Tuesday; Remember, Shrove Tuesday,
## March 4th,
## For the Benefit of Mr. H. G. BROOKS,
### The Protean Witness!

GRAMMER, Printer, 8, Princes St., Little Queen Street, Holborn

**ILLUSTRATION 11.** Handbill advertising the Judge and Jury Society at the Cyder Cellars.

truly Rabelaisian character, fast approaching 20 stone in weight, he was the epitome of good humour, dispensing laconic comments while sipping brandy and puffing on a cigar. He was cheered on in his impromptu and improper asides by an all-male audience that usually included a sprinkling of celebrities. A commemoration of the society's most eminent patrons in the form of an oil painting also served as an advertisement for the entertainment. Archibald Henning's group portrait, hanging in the front window of the Garrick's Head, depicted the bewigged Lord Chief Baron looming over an audience that included the young novelist Charles Dickens; the politician Sir Robert Peel; England's most famous general, the Duke of Wellington; the prize-fighter and comic singer Sambo Sutton; and the actor William Betty, billed in his youth as 'The English Roscius', but by then sinking into an undistinguished middle age.

Mock trials may have been popular with many men about town, but they were also widely condemned. To Ewing Ritchie the language used in the Judge and Jury Society seemed almost as bad as the deeds that were discussed:

> the Judge and Jury Clubs make you familiar with the manners of the stews: and I solemnly believe that in Sodom and Gomorrah nothing more filthy could have been talked about, and that this side of Pandemonium there is nothing more debasing or debased. If you wish to see your son thoroughly depraved, send him to a Judge and Jury Club. In a little while he will come back to you with every noble principle blotted out, with a mind stored with pollution, and with a fitting phraseology, ready to run a mad career of debauchery and vice.[13]

Away from the entertainments Nicholson combined reasonable prices with good standards of catering. 'Excellent bed chambers' were available for 1s 6d and patrons dined off damask table cloths using silver cutlery. An advert in the form of a trial transcript emphasised the 'criminally' low charges made for refreshments:

> *Attorney-General.* – Another object of the act of Incorporation was the preventing of cheap dinners to the poor of unwholesome meat.
> *Lord Denman, C. J.* – What, Mr Attorney, is the precise object of your application?
> *Attorney-General.* – Nicholson, to whom we ask the *mandamus* should issue, vends not in a public window, and as my affidavit shows, vends at a very cheap rate.
> *Lord Denman, C. J.* – What do you call cheap?

*Attorney-General.* – He vends a plate of meat for fourpence.
*Lord Denman, C. J.* – Indeed!
*Patterson, J.* – Is it possible?
*Coleridge, J.* – Astonishing!
*Williams, J.* – Where did you say Nicholson lived?
*Attorney-General.* – At the Garrick's Head, my lord, in Bow Street. My affidavit says that he supplies a large plate of meat for sixpence and vegetables at a penny a plate each sort.
*Lord Denman, C. J.* – And what of bread?
*Attorney-General.* – A penny, my lord.
*Williams, J.* – Supposing I had one of his maximum plates, say boiled beef, what charge does he affix for peas-pudding?
*Attorney-General.* – We are silent respecting pudding.[14]

It was not long before 'Lord Chief Baron' Nicholson's name was prominently displayed at major events throughout England. His canvas pavilion became a familiar feature at race meeting and fairs across southern England, providing food, drink and a platform for dancing. The success of this egalitarian enterprise seems to have persuaded Nicholson that a bright future awaited an entertainment complex that offered alfresco and indoor entertainment and catering at prices that would attract a large cross section of society. In 1843 he purchased a 12-acre parkland site close to the Thames in West London. Originally named Chelsea Farm, the estate had belonged to Lord Cremorne before it had been converted into a venue for sporting activities in the early nineteenth century. There were several long-established pleasure gardens on the fringes of London, but Nicholson conceived Cremorne as a larger and better organised establishment, a brasher and cheaper alternative to the long-established Vauxhall Gardens on the opposite bank of the river. Once popular with royalty and the aristocracy, Vauxhall Gardens had become a shadow of its former self, trading on recollections of its eighteenth-century grandeur to charge what many considered to be extortionate prices. Forty years later Edmund Yates wrote of Cremorne:

The gardens were large and well laid out; some of the grand old trees had been left standing, and afforded pleasant relief to the town eyes which had been staring all day at brick and stucco, while their murmuring rustle was pleasant to the ears aching with the echo of city traffic. There were plenty of amusements – a circular dancing platform, with a capital band in a large kiosk in the middle;

a lot of *jeux innocens*, such as you find at a French fair; once a week a balloon ascent; and a very good firework display. The admission fee was one shilling; there was a hot dinner for half a crown, a cold supper for the same money; and it was not considered necessary, as at Vauxhall, to go in for expense; on the contrary, beer flowed freely; and it was about this time, I think, and at Cremorne, that the insidious 'long' drinks – soda and 'something' – now so popular, first made their appearance. Occasionally, there were big banquets organised by certain 'swells,' and held there, when there would be heavy drinking, and sometimes a row – on Derby night, once, when there was free fight, which lasted for hours, involving the complete smash of everything smashable; and I mind me of another occasion, when a gigantic Irishman, now a popular M.P., sent scores of waiters flying by the force of his own unaided fists. But, on the whole, the place was well and quietly conducted, and five minutes after the bell for closing rang – just before midnight – the gardens were deserted. There was a general rush for the omnibuses and cabs, which were in great demand, and for one or two seasons there was a steamboat which left the adjacent Cadogan pier at the close of the entertainment, and carried passengers to Hungerford Bridge, and which was very popular.[15]

Cremorne's clientele attended in two distinct shifts. Throughout the day and early evening patrons consisted mainly of family groups and couples present to eat, drink and enjoy the various entertainments. As night fell, hundreds of prostitutes arrived to fraternise with a larger number of single men. Activity was largely confined to the area around the dancing platform, although of the 1,000 visitors counted by William Acton in 1857 only about 200 were engaged in dancing. Such a social dichotomy was cleverly exploited by Nicholson who promoted the wholesome and respectable side of his various catering and entertainment ventures in his official advertising while elaborating on their insalubrious aspects in a series of prurient booklets. In several editions of *The Swell's Night Guide*, available from a notorious publisher of pornography, the 'Lord Chief Baron' happily discussed the 'Paphian Beauties' and 'Fancy Ladies' who visited his establishments. He was, on the other hand, quick to disassociate the Garrick's Head from any blame when a young chemist's assistant committed suicide after visiting the concert room with a prostitute he had picked up at the Adelphi Theatre.[16]

As with many of Nicholson's ventures, a financial crisis brought an early end to his connection with Cremorne. He had borrowed heavily to create the attraction and, despite large attendance figures, was forced to sell to Simpson, his publican colleague. Upset but undeterred, he continued to present other entertainments while finding time to add to his literary output. He had always been a prolific journalist and his books included an autobiography; works on prize fighting, and London life; and *Dombey and Daughter*, a part-issue novel capitalising on the success of Charles Dickens' *Dombey and Son*. Nicolson's fluctuating fortunes resulted in the Judge and Jury Society following an erratic circuit. When he fell out with Simpson over the sale of Cremorne in 1844, proceedings were transferred to the Coal Hole, Fountain Court, 103 Strand. After two years the Society returned to the Garrick's Head, moving on to the Justice Tavern, 36 Bow Street, in 1849, then back to the Coal Hole in 1851, and finally ending up at the Cyder Cellars in 1858. Despite the popularity of his mock trials, Nicholson was keen to introduce fresh novelties, particularly if they stood any chance of provoking public controversy. Send-ups of elections and parliamentary debates were sure to irritate and delight the political classes, while the *poses plastiques* or *tableaux vivants* in which naked (or seemingly naked) female models imitated classical statues or famous paintings struck many commentators as semi-pornography rather than a tribute to high art.

In 1849 'handsome as a peacock' Eliza died in Boulogne, leaving 'Nick' to bring up two young daughters alone. There was no slackening in his pace of life; no reduction in his consumption of cigars and brandy. His many ventures earned him large sums of money, but he invariably found himself in debt and a frequent visitor to the court of bankruptcy. Although a large target, the 'Lord Chief Baron' was resilient, a substantial bastion around which an alliance of the amoral, the venial and the subversive grouped to repel the assaults of social reformers and legislators. When he died on 18 May 1861 of dropsy and heart disease, appropriately at the Gordon Tavern in the Piazza, Covent Garden, a decade of metropolitan revelry was yet to unfold. Yet, even during the sinning 1860s, the 'flash' way of life that he so skilfully represented was clearly doomed. Within a year of his death both the Coal Hole and the Cyder Cellars had their entertainment licences refused because of complaints to the magistrates about the indecency of the *poses plastiques*, comic songs and mock trials.

Nicholson's Judge and Jury Society did not cease with the closure of its old court rooms. Even before the final judgement had been passed on the Cyder Cellars, 'The Protean Witness' had taken the Society on tour, eventually gathering together several original performers from the entertainment world to appear nightly at 404 Strand, close to the Adelphi Theatre. Henry G. Brooks put aside shawls and bonnets to assume the wig and gown of the 'Lord Chief Baron', while he was joined by Mr Lush, Mr Thomas, Mr Bullock and Mr R. Phillips, 'the world renowned delineator of "Skittles"' (i.e., Catherine Walters, the most famous of Victorian courtesans). Renamed 'The Hall of Justice', what had been the Adelphi Rifle Gallery was provided with a stage and proscenium on which *Poses Plastique* were displayed, while Brooks delivered an 'explanatory comic lecture'.[17]

In 1865 'The Hall of Justice' moved to 21 Leicester Square, three doors away from the famous Alhambra Music Hall. That the Judge and Jury entertainment was conducted along Nicholson's old, improper lines was demonstrated in January 1869 when Brooks was fined 40s for permitting disorderly conduct against the terms of his licence as the keeper of a refreshment house. A police

JUDGE AND JURY ASSEMBLY, IN THE STRAND.
DRAWN AND ENGRAVED BY OUR OWN ARTIST.

**ILLUSTRATION 12.** Henry G. Brooks presides over the 'Temple of Justice' in the Strand, 1864.

inspector reported that the entertainment consisted of 'a mixture of ribaldry and obscenity, interspersed with double *entendres*'.[18] Within a few days Brooks was again in court charged with 'unlawfully, and by words, gestures, and actions, representing a certain lewd, obscene and indecent performance, whereby a public nuisance was occasioned against the peace'. In an attempt to rid London of such a long-running nuisance, the magistrate Mr Knox was prepared to cut Brooks a deal. He could either be found guilty and serve a prison sentence or agree to remove the objectionable element from the society's performances – 'make everybody laugh if you like, but don't combine amusement with obscenity'.[19] The protean defendant immediately agreed to the proposal thanking the magistrate for his kindness. In Brompton Cemetery Renton Nicholson must have turned in his ample grave.

Henry G. Brooks's first appearances in court prompted *The Saturday Review* to complain about an inconsistent legal approach to 'public indecencies' that stretched back into Nicholson's heyday:

> Last Monday Mr Knox took evidence and fined a fellow named Brooks for permitting Poses Plastiques, Tableaux Vivants, or whatever they are called, and for presiding over or keeping what is called a Judge and Jury Club – that is, a mock trial, the staple of which is filthy language, or, as Mr Knox calls it, 'broad and disgusting bestiality.' We shut our eyes and wonder where we are. Is it, or is it not, true that there was such a fellow as Chief Baron Nicholson? Was, or was not, his portrait as familiar to all London people as the lion on Northumberland House? Did he not go on for years unchecked in his dirty trade? [...] If that huge Satyr, Baron Nicholson, was allowed to rot in the odour – and a very nasty odour it was – of obscenity, unpunished, then Mr Henry Brooks is rather hardly dealt with. It cannot be that the meshes of the law were not strong enough to retain the bloated carrion-fly of the days gone by while it has contrived to catch the small midge Brooks, for the law was the same, the offence was the same, the sort of house in which the offence was committed was the same.[20]

*The Saturday Review* was pushing at an open door. Constant agitation from pressure groups and periodicals, and a greater willingness from politicians to tackle social issues soon led to legislation that brought night houses – and night life – under far stricter control. With the writing on the wall in 'Modern Babylon', Brooks had little choice other than to accept Mr Knox's proposition. The days of his 'Hall of Justice' were numbered; he had been tried and found wanting and the courts and licensing authorities seemed determined to change the nature of public entertainment. Even 'Lord Chief Baron' Nicholson would have struggled to make his way in such a hostile climate.

Renton Nicholson's libertine philosophy and dubious business enterprises embodied the post-Regency, inner-London world that the Victorian establishment was intent on breaking up. He had been able to succeed – and to fail – in so many ventures because 'flash' society was relatively cohesive, making his talents and those of his loyal henchmen easily transferable. Whether he ran a newspaper, sold food and drink, wrote novels or presided over a mock court, 'Nick' carried with him the same loyal customers. He, in turn, did his customers the honour of writing about them, of representing their lifestyle as a riotous rejection of killjoy authority. Many of his contemporaries felt that he made poor choices and that he could have become a nobler and more respected character, but he was driven as much by financial expediency as by a roguish disposition. He would have seen no inconsistency in the sympathy he expressed for prostitutes and the relentless exploitation of sex by which he made a living. Cement Scott, the theatrical journalist, recalled him as 'a plebeian Falstaff turned tapster; humorous, handsome, obese, sensual, impudent; a rooker of the rich and the soul of good nature to the poor'.[21] The theatrical newspaper *The Era* that had chronicled his roguish progress since the 1830s published a sympathetic obituary:

> The charity he exercised will cover, let us reverentially hope, more sins than are to be placed on the account of the one that has gone from amongst us, and who will be long missed from his accustomed haunts.[22]

# 5

# OLD STOCK AND FANCY GOODS

'Old Stock' had seen better days and nights. Like many of the raggedly dressed women employed to keep a watchful eye on prostitutes, she had also been on the game. In an interview conducted on behalf of the social investigator Henry Mayhew in the late 1850s, she remembered the time when she had possessed her own house, servants and 'heaps of men sighing and dying' for her. Now she did odd jobs in a brothel, hoping to pick up a few pennies which she immediately spent on drink. She was philosophical about her fate, commenting that 5s would keep her 'jolly for a week'. 'Talking of giving a woman five bob reminds me of having fivers given me', she continued, 'I can remember the time when I would take nothing but paper; always tissue, nothing under a flimsy. Ah! Gay women see strange changes; wonderful ups and downs, I can tell you.'[1]

As the busiest, most cosmopolitan street in the metropolis, the Strand had provided the setting for the ups and downs of countless gay women. Victorian statisticians exhausted themselves in attempting to calculate the number of 'unfortunates' in London, but despite widely varying estimates it is clear that at any time during the period the total stood at many thousands. Most prostitutes had previously worked as servants, shop assistants or workers in poorly paid occupations such as millinery and dress-making, while a large number of 'Dollymops' operated as occasional or part-time prostitutes to supplement their earnings. Prior to the Criminal Law Amendment Act of 1885 many girls became prostitutes in their early teens. French journalist Max O'Rell wrote in 1883:

The police des moeurs [vice squad] does not exist in London and the capital of this country, so moral and so Christian, exhibits sights too heartrending to imagine. Girls of fourteen or fifteen, with dyed hair, and wan-looking faces, daubed with paint, stand about drunk and in rags, soliciting the passers-by for a vile wage.[2]

An overwhelmingly economic imperative for entering the profession was often obscured by melodramatic accounts invented to gain sympathy from clients or social investigators. Mayhew explained that 'loose women generally throw a veil over their early life, and you seldom, if ever, meet with a woman who is not either a seduced governess or a clergyman's daughter; not that there is any truth in the allegation'.[3] A very few high-earning prostitutes managed to preserve their wealth, while others saved enough of their earnings to set themselves up as procurers or brothel-keepers. Many found their way back into conventional society. William Acton, an eminent doctor and writer on sexual health, shocked many of his readers in 1857 by considering that prostitution was 'a transitory state, through which an untold number of British women are ever on their passage'.[4] Like all professions, prostitution possessed a hierarchical structure. Writing in The Town at the start of the Victorian period, Renton Nicholson allocated theatre whores a 'second-class' position:

> they are looked down upon by the first-rate women who ride about in the carriages of noble protectors. Then the theatre-women think themselves degraded by comparison with those who do the excessively swellish on the pave. The dashing Cyprian who treads the aristocratic pavement of Regent Street by day scorns an alliance with those who do the same thing at night and the well-dressed street harlot looks with pitiable contempt upon the ragged, low-life characters.[5]

Not all prostitutes lived long enough to become 'Old Stock'. Illness, drugs and alcohol took a heavy toll. Although most deaths went unreported, the case of a 25-year-old woman who died in a workhouse in 1856 caused public outrage. It may have surprised Mayhew to learn that Louisa Regan had, in fact, been employed by a noble family as a governess. The daughter of an ex-proprietor of the Cyder Cellars, Louisa had received a good education but 'fell into bad habits, and latterly lived a very dissolute life'.[6] She had been homeless for two weeks when police sergeant Gentry discovered her slumped, close to the Cyder Cellars, in Brydges Street. It was a cold, wet morning and realising the seriousness of her condition the sergeant arranged for her to be conveyed to nearby King's College Hospital. After waiting for more than an hour she was refused treatment on the surprising grounds that she was ill. It was thought that that she might be suffering from tuberculosis, an infectious disease that the hospital had no facilities to treat. The police next took her by cab to the Strand Union Workhouse, Cleveland Street. Despite her 'very deplorable state', the workhouse staff made little effort to provide her with stimulants or nourishment. Eight hours after being found in the street she died in the sick ward, in the words of the Morning Chronicle, 'like a poisoned rat on a dung-heap'.[7] Both hospital and workhouse were severely criticised by a coroner's jury and by reports in a number of newspapers. Such passionate discussion of 'the great social evil' would temporarily reignite with successive suicides or murders, but would just as quickly subside until the next pitiful case occurred.

Many prostitutes were encountered in the public environment of theatres, music halls, dance rooms and taverns, but others waited for clients to seek them out in specific locations. During the early and mid-eighteenth century a large concentration of brothels was to be found in a network of ill-favoured streets running off the eastern end of the Strand close to Temple Bar. Shire Lane, 'a dingy, disreputable defile',[8] accommodated several 'houses of ill-fame'. It was in one of these in 1851 that a Birmingham businessman named Digby Anstice was robbed of £35 by a posse of prostitutes – Ann Mingay alias Lady Mansfield; Julia Divine alias Rosy Julia; Jane Owen alias Black Jenny; and Ellen Smith who alas had no alias.[9] Adjacent to Shire Lane was Newcastle Court, remembered by John Diprose in 1868:

> There might be seen in the broad glare of day, sitting at the parlour window of nearly every house, abandoned women, young and old, decked in tawdry finery, bloated with gin and debauchery, lavishing enticing smiles, and bandying obscene expressions to entice the unwary passer by. The scenes enacted by night were of the most horrible description and at last its abominable notoriety became so glaring, the public authorities were compelled to indict the occupants, which they did, and the vicious inhabitants were turned out; but only for some of them to remove their shocking mode of living to Wych Street. One of the frail sisterhood, whose magnitude of height and rotundity may be better conceived than described,

when we state that her weight was above twenty stones, bore the cognomen of 'The City Barge.'[10]

Shire Lane and Newcastle Court formed part of 'the Carey Street site', an area demolished in the mid 1860s to make way for the construction of the Royal Courts of Justice. The narrow alleys with overhanging upper stories only a few feet apart accommodated a population of some 3500 costermongers, prostitutes and 'an immense number of those parties who go about singing with black faces – "niggers" as they call themselves'.[11] With the levelling of the area, brothels became more widely dispersed, occupying various premises in the general vicinity of the Strand. In two months at the end of 1872 prosecutions were brought against the owners of three 'disorderly houses' that ostensibly functioned as coffee shops. The Library Coffee House, at 24 King William Street stood next to the Charing Cross Theatre, while the Britain Coffee House was close to Trafalgar Square at 2 Agar Street. At the other end of the Strand Colliver's Hotel and Coffee House, 26a Holywell Street, had been a brothel for 16 years and was observed to be visited by 70 prostitutes in a two-week period.[12]

A principal venue for meeting prostitutes was provided by the dance rooms or night houses that flourished from early in the century until the 1870s. Opposite the main entrance of the Theatre Royal, in Brydges Street (later to become part of Catherine Street), Mother Hoskins' or Mother H's, had a window filled with an enticing display of food. Inside, a grand dance and dining room extended back the depth of two houses to Charles Street (later Wellington Street). Mrs Hoskins, who ran the establishment during the 1820s, made a lasting impression on the young Renton Nicholson:

She was the ugliest woman I ever beheld; but she dearly loved paint, dress and decorations. Her attire was in the highest style of fashion, generally black velvet or satin, jewellery in profusion, silk stockings, and very neat kid shoes. She had rather a pretty foot and ankle.[13]

As at most night houses, the prices charged at Mother H's were high and sometimes dishonestly applied. In 1849 'J. R. Gr–n', a correspondent to the briefly resurrected The Town, complained that he, together with two male friends and two prostitutes they had picked up at the Haymarket Theatre, were charged £15 6s for food, drink and cigars. The bill, including 16 bottles of champagne, four bottles of sherry, five brandies and sodas, and three bottles of stout, was challenged, and after the intervention of a solicitor, was reduced to £6 5s 6d (for a modest nine bottles of champagne, three bottles of sherry, three brandies and soda and two bottles of stout). Mr 'Gr–n' considered that the final reckoning was still substantially more than he would have been charged by the finest tavern in London.[14]

Mother H's bad reputation was challenged by that of its neighbour, Jessop's, a former amateur theatre at 11 Catherine Street which was described in the 1840s as 'the most disgraceful and iniquitous night saloon in London'.[15] Much of the worst behaviour took place in the early hours of the morning when patrons were extremely drunk. At about 10.30 p.m. on the evening of Friday 28 July 1854, a 22-year-old clerk named Charles Douglas Nash met Eliza Graham, a prostitute, at Cremorne. They went on to a public house and then to Jessop's where Nash started gambling with 'a man of colour',[16] tossing coins for bottles of champagne. After helping to consume about 12 bottles the 'man of colour' left and another prostitute attempted to wrest Nash from Eliza's grasp. When the newcomer grew violent and abusive she was thrown out of the establishment. Eliza and Nash left Jessop's at around 5 a.m. only to encounter the hostile prostitute who resumed her assault. The young clerk was knocked to the ground, fracturing his skull. He died soon after in Charing Cross Hospital, the assault arousing only minimal coverage in the press.[17] Another violent altercation occurred four years later when, at 4.30 on a July morning, police found three prostitutes who had just left Jessop's screaming and fighting, cheered on by a circle of 'gentlemen'. Ann James, Elizabeth Williams and Jane Williams were brought before Mr Jardine at Bow Street Police Court. The magistrate was more disgusted by the problems that the night house created than by the conduct of the women:

> One can't help pitying them. They are tempted into these abominable places, which are kept open all night to encourage idle people to get drunk, and then they are set on to fight by these brutal men. They are liable to be sent to gaol, but I shall not punish them. They may go.

By the 1860s both Mother H's and Jessop's had closed and the main night houses patronised by prostitutes were the Argyle Rooms in Coventry Street, Piccadilly, and the Casino, High Holborn. As the social reformer Ewing Ritchie indicated, the area around the Theatre Royal and the Lyceum had lost much of its kerb appeal as better-class prostitutes moved to the more elegant surroundings of the Haymarket, Leicester Square and Regent Street:

> The West is the more fashionable quarter, and the glory of Catherine-street is fled. Almost every house you come to is a public-house or something worse. Here there is a free-and-easy after the theatres are over; there a lounge open all night for the entertainment of bullies and prostitutes, and pick-pockets and thieves, greenhorns from the country or London born; here a dancing saloon, which we are told in the advertisements no visitor should leave London without first seeing, and there a coffee house, where expelled from gayer places of resort, half intoxicated men and women take an early breakfast.[18]

'Old Stock' was becoming one of a vanishing breed when interviewed for Mayhew's great social study. During the early Victorian period it had been common for older women to be employed to trail prostitutes whose eye-catching clothes were supplied by a bawdy-house keeper. The disturbing vision of an attractive young 'dress lodger' followed by a ragged harbinger of her future decay was not unusual. Ewing Ritchie wrote:

> As you walk along the Strand any time in the afternoon and evening, have you not seen (to our shame it is said) a sight not visible in the chief thoroughfare of any other capital in Europe? The sight I allude to is that of girls, whose profession is but too evident from their appearance, stopping almost every man they meet, mildly, perhaps, in the early part of the evening – but, under the influence of drink, with greater rudeness and freedom as the night wears on. These girls, as you observe, are dressed in finery hired for the purpose; and following them, as a hawk its prey, you will perceive at a respectful distance old hags, always Jewesses, whose business it is to see that these girls do not escape with their fine dresses, and that they are active in their attempts to entrap young men void of understanding. Well, these women all live in the neighbourhood of Catherine-street.[19]

Sometimes the 'dress lodger' was held as a virtual slave in a brothel, working only for food and accommodation, but increasingly the arrangement became merely one of costume hire for which the wearer paid a large percentage of her earnings. Women became less likely to abscond with their rented dresses and the need for 'Old Stock' and her compatriots was greatly reduced.

The modus operandi of prostitution might have altered as the century progressed, but customers remained very much the same. 'Old Stock' was the parasitical appendage of a young prostitute who worked the Strand:

> We, that is me and Lizzie, the girl I'm watching, came out tonight at nine. It's twelve now, ain't it? Well; what do you think we've done? We have taken three men home, and Lizzie, who is a clever little devil, got two pounds five out of them for herself, which ain't bad at all. I shall get something when we get back. We ain't always so lucky. Some nights we go about and don't hook a soul. Lizzie paints a bit too much for decent young fellows who've got lots of money. They aren't our little game. We go in more for tradesmen, shop-boys, commercial travellers, and that sort, and men who are a little screwy, and although we mustn't mention it, we hooks a white choker [a clergyman] now and then, coming from Exeter Hall. Medical students are sweet on Lizzie, but we ain't in favour of the bar.[20]

Clearly not all punters were, as Ewing Ritchie suggested, 'young men void of understanding'.

In 1858 a curious case was heard at Bow Street Police Court in which a dress-lodger watcher, Hannah M'Carthy, was found guilty of attacking 'The Protean Witness', Henry G. Brooks. When 'Lord Chief Baron' Nicholson selected 'The Great Social Evil' as a subject for the Judge and Jury Society at the Cyder Cellars, the role of a dress-lodger watcher was allocated to Brooks. It was a convincing performance, bearing every sign of having been founded on an original model. Hannah M'Carthy was convinced that she was personally being held up to ridicule. At 9.30 on the evening of 2 May 1858 she took time off from her observational duties to castigate the comedian who was talking to a friend at the corner of the Strand and Wellington Street. She accused him of blackening her reputation by 'taking her off', and to emphasise the sincerity of her beliefs she became increasingly violent and abusive.

Eventually, she was arrested and taken to Bow Street Police Court where the magistrate sentenced her to a fine of 40s or one month's imprisonment. Called for the prosecution, the 'Lord Chief Baron' offered the somewhat tongue-in-cheek evidence that he had often been annoyed by women of the same 'degraded class'.

An evening spent with 'Baron' Nicholson and a subsequent encounter with a pair of 'soiled doves' was to lead to William Slater making an unexpected court appearance. On 24 January 1853, Slater had been to visit his old friend Francis Graham, the landlord of one of London's most ancient pubs, the Old Bell Tavern in Fleet Street. After a few drinks the pair went to the Coal Hole, arriving

ILLUSTRATION 13. Staged scene of a 'fast' young woman leaving a public house, c. 1862.

just in time for the summing up in a case: 'it was not something very indecent' remembered a clearly disappointed Graham. The friends had a jovial time, enjoying a supper washed down by glasses of stout. They were honoured when 'Lord Chief Baron' Nicholson condescended to take a glass of sherry with them. At about 2 a.m. they walked back along the Strand to Fleet Street. It was in the vicinity of Temple Bar that they met two prostitutes, Hannah Healy and Ann Jackson. The latter remembered Slater as a 'gent with specs' who caught her by the shawl and invited her to share a brandy and water. Slater and the ladies went into the Crown, 1 Crown Court, bidding farewell to Graham who had wisely decided not to join the party. Like many central London pubs, the Crown kept extremely late hours, catering to journalists and, according to its landlady, 'many women'.[21]

Hannah and Ann toasted their short-sighted, tipsy host. His thick watch-chain marked him out as a man of some substance, while a bulge in his waistcoat pocket indicated the presence of coins, possibly gold sovereigns. Taking a cab back to the Strand they visited one, two or possibly three more pubs. At one establishment, Ann remembered, Slater treated four ladies who were standing at the bar. Lapsing into unconsciousness in the carriage, he later felt that he been sedated by something put into one of his many drinks. When he eventually found his way home to Blackfriars Road at around 5 a.m., Slater discovered that £8 10s was missing from his pocket. Next day he complained to the police who arrested Hannah Healey in the Sun public house close to her home in Clements Lane, another of the Strand's disreputable tributaries. The trial of the two women at the Old Bailey was just the sort that the patrons of the Coal Hole would have relished, although Francis Graham understandably preferred the latter location: 'they do not listen to a dry trial as they do here', he told the judge, 'but have something to comfort them, and "the chief" baron had something to drink and a cigar'. Unconvinced that Slater had been drugged by anything other than a large amount of alcohol, the jury found Hannah and Ann not guilty. They were unaware that three years earlier Hannah had been convicted at Clerkenwell Assizes of stealing a handkerchief and ten gold sovereigns.[22]

The rich pickings that could be had by supplying upmarket prostitutes with luxury items was highlighted by an 1870 court case in which a Strand trader attempted to recover a debt from Kate

**ILLUSTRATION 14.** Mabel Grey and Kate Cooke.

Cooke, one of London's leading courtesans. Born in around 1842 in very poor circumstances, Kate became an equestrian performer in her teens, living for a time with a circus showman called Cooke. Tiring of his abusive behaviour, she married a commercial traveller,

George Manley Smith, in Glasgow in July 1863, only to be deserted after five months. The following year she arrived in London where she stayed in a brothel run by a Mrs White, in Sunderland Street, Pimlico. Within a few hours she had become indebted to Mrs Rosalie Bernstein, a widow who supplied the six women in the house with fashionable clothing to be paid for in instalments or by grateful customers. Mrs Bernstein kept a 'fancy shop' in the Strand patronised by prostitutes and men who wished to make their acquaintance. Naturally, a premium was added to any presents that gentlemen might purchase for the 'gay' women they were seeking to impress. There was soon no shortage of admirers to escort Kate to nightspots such as the Argyle Rooms, Cremorne and the Holborn Casino. Often Mrs Bernstein would tag along, no doubt bearing news of the latest fancy goods to be had at her Strand emporium.

Kate joined a select group of exclusive courtesans at a time when their influence on society was becoming a hotly debated issue. Their increasing celebrity status and well-publicised relationships with members of the nobility led to predictions of a decadent London meeting the same fate as its ancient counterparts, Babylon and Rome. Across the Channel, Paris provided a contemporary example of the consequences of moral degeneration. With the collapse of the Second Empire and the defeat of France by Germany in 1871, the attention paid to inhabitants of the demi-monde was regarded as a sure sign that if action was not taken Britain would soon suffer similar humiliation. It was not always easy for the 'Frail Sisterhood' to appreciate the delicacy of their position. Kate's close friend Mabel Grey was a young Irish shop girl-turned-*grande-horizontale* whose make-up, hair styles and fashionable clothes were emulated by a cosmopolitan public. But she caused outrage in 1869 when she threw a post-Derby banquet and ball at the St James's Hall, Piccadilly, for fellow prostitutes, accompanied by gentlemen who paid £10 for the privilege of escorting them. In the same year a version of the musical burlesque *Sandanapalus*, featuring Muriel, Kate Cooke and Nellie Clifton (perhaps the Irish prostitute who had been involved with the Prince of Wales in 1861), also met with widespread disapproval.

In July 1866 Kate found a wealthy patron to install her in her own home at 14 Victoria Grove, South Kensington. As bad luck would have it, her 'protector' died after only six weeks, leaving an unpaid furnishing bill with Mrs Bernstein that totalled several hundred pounds. The two women came to an understanding with Kate agreeing to pay £5 a week and a new gentleman friend contributing £364. Up until 1867 Kate appears to have made sure that Mrs Bernstein's excessive bills were regularly paid, either by herself, or more frequently, by her most recent lover. But soon after her friend and supplier married Charles Ochse, Kate's account began to move deeper into the red. Finally, Mr Ochse went to court in an attempt to recover £665 2s 4d for goods supplied during the period June 1867 to May 1869. Details from the account provide a vivid insight into the wardrobe of a successful Victorian courtesan:

> One pair of drawers trimmed with real lace, £1 12s; two chemises trimmed with real lace, £2 16s; six French under petticoats, 34s 6d; a satin petticoat, £8 8s; striped silk stockings, 21s; a morning wrapper, £4 10s; another morning wrapper, £16 18s; a real lace morning wrapper, £25; a velvet mantle, £25; a silk jacket, £25; a second silk jacket, £12 12s; a green satin dressing gown lined with silk, £15 15s; a violet velvet and satin costume, £29 8s; a pink and white costume, £10 10s; a velvet jacket trimmed with chinchilla, £35; a blue silk dress, £32; a black silk spangled fan, £1 10s; an opera cloak, £15 5s; two parasols, £3; and an ivory handled parasol, £6 10s.

The last expensive item prompted the judge to remark that 'unless it was a special parasol it would be rather dear'.[23]

Charles Ochse knew a thing or two about the avoidance of debt, for he had previously fled Paris to escape a two-year prison sentence imposed on him as a fraudulent bankrupt. Perhaps a lack of familiarity with English law had not prepared him for Kate's defence, that the goods had been supplied to enable her to follow a career as a prostitute. She was able to produce letters from Rosalie Ochse which clearly demonstrated an understanding of the means by which she would settle her bills:

> My dear, I really must seriously beg of you to let me have the £100 you promised me for certain at Christmas. I cannot wait any longer. I am sure if you ask the colonel he will give you it, if he did promise it to you.[24]

In the face of such evidence Mr Justice Blackburn ruled that 'if articles were furnished for the purpose of enabling a woman to carry on the avocation of a prostitute, the law would not assist the persons furnishing the goods'. Consequently, Kate left the court with her debt, if not her reputation, wiped clean. She was to find a fresh source of income later in the year when she met a young army officer with a title and a large fortune. During the next two decades Charles and Rosalie Ochse made many similar court appearances in usually futile attempts to retrieve money from wayward customers. On one such occasion they registered a claim of £1,148 on the estate of William Harry Vane Milbank, grandson of the Duke of Cleveland, who had bankrupted himself by 'protecting' Mabel Grey.

Although those supplying 'fancy goods' to 'fancy women' continued to make a lucrative, if precarious, living, another service industry found its profits in sharp decline. In 1872 the Licensing Act radically altered the milieu inhabited by prostitutes and their clients. Pubs and bars which had previously been free to set their own times were compelled to close by midnight or 12.30 a.m. and heavy fines were introduced for keeping a 'disorderly house'. The Act instructed:

> If any licensed person knowingly permits his premises to be the habitual resort of or place of meeting of reputed prostitutes, where the object of their so resorting or meeting is or is not prostitution, he shall, if he allows them to remain thereon longer than is necessary for the purpose of obtaining reasonable refreshment, be liable to a penalty not exceeding for the first offence ten pounds, and not exceeding for the second and any subsequent offence twenty pounds.

Soon after the Act was passed, the police raided The Lyceum Tavern, 354 Strand at 12.25 a.m. A number of customers found consuming champagne, oysters and chops were arrested and fined. The landlord, who claimed that he thought patrons were allowed to finish food and drink ordered before midnight, was severely admonished and dismissed, but with only a small penalty.[25]

A number of clubs were set up to fill the void created by the enforced closure of licensed premises, but the general effect of the act was to limit the numbers of people on the streets in the early hours of the morning. In 1892 the journalist and playwright, Joseph Hatton, remembered 'the good old days, before Mr Gladstone passed the Early Closing Bill':

> If you lived beyond the regions of Regent and Oxford Streets, and wended your way home at strange hours of the morning, your path

would be strewn with the wreckage of Music Hall and Finish, with 'rollicking rams' and 'Champagne Charlies,' with bedraggled silks and satins, with noisy fares in rickety cabs, and all the glories of the night's fun and frolic.[26]

After 1872, however, the crowds of fun-seekers in central London usually dispersed by 1 a.m. Some prostitutes found their way into 'cock and hen' clubs, but others were left looking for clients on sparsely populated streets. The social commentator Robert Blatchford described a conversation with two young prostitutes in the Strand during the 1890s. It was past midnight and heavy sleet was being driven on a penetrating wind. Alice, 17, and Marian, 20, were well dressed, but their thin shoes were no protection against a layer of freezing slush. Blatchford had been talking to a policeman at the corner of Wellington Street (where Hannah M'Carthy and Henry G. Brooks had had their altercation 30 years previously) when the elder of the women approached him in a familiar manner – calling him 'dearie' – and asked him what he was doing out so late. When he explained that he was about to go home, she whispered an explicit sexual proposition. He replied:

'My girls this is a bitter cold night and you both have bad coughs, and your feet are wet. Would you not be better in bed?'
The younger woman responded 'We can't go home without money. They wouldn't let us in.'
Marian added: 'I have a baby. It has no milk. I must have the rent and something for the baby. If I had a shilling, the woman would sell me some milk and a bit of coal.'
'Are you so very poor?'
'We are awfully hard up. We have been out in this weather since five this afternoon, and not got a penny but what you gave us. We were out till three last night.'
'It's hard times. The Strand last night had no one in it but policemen and girls. It was pitiful to see it.'
'Would you like to go home? If I give you both some money will you go home and stay there till morning?'
'We shall be very glad. You are very kind.'
'I knew you were kind. Marian said you had a stern face, and she was afraid to speak to you. But I knew you were kind.'
'You are a good man, aren't you?'[27]

# 6

# THE IMPORTANCE OF BEING ERNEST...
# AND FREDERICK

Musical burlesque, as presented at the Strand and Gaiety Theatres, was given a special dispensation to be naughty as long as it remained nice. It had an unofficial licence to prod and pick at Victorian sensibilities providing that no major discomfort or offence was caused. Such velvet glove satire was usually achieved by means of inversion and abasement. As with pantomime, appearances were not always what they seemed. Grand themes from an epic past were provided with commonplace and contemporary settings. Heroes and villains were presented as equally ridiculous and laughable. Traditional aspects of femininity and masculinity were subverted by actresses appearing as men and actors as women. Such a disruptive view of the world was amusing while confined to the stage, but when it migrated to the audience there was cause for serious concern. In 1870 fears of a social meltdown were prompted by the arrest of Ernest Bolton and Frederick Park after attending a performance at the Strand Theatre dressed in women's clothing. No less a figure than the Attorney-General predicted the possibility of a 'plague' of homosexuality which, 'if allowed to spread without check or hindrance, might lead to serious contamination of the public morals'.[1]

Stella and Fanny, as presented by Ernest and Frederick, were well known around town during the late 1860s. Wearing gaudy dresses and adorned with excessive amounts of powder and rouge, the 'sisters' were frequently seen at places of amusement such as the Argyle Rooms, Evans's Hotel, the Holborn Casino, Highbury Barn and Cremorne. Adopting the costumes and mannerisms of prostitutes, they promenaded the streets of central London winking at men and cooing to attract attention. A favourite resort was the Burlington Arcade where they cruised alongside a contingent of 'heavy-chignoned brief-skirted women [who] paraded themselves as the Western counterpart of an Eastern slave-market'.[2] With delicate features and curling dark hair, Ernest was every inch a languid Pre-Raphaelite beauty. Judging from surviving photographs Frederick was less comfortable in skirts, his upright stance and solemn expression conveying awkwardness and self-consciousness (or perhaps just awareness that he was the less pretty of the two).

Both came from middle-class homes. Ernest gave up his job as a clerk in a bank in January 1867 when he was in his late teens; Frederick was a law student articled to a respectable firm of solicitors. By 1867 Ernest had come to the notice of the police when wearing drag in Regent Street with an acquaintance named Martin Luther Cumming and, later, with another man known as 'Lady Jane Grey'. In the same year he and Cumming were arrested in the Haymarket after brawling with a group of prostitutes who considered that they were attempting to steal their customers. Soon Ernest and Frederick were at the centre of a like-minded group who frequently met and exchanged chatty, affectionate letters signed with feminine pseudonyms. Even when dressed in male attire Ernest and Frederick frequently caused offence. Their powdered faces and mincing gait marked them out as 'Mary-Anns', i.e., homosexuals, and their continual flirting with other men led to them being ejected several times from public buildings and arcades. At the Alhambra Music Hall, Leicester Square, they fell foul of a usually tolerant management on several occasions. In 1868 they were forced to leave after their appearance in drag had caused a disorderly scene, and soon after their apparently indecent behaviour, again in female costume, led to another expulsion. On many subsequent visits they attended in male evening dress, dress worn with such insouciance that some theatregoers took them to be women in men's clothing. Of a large group of apparently homosexual men who regularly attended the Alhambra, Ernest and Frederick were the worst behaved. Performers on stage must have considered them to be the audience from hell as they constantly sought to draw attention to themselves by waving to acquaintances, blowing kisses and leaning out of their private box to light cigarettes from wall-mounted gas lamps. It appears that they were frequently drunk, consuming large quantities of champagne and brandy and soda.

With an expensive lifestyle to maintain, Ernest must have been overjoyed to strike up a relationship with free-spending Lord Arthur Pelham-Clinton, third son of the Fifth Duke of Newcastle. Eight years older than Ernest, Lord Arthur had spent most of his life closeted in all-male institutions. From Eton College he had joined the Royal Navy, seeing active service during the Indian Mutiny while still a midshipman. After leaving the service as a lieutenant, he was elected to Westminster as MP for Newark. Lord Arthur was enchanted with his new young friend, lavishing presents on him and employing a hairdresser to visit him daily. By 1868 Arthur and Ernest were sharing rooms at 36 Southampton Street, Strand, where they played an elaborate game of 'husband' and 'wife'. Frederick was welcomed to their home as a slightly less vivacious, but more sagacious 'sister-in-law'. Not everyone joined in the conceit. When an impertinent servant charged Ernest with being a man, he apparently replied 'I am Lady Clinton, Lord Arthur's wife', an assertion that was supported by a wedding ring and crested visiting cards which announced him to be 'Lady Arthur Clinton'. It was to prove a short marriage for within a few months Lord Arthur was declared bankrupt with debts and liabilities amounting to a massive £70,000. Thereafter he and Ernest and Frederick went their separate ways.

Lord Arthur and Ernest not only played male and female roles in the privacy of their lodgings. They replicated their domestic arrangement onstage in two short sketches *A Morning Call* and *Love and Rain*. An appearance before a large London audience took place at the Egyptian Hall on 2 September 1868 when they participated in a show held on behalf of the famous ventriloquist, Frederick Maccabe, who was giving up his management of the famous Piccadilly theatre after a two-year tenancy. Their time and theatrical talent was given for free at Maccabe's benefit, but the following month they were paid nearly £30 for a three-day engagement at the Spa Saloon, Scarborough.

Theatrical appearances, whether amateur or professional, provided a convenient showcase for the exhibitionist tendencies of Ernest and several of his friends. Cumming, his Regent Street cruising partner, was said to be a talented actor, while another close acquaintance, Amos Westropp Gibbings, had gone to the expense of hiring St George's

Hall, Langham Place, to present his interpretation of Lady Teazle in Sheridan's *The School for Scandal*. In January 1869 Ernest lured Frederick onto the stage of the Theatre Royal, Stock, where they adopted the theatrical pseudonyms of Ernestine Edwards and Mabel Foster to appear in H. J. Byron's comedy *One Hundred Thousand Pounds*. During the performance 'Ernestine' charmed the audience with mezzo soprano renditions of the parlour ballads 'My Pretty Jane' and 'Fading Away':

> Rose of the garden,
> Blushing and gay,
> E'en as we pluck thee,
> Fading away!

Frederick dropped out of theatrical performances, leaving Ernest to embark on an extended tour partnered by the actor Charles James Pavitt. Their 'Drawing Room Entertainment' was presented in the spring and early summer of 1869 at public halls and small theatres throughout Essex. Commencing at the National School-Room, at Rayleigh, their programme usually consisted of 'a short opera, a humorous duologue and a laughable sketch', with Ernest, of course, playing all female roles. Along with honing Ernest's histrionic talent, the shows provided a welcome source of income, £35 being taken at the box office during a two-night stay in Bishop's Stortford. While touring in *A Morning Call*, *The Power of Gold* and various potted operas, Ernest seldom missed the opportunity of being photographed in the female costume he wore onstage.

The portrayal of women by men and men by women was not unusual on the Victorian stage. Occasionally, actresses like Charlotte Cushman and Sarah Bernhardt attempted serious masculine roles, but usually male impersonation had been an excuse for burlesque and music-hall performers to dress in a revealing, hybrid costume of stylised male jacket and well-padded tights. The *raison d'être* of actresses and singers such as Madame Vestris, Mrs Keeley, Nellie Farren, Nelly Power and Vesta Tilley had been to gently satirise masculine characteristics while eliciting admiration of their own feminine attractiveness. Male representations of women were more denigrating, usually confined to the old hags, vindictive harridans and avenging harpies so convincingly portrayed by 'The Protean Witness', Henry G. Brooks. The pantomime dame, whose bulbous and bibulous figure provided a template for much female

**ILLUSTRATION 15.** Unidentified male impersonator, possibly Nellie Power.

impersonation during the second half of the century, appears to have originated with a more considered performance. On 1 April 1861 the Strand Theatre presented a burlesque *Aladdin; or, the Wonderful*

*Scamp* in which James Rogers (1821–63) portrayed 'the miserable mother' in what was described as 'a very artistic and amusing performance, without being carried beyond the proper bounds of travestie'.[3] The Aladdin to Jimmy Roger's Widow Twankay (to become Twankey in later pantomimes) was a truly wonderful scamp being played in fetching silk trousers by Marie Wilton.

Ernest troubled some members of the audience because he attempted to give an impersonation of a female rather than appearing as a female impersonator. Although attracted by the exaggerated characteristics displayed by prostitutes, he aimed in his stage roles to create a convincing impression, rather than a grotesque caricature, of femininity. From its first production at the Theatre Royal, Drury Lane, in 1851, the role of Fanny Chillingtone in George Dance's one-act comedy *A Morning Call* had, understandably, been played by an actress. Part of the humour of the piece, in which a male and a female character battle for sexual supremacy, was an episode in which both adopt elements of the other's clothing:

> Sir E. Good; I am the slave of the ring, ready to obey you in all things. I entreat you make trial of your power.
> Mrs C. You shall be indulged. Fetch my bonnet and shawl (*he goes for them*) and while you are about it, bring your own hat. (*he returns with them.*) Now put that on. (*he is about to put on his hat.*) No, no, put on my bonnet.
> Sir E. Not your bonnet!
> Mrs C. Yes, and shawl. (*he puts on the bonnet and shawl.*) Good, now give me your hat. (*he gives it to her.*)
> Sir E. What next, I wonder.
> Mrs C. Now, Sir, according to your own modest account, ladies have been making love to you all your life. I am curious to see how a lady looks when she so demeans herself; (*putting on his hat*) fancy me the fascinating man, which you evidently fancy yourself. Down on your knees, and – I leave the rest to you.

The spectacle of a man playing a woman dressing as a man proved distasteful to at least one critic. Writing of Ernest's Egyptian Hall appearance, *The Era* commented:

> As may be imagined, this was a strange performance, and a dramatic vagary that altogether defies criticism. Mr Boulton's make-up was perfect, and though it is, perhaps, not particularly complimentary to

say that he looked astonishingly like a 'fine lady', it is the simple truth. There is an inevitable unpleasantness in any attempt of this kind when burlesque does not furnish the excuse, but at the same time as a piece of acting Mr Boulton's Mrs Chillingtone was by no means bad.[4]

Although stage appearances seem to have dried up later in 1869, Ernest and Frederick's theatrical performances continued from the other side of the footlights. In their frequent visits to theatres and music halls they invariably attracted attention to themselves to the detriment of stage performers. Pursuing a life of abandon, gay or otherwise, they came increasingly under police surveillance. When they appeared in drag, it was considered that they were either practising homosexuals looking to recruit others or were blackmailers conniving to entrap straight men. They were considered a public nuisance, but within a society that tolerated widespread episodes of violent 'lark', 'freak' and 'frolic', their provocative antics were not sufficient to mark them out as a major cause for concern. On 6 April 1870 they hired a carriage to take them, dressed as women, to Hammersmith, West London, to watch the University Boat Race. Unfortunately, the bridge was too congested for their vehicle to park and there were no other suitable vantage points from which they might be seen and admired by the crowds. After stopping at a pub and a confectioner's shop, they continued on to Haxell's Hotel in the Strand (scene of the infamous clergymen's boot swapping incident) where they were to attend a ball the following evening.

Haxell's Royal Exeter Hotel was a plain-fronted, matronly building which enfolded the entrance to Exeter Hall in its capacious wings. The private ball, which started at 9.30 p.m., was a routine sort of event for Ernest and Frederick. They appeared in drag with four other men, joining seven women and 35 men in conventional evening dress. Their host, 22-year-old Amos Gibbings otherwise known as Charlotte, wore a mauve silk dress. After a good many bottles of champagne had been consumed, a woman fainted and had to be revived by someone said to be connected to the medical profession. One of the men dressed as a woman slapped a 'gentleman's' face when he asked Miss Agnes Erle (a real woman) for her address. Ernest, wearing a white silk ball gown trimmed with pink roses, sung his favourite ballad 'Fading Away' – several times. Perhaps it was Stella's repeated performances which necessitated the cancellation of a number of the 20 planned dances, a move which led to several tipsy men mounting a noisy protest. Finally drawing to a close at 3.30 a.m., the event so pleased Charlotte that he thought he might hold another the following month.

Ernest and Frederick attended the theatre several times during the month. On Friday, 22 April, they travelled across the Thames to the famous 'transpontine' Royal Surrey Theatre, Blackfriars Road, where Charles H. Ross's *Clam* had just opened. Billed as a 'romantic Drama of London Life, depicting many favourite resorts',[5] the production featured a cross-dressing actress as its eponymous heroine. Agnes Burdett played Josephine Weatherwell, a young woman forced by complex circumstances to masquerade as a teenage boy. Assuming the nickname Clam, she wore tattered clothes to become the leader of a gang of street urchins, also appearing in midshipman's uniform in a scene set at Cremorne. While watching the play, Ernest and Frederick who were dressed in their own colourful interpretation of male attire struck up a conversation with a 23-year-old solicitor named Hugh Alexander Mundell. If an illustration in *The Days' Doings* is an accurate portrayal, Hugh was a pedigree 'Jolly Dog', resplendent in top hat, high starched collar, monocle and shaggy 'Dundreary' side whiskers.[6] After observing them for some time, he expressed his interest to the actor Boothroyd Fairclough: 'Come into the dress circle and see two women who are dressed as men. It's a great make up and worth seeing.'[7] Ernest, Frederick, Boothroyd, Walter and the theatre's stage manager Mr Ross chatted for some time, after which the party visited the backstage area. Delighted to be the centre of such attention, Ernest and Frederick went onstage, mingling with the crowd of merrymakers in the Cremorne scene. At the play's conclusion Ernest, Frederick and the besotted Hugh walked across Waterloo Bridge, a painted backcloth of which had featured in the production. Ernest and Frederic maintained they were men, but Hugh was not convinced. After arranging to see *Clam* again the following Tuesday Hugh told them: 'I thought you were women dressed in men's clothes.' Then, with a helping hint on manly deportment, he added: 'When you walk you should swing your arms to look more like men.'

When Hugh Mundell returned to the Surrey Theatre the following week his suspicions were seemingly confirmed. This time two ladies, with a male guest, were there to greet him and accept the roses he proffered. After watching the play from a private box they drove in a brougham to the Globe Supper Rooms in Coventry Street, near Piccadilly Circus. When the gentlemen were dropped, Stella and Fanny went on to visit three public houses, each time treating their driver to a glass of ale. Earlier in the evening Stella had slipped Hugh a mysterious envelope which contained the disturbing message that the ladies were still men.

Either an eternal optimist or, like Osgood Fielding III in *Some Like it Hot*, an advocate of the 'no one's perfect' philosophy, Hugh continued to socialise with his fascinating new friends. On Thursday, 28 April he called at Frederick's lodgings at 13 Bruton Street, Berkeley Square. During a fun-filled afternoon during which Ernest sung and played the piano, they decided to visit a burlesque *Sir George and a Dragon* at the Strand Theatre. To prepare for the evening Ernest and Frederick went to 13 Wakefield Street, Regent Square, where they stored many of their female clothes. Ernest elected to wear a cherry-coloured, silk evening dress, with bare shoulders and arms complemented by several items of flashy jewellery, while Frederick selected a low-cut, green satin dress with white kid gloves. As they stepped into the cab taking them to the theatre, they were unaware of a police detective William Chamberlain watching from nearby. He had had his eye on them for some time.

*Sir George and a Dragon* by F. C. Burnand was a typical Strand burlesque. Sir George was portrayed by the music-hall singer Lizzie Dashwood, while other male characters were also played by women. *The Examiner* noted that:

> the heroes themselves are represented by a band of very charming young ladies, whose faces and limbs are models of beauty and symmetry; that the very small quantity of clothing they wear is extremely becoming; that they sing and dance to perfection.[8]

In past years a major feature of the Strand burlesques had been the female impersonations of its actor-manager Jimmy Rogers. He had been dead for some years, but a talented newcomer, Edward Terry, had stepped into his feminine footwear. In *Sir George and a Dragon* his playing of the sorceress Kalyba was extremely well received, *Reynolds's Newspaper* commenting: 'his "get up" is marvellous, and till the deep tones of a masculine voice dispel the illusion, the deception of sex is perfect.'[9]

**ILLUSTRATION 16.** Unidentified female impersonator, probably Edward Terry.

As usual, the presence of Stella and Fanny in their private box, accompanied by Hugh and their friend Cecil 'Sissy' Thomas, distracted some members of the audience. It was difficult not to be noticed as, according to John Hollinshead, the theatre was 'a stuffy little house in which its audience and the actors could almost shake hands across the footlights'.[10] Detective Chamberlain positioned himself in a refreshment bar where he observed the cross-dressing suspects drinking brandies. Towards the end of the performance, at around 10 p.m., Superintendent James Thomson arrived at the theatre where he witnessed Stella sitting with her back to the stage, waving a fan and nodding to gentlemen in the stalls. The police closed in as the group left the theatre and hailed a cab. As they got into the vehicle Sergeant Frederick Kerley entered with them, causing the alert Thomas to leap out, quickly losing himself in the crowd. The remaining three men were arrested inside the cab and, rather than conveying them on their anticipated tour of London's nightspots, it took them directly to Bow Street Police Station. Frederick blustered to Sergeant Kerley that he might as well release them as no charge would be made. Ernest, who at first gave his name as Cecil Graham, appeared to be more desperate. He offered the sergeant 'any amount of money' to let them go. Any fears that either man might have harboured were soon to prove horribly justified.

The establishment had finally run out of patience with Ernest and Frederick. Mindful of the British public's 'periodic fits of morality', the police decided that the pair should feel the full force of the law; their ultimate punishment intended to discourage similarly minded individuals. Following a night in the cells they were brought – still wearing their costumes from the night before – for a preliminary hearing before the magistrate Mr Flowers at Bow Street Police Court. Hugh, who appeared to be more of a dupe than duplicitous, was released on bail, but the case against Ernest and Frederick was considered serious enough for them to be remanded in custody. Initially, they were charged under the Vagrancy Act with frequenting the Strand Theatre with intent to commit a felony. Later, the indictment was altered to: 'did with each other and one another feloniously commit the abominable crime of buggery,'[11] a crime that until 1861 had carried the death penalty. They were further charged with conspiring with other persons to commit buggery; with inducing and inciting other persons to commit buggery; and by disguising themselves as women to 'openly and scandalously outrage public decency and corrupt public morals'.[12] It appears that police action had caused the 'outrage' to be continued into the first court appearance. When Amos Gibbings arrived at Bow Street carrying

male clothing for the defendants to change into he was turned away.
As it was, Ernest and Frederick were compelled to make the crossing
from the police station to the court in their dishevelled dresses, their
progress rendered painfully slow by a jeering, jostling mob.

Back in the station they were subjected to a humiliating and
unlawful medical examination conducted by a police surgeon, Dr
James T. Paul. Forced to remove all their clothes, including stockings
and ladies' drawers, they were instructed to lay naked across a wooden
stool. Paul considered Ernest's anus to be dilated, its weak muscles
indicating that he was a practising homosexual. The same verdict was
delivered on Frederick with the addition that extensive discolouration
indicated a recent syphilitic sore. The 'abnormal' size of Ernest's penis
was also taken by Paul to be a sure sign of homosexuality.

Back in Bow Street Police Court on 6 May, Hugh Mundell's status
was changed from defendant to witness. In a hearing that continued
throughout May, details of Ernest and Frederick's lifestyle, their
friendships with other men, and their Wakefield Street hideaway –
stuffed with woman's clothing, cosmetics, photographs and personal
correspondence – were revealed to the court and to the wider world.
Inevitably, others were implicated and warrants were issued for the
arrest of six men, including Martin Luther Cumming, Cecil Thomas
and Lord Arthur Pelham-Clinton. The crowds who besieged the court
to gain a glimpse of the accused pair were not universally hostile.
Interspersing the howls of abuse, there were frequently bursts of
applause from courageous or foolhardy supporters. Applications for
admission to the court room so far exceeded its limited capacity
that the manager of an unnamed Strand theatre ironically suggested
that another row of stalls should be added, with seats bookable a
fortnight in advance.[13]

Public interest in the case was catered for by a plethora of cheap
literature such as The Unnatural History and Petticoat Mystery of Boulton and
Park, a penny pamphlet published at 5 Houghton Street, Strand, and
'The Funny He-She Ladies' a comic song issued from the London
home of broadside ballads, Seven Dials, Charing Cross:

> At Wakefield Street, near Regent Square,
> There lived this rummy he-she pair,
> And such a stock of togs was there,
> To suit those he-she ladies.

There was bonnets & shawls, and pork pie hats,
Chignons and paints, and Jenny Lind caps,
False calves and drawers, to come out slap,
To tog them out, it is a fact.

This pair of ducks could caper and prance,
At the Casino they could dance,
Ogle the swells and parle vou France,
Could the pair of he-she ladies.
They'd sip their wine and take their ice,
And so complete was their disguise,
They would suck Old Nick in and no flys,
Would the beautiful he-she ladies.

A poetic effusion of a more literate, but coarser nature appeared
in a pornographic magazine, *The Pearl*:

There was an old person of Sark
Who buggered a pig in the dark;
The swine in surprise
Murmored: 'God blast your eyes,
Do you take me for Boulton and Park?'[14]

It soon became apparent that the police and the attorney-general
had dug themselves into a deep, unsavoury hole. What had originated in a straightforward attempt to slap the limp wrists of a couple of Mary-Anns had now become a test of the moral fibre of the
nation's manhood. If it was feared that an unchecked Ernest, Frederick and their circle of friends would rapidly spread the 'blight'
of homosexuality, it must follow that there were many receptive
men ready to become 'infected'. With no major conflicts since the
Crimean War and the Indian Mutiny back in the 1850s, a concern
was often expressed that the younger generation was manifesting
signs of softness, even effeminacy. With antagonistic foreign nations
and resentful British colonies closely following the case, was it really
wise to suggest that homosexuality was such a danger?

In July 1870 the attorney-general withdrew the charges of
buggery and after two months in prison Ernest and Frederick
were released on bail. The trial was postponed, leaving three of the
accused sufficient time to find hiding places away from the not-too-
rigorous reach of the police. Soon after receiving the warrant for his
arrest, Sir Arthur Pelham-Clinton was reported to have died from

exhaustion following an attack of scarlet fever. There were many who thought that he had done the honourable thing and committed suicide; others considered that his death was a hoax and that he had removed himself to one of the Empire's further flung outposts. Whether the result of fatality or flight, Sir Arthur's disappearance further lessened the potential for an extended courtroom drama.

With all the trappings of a state trial, the case against Ernest, Frederick, John Safford Fiske and Louis Charles Hurte was finally heard in the ancient Court of Queen's Bench on 9 May 1871. Fanny and Stella had been banished, their existence only acknowledged by the extravagant floral buttonholes worn by Ernest, now sporting a slight moustache, and Frederick, who had grown whiskers and become rather stout. Located in a corner of the medieval Westminster Hall, the courtroom must have seemed intimidating to the defendants. But it rapidly became obvious that they had little to fear from a crown prosecution that was ill-prepared and half-hearted. Having dropped the charge of buggery, the attorney-general now had to convince the jury that the accused had conspired to indulge in buggery or had attempted to persuade others to commit the crime. He was at pains to point out that the act of wearing female clothes was not in itself a manifestation of homosexuality:

> It is fair to them to remember that they frequently acted the parts of women in private theatricals, and he need not say that to assume a woman's dress for that purpose was no offence whatsoever. Nay, even if it went further – if, being possessed of female dress for the purpose of acting, they had indulged in frolic or masquerade in the streets in female attire, and that was all, that would not make them amenable to such a charge as the present.[15]

The police's attempt to establish signs of anal sex was severely criticised by the judge, Lord Chief Justice Sir Alexander Cockburn. He warned Dr Paul that being a police surgeon did not entitle him to take the law into his own hands. He might find himself in 'very unpleasant circumstances' if he continued to act in such a careless way: 'You had no more authority to call upon these young men to undergo this revolting examination than if you had sought a man in the street and asked him to unbutton his breeches.'[16] Dr Paul also found his medical judgement under fire from several medical experts who completely refuted the findings of his illegal examinations.

Other witnesses for the prosecution were similarly ineffective. Hugh Mundell insisted that Ernest and Frederick had behaved in a proper fashion and that it was he who had made uninvited advances to them. A beadle, George Smith, who testified to their improper behaviour in the Burlington Arcade, was shown to be a drunkard who accepted bribes from prostitutes. And various police officers who had been stalking the defendants for at least a year could testify to nothing more than rowdy behaviour and cross-dressing. Frederick's lawyer Sergeant Parry argued that the wearing of women's clothes was merely a joke in poor taste, utilising costumes procured for theatrical performances:

> In former times these characters were always performed by a man; yet it was a remarkable fact that in the immoral reign of Charles II, when this was frequent, no immorality appeared to have attached itself to the practice. That young men had performed female characters in many towns, openly and were actually invited to parties after the performances, and desired to retain their female costume. Nay, the practice of men performing female characters prevailed at this moment upon the stage, even with the sanction of the Lord Chancellor. The things were done, and, if so, why should guilt be inferred against these young men because they did so?[17]

The witnesses for the defence proved more persuasive, the most effective being Ernest's mother who had been carefully schooled by the solicitor, George Lewis. Her performance as a caring mother fully aware of her son's unusual interests was as good as any given by Ernest. With this 'Angel in the House' reassuring the jury that Ernest's idiosyncrasies were merely a boyish quest for admiration, the fear of an impending moral plague began to recede. Sensing the likelihood of an acquittal, the Lord Chief Justice was able to place the cause of justice over concerns about international disgrace in his summing up:

> In the eloquent speech of my learned brother, Sergeant Parry, a speech which addressed itself with manly energy, with all the simple beauty of real genuine oratory [...] there was one observation in which I could not concur – that part in which he asked you to be careful how you convicted the defendants lest you should cast a stain upon the national character. I agree in the remark of the Attorney-General upon that observation – that it would be fatal to the character of this country if guilt, when detected and proved, were allowed to pass unpunished. The first and the greatest attribute

of a great nation is its moral character, and the next, even if it be not
of co-equal importance, or indeed, involved in the former, is the
regard for truth and justice. If you are satisfied of the guilt of these
persons pronounce it; be not afraid of the consequences.[18]

It took the jury only 53 minutes to find the defendants not guilty.
When the verdict was announced Ernest, forgetting his new-
found masculinity, swooned like the heroine of a melodrama.
Outside the court the crowds cheered, relieved no doubt that after
a close examination the stain upon the national character had been
scrubbed clean. It was an obdurate blot, however, reappearing on
several occasions to embarrass Victorian society.

In 1884 newspaper allegations were made that homosexual
practices were widespread at Dublin Castle, the seat of British
Government in Ireland. After failing to win a libel case the secretary
of the Irish General Post Office, Gustave Coventry, was charged with
sodomy, but acquitted. Seven years later, in 1889, an investigation
into the extra-mural earnings of a number of London post office
telegraph messengers resulted in a raid on a male brothel in Cleveland
Street, a shabby area to the north of Oxford Street. The Prince of
Wales' Assistant Equerry Lord Arthur Somerset was revealed as one
of the establishment's aristocratic patrons, with veiled suggestions
that Queen Victoria's grandson Prince Albert Victor, the Duke of
Clarence, was also involved. In 1895 the prosecution of Oscar Wilde
demonstrated that the homosexual underworld was still very much
active. By the mid 1880s sexual relationships between men had
become more hazardous than at the time of Ernest and Frederick's
trial. A last minute clause inserted into the 1885 Criminal Law
Amendment Act by Henry Labouchere made any acts of indecency
between males, even those performed in private by consenting
adults, serious criminal offences.

The names of Boulton and Park were invariably evoked at each
breaking scandal, despite being exonerated of any crime. The
notoriety which kept them together before the trial appears to have
forced them apart after their legal ordeal. Frederick broke away from
his overshadowing friend to start a new life in the United States where
he appeared as Fred Fenton, comedian and female impersonator.
His death in 1881 was probably caused by syphilis. Ernest took
another partner, Louis Munro, and continued to tour theatres and
concert halls in old roles and new dresses. When Louis left, Ernest's

brother Gerald was recruited to play the male lead in drawing room 'comediettas' such as *My New Housekeeper* and *Complications*. They remained together until Ernest's death in 1903, changing their stage name from Boulton to Byne and finally to Blair.

In his *Fanny and Stella; the Young Men Who Shocked Victorian England*, Neil McKenna speculates that Oscar Wilde might have made an oblique reference to Boulton in his play *Lady Windermere's Fan*. The characters in the 1892 comedy include an acerbic dandy called 'Cecil Graham', the same name that Ernest gave to Inspector Thompson when arrested at the Strand Theatre (Frederick also sometimes presented himself as Fanny Winifred Graham). It is an intriguing theory, for Wilde could easily have come across Ernest on his excursions into the gay London underworld. Had he not encountered either Ernest or Frederick in the flesh, he would probably have read about their real or fictionalised exploits in a pornographic novel, *The Sins of the Cities of the Plains*, published in 1881.[19] Wilde might also have chosen to celebrate Ernest in his most famous play *The Importance of Being Earnest*. It has often been asserted that 'earnest' was Victorian slang for homosexual. If so, had the term come into use because of Ernest Boulton's fame? Or was Wilde merely paying homage to one of the best known 'uranistes' of the time?

There are further curious twists to the plot. As well as being Wilde's fictional creation and Ernest's hurriedly adopted alias, Cecil Graham was the name of a musically inclined young homosexual summoned from London to Dublin to give evidence in the Coventry trial of 1884. Still more curious is that Cecil Graham was joined in the witness stand by Jack Saul who had earlier described having sex with both Ernest (on a piano stool) and Frederick in *The Sins of the Cities of the Plains*. Frederick had been long dead by the time Wilde's *The Importance of Being Earnest* came to be written, but the plot dictated that the central character should be called both 'Jack' and 'Ernest'. The former name was condemned as being 'more than usually plain',[20] while the latter was 'divine' with 'a music of its own'.[21] At one point in the play the fearsome Lady Bracknell declares, 'I feel bound to tell you that you are not on my list of eligible young men, although I have the same list as the dear Duchess of Bolton'.

# 7

# SAM AND MAUD

When George Samuel Cooke met Maud Merton in the Strand in 1891, he had not lived in London for long enough to lose his soft East Anglian accent. He had spent his early adult years as an agricultural labourer and as a fisherman, eventually leaving the open farmlands and stormy North Sea to seek his fortune in the capital. His robust physique and congenial personality marked him out as an ideal candidate when he enlisted in the Metropolitan Police Force in June 1888. Twenty-year-old Maud Merton had just embarked on a very different type of career when she first encountered Sam in Brewers Lane, a narrow alley running alongside Charing Cross Station. She had quit her job as a barmaid and was working as a prostitute. It was inevitable that policemen and prostitutes grew to know each other as they pursued their business in the streets. Both had regular 'beats' which often ran in parallel or overlapped. Prostitution was tolerated as long as it did not become an overt nuisance, the police often co-operating with 'women of the town' for financial or sexual rewards. It seems likely that Sam Cooke and Maud Merton were not the only members of their respective professions to embark on a long-term relationship. Theirs, however, was the only such affair to end in complete tragedy.

Sam was born in 1866, the only son of a farm bailiff. By his early teens he was working with his father at Hill Farm, Depwade, on the Norfolk/Suffolk border, but after a few years he decided to try his luck as a fisherman sailing out of Yarmouth with the hope of one day acquiring his own boat. During three years at sea he suffered a number of mishaps, the worst being when he was washed overboard and rescued unconscious from the waves. At the age of 22 he joined L Division of the Metropolitan Police based in

Lambeth, transferring after six months to A Division, where he was assigned to duties at the House of Commons. After two years at Westminster, he was posted to Bow Street from where E Division had the doubtful honour of maintaining law and order in central London. He proved himself to be an exemplary constable: steady and sober with a special aptitude for regulating street traffic. Of the 100 police officers billeted at the Bow Street Section House, Sam was one of the best. Maud's background was more obscure. She told Sam that her mother lived in Finchley or Holloway, North London, and that she had worked as a barmaid at the Clarence public house in the same area. A landlady received a different story. Her father had been murdered, her mother was dead and she had worked at the Peacock in Islington, until becoming pregnant by the manager.[1]

It is possible that Sam's intentions towards Maud were relatively honourable, given that he was physically attracted to her. He may have felt that it was possible to divert her from the way of life that she had started to lead. If he had such hopes of reclamation, he was soon to be disappointed for even as their affair developed she continued to see other men. By the beginning of 1892 he had often visited her at her lodgings in Quin Square, Waterloo Road, Lambeth. Conveniently situated on the south side of Waterloo Bridge, the area provided accommodation for hundreds, if not thousands, of prostitutes who commuted to work in central London. Over the next few months Maud moved several times within Lambeth, changing not only her address but her name, from Merton to Croucher, then Smith and finally to Cooke. At 13 College Street, Sam and Maud paid a weekly rent of 6s for a furnished room, their landlady, Emma Felmore, remembering a strained and violent relationship:

> The quarrels were very frequent and would last a considerable time, and there was loud talking – I could hear it all. I was in the next room. I did not hear both voices. She would not answer – he used to want her to answer him, and she would not – there would be a dreadful noise as if he was pushing her about the place.[2]

Sam appears to have become jealous and exasperated, beating her when another constable said that he had seen her 'larking about in the Strand'. Their destructive affair reached crisis point in April 1893 when Maud presented herself at Bow Street Police Station. For a known prostitute to make a complaint against a police constable

**ILLUSTRATION 17.** Approached through an archway from the Strand, Brewers Lane was a haunt of sandwich board men and prostitutes. Illustration from *The Graphic*, 1894.

was a brave, but foolhardy action. She insisted on making a statement that implied Sam had lived off her earnings:

> I, Maud Merton, alias Cooke, of no. 8 Tenison Street, York Road, Lambeth, have known Police Constable 130E George Samuel Cooke for the last year and ten months. I first became acquainted with him when he was in Brewers Lane, Strand. I had been on the street then as a prostitute for three or four weeks. He frequently came to me

when I resided at 168, Quin Square, Waterloo, and at 24 Stangate Street, Lambeth, where I passed as Mrs Cooke, and in October last he has stayed at the latter address with me; I kept him. He was on annual leave, and passed off as a waiter. He has often struck me, and one night he caught hold of me in Southampton Street and shook me by the throat. That would be about Christmas. Since then he came to my lodging, 13 College Street, and beat me, but for what I don't know. I left that lodging shortly after because I was ashamed to stay there through him. Last Thursday, the 20th, he came to my lodging and took away all my letters from my box, and my key. I met him in the Strand yesterday afternoon and asked him for it; he refused to give it me. I then came to Bow Street and complained of his conduct, but I refused to give his name and number. He knows I am a prostitute walking the Strand for my living.[3]

Despite an allegation which would normally have resulted in him being dismissed from the service, Sam was considered to be such an excellent officer that he was treated with leniency. He was suspended from duty for a week and then reassigned to the less prestigious X Division operating out of Notting Dale Police Station, West London. It was a move calculated to extricate Sam from Maud's supposedly bad influence. At the same time as Sam's exile to the drab, poverty-stricken streets of North Kensington, the police attempted to rescue Maud from her life of prostitution. A sub-commissioner found her respectable lodgings and arranged for her to receive a payment of 15s a week until suitable employment might be found. Within a short time she was back at Bow Street Police Station drunk and disorderly and charged with importuning men in the Strand. In court Maud successfully pleaded for another chance. A missionary promised to find her a place in 'a home' and she was discharged.

The attempts to bring about a lasting separation between Sam and Maud were unsuccessful. Over the next few weeks they continued to meet, although their relationship was as ill-tempered as ever. For some reason she was infuriated when he gave his (not her) address to her former lover, Corporal Edward Atkins of the 4th Dragoon Guards. A few nights later she was again irate when she found a letter from another woman in Sam's pocket. In the short time he had been based in North Kensington he had met a local maid servant and become engaged to be married.

At 8 o'clock on the evening of 6 June 1893, Maud arrived at Notting Dale Police State, asking where she might find Sam. She was respectably dressed in dark clothes, with kid gloves and an umbrella. It was approaching midnight when she finally caught up with PC X365 close to the prison situated on the edge of the vast, featureless common known as Wormwood Scrubs. Sam's heart sunk as she approached him. As usual they argued:

'What are you doing here?'
'I am going to stop here until you are off duty.'
'There will be another policeman here directly.'
'I should like to see him. I would tell him something.'
'You clear off.'
'I shall not.'

He broke away, walking onto the open expanse of the Scrubs. She followed him into the darkness, intent on pursuing their endless quarrel. As she approached Sam took his truncheon from his pocket and slipped it into his tunic sleeve.

'Are you going?'
'No, I am going to stop and annoy you till Sunday and then you can fuck yourself.'[4]

They were Maud's last words. Removing the hidden truncheon, Sam struck her violently on the side of the head. As she lay on the grass he hit her several more times. Then he placed his muddied boot on her throat and held it there until her pained gurgling subsided. Although he initially denied the murder, he later confessed: 'I thought nothing of killing her. I have been much happier since she has been dead than I was before. She was always annoying me and I was in misery.'

At his trial Sam shocked spectators by adopting a casual approach to the proceedings. He had faced death before and awaited his fate with good-humoured resignation. Although a guilty verdict was inevitable, there was an outside chance that his life might be saved. But despite the jury's recommendation of clemency, the judge imposed a capital sentence. A large section of the press and general public felt that Sam had been provoked beyond the point of self-control. Petitions calling for mercy were delivered to the Home Secretary, the future Prime Minister Herbert Asquith, including one from Yarmouth bearing 11,000 signatures. His unnamed fiancée spoke of his gentlemanly character: 'he always acted as a true man towards me, being kind and considerate, never seeking to take the slightest liberty in any way'.[5] When Asquith rejected all appeals she wrote to her last hope, Queen Victoria:

> May it please your Majesty. I have learnt last night the awful news that my sweetheart Constable George Samuel Cooke, who was to be my husband in October next, has to suffer the extreme penalty of the law on Tuesday morning. Both the Coroners and the Old Bailey Jury recommended him strongly to your Most Gracious Majesty's mercy, and I now, in my despair, approach the throne. I know your Majesty has a heart for the sufferings of your humblest subject. I therefore beg, even now at the last moment, to ask your Most Gracious Majesty's interception on behalf of the man I plighted my troth to. Think, your Majesty, of the happiness of your beloved grandson, whose marriage with the Princess May gladdened my heart as well as that of the entire nation, but joy in my case has given way to the darkest of sorrow, sorrows so overwhelming that I scarcely know what I do, sorrow which has even taken the liberty of appealing to your Most Gracious Majesty on behalf of my wretched lover in Newgate. I beseech your Most Gracious Majesty to spare his life and save an unhappy girl from destruction.[6]

It was not a good time to be pleading for the life of a policeman convicted of murder. Since the creation of the Metropolitan Police Force in 1829 the inappropriate conduct of the constabulary had been continually criticised and lampooned. They were said to spend an inordinate amount of time chatting to female servants; they solicited gifts of food and drink; and they were willing, for a small 'consideration', to turn a blind eye to criminal activities. A widespread belief that they robbed intoxicated gentlemen of their gold pocket watches provided the inspiration for the music-hall song, 'If You Want to Know the Time, Ask a Policeman'. More seriously, there had been a humiliating failure to capture the Whitechapel murderer and disturbing rumours of institutional corruption. Although Sam's victim was a common prostitute, concern about the reputation of the police force militated against his reprieve.

At 10 o'clock on the evening of 24 July 1893, Sam went to bed in the condemned cell at Newgate Prison. He slept fitfully and ate little of a breakfast of bread and eggs. After thanking the warders for their consideration he was led briskly to the adjacent scaffold. Taking his height and weight into account the public executioner allowed a drop of six feet three inches which ensured that Sam's death, unlike Maud's, was instantaneous. Outside Newgate a crowd of several thousand people of all classes had gathered as the execution time approached. At 9 a.m. the traditional bell was rung to announce that sentence had been carried out. A drunken woman claiming to be a relative of Maud was moved on by the police and a group of prostitutes danced a celebratory cancan in the road.

# 8

# KICKING OVER THE TRACES

Lottie Collins lost her drawers.
Will you kindly lend her yours?
Just to keep the draft away.
Ta-ra-ra-boom-de-ay!

Generations of young girls chanted the playground song with no idea who Lottie Collins was or why the loss of her underwear possessed any special significance. Unbeknown to them, their cheeky favourite was a parody of one of the most notorious and influential songs to emerge from the British music hall. Some 20 years after its introduction at the Tivoli Music Hall in the Strand, chroniclers of the period recollected Lottie Collins' song, 'Ta-ra-ra-boom-de-ay', and its accompanying dance as an anthem of rebellion against Victorian mores, a harbinger of modernity and the blazing fuse that ignited the explosive decade known as 'The Naughty Nineties'.

At the close of the nineteenth century, the debate for and against 'Ta-ra-ra-boom-de-ay' resulted in a cathartic airing of many of the concerns that surrounded one of the nation's favourite entertainments. Victorian attitudes towards dance and dancing had always been ambivalent. At home or at private balls, dancing provided not only a pleasant social activity, but an opportunity for young, unmarried people to meet in a strictly supervised environment. On formal occasions the physical and emotional excitement of dancing with members of the opposite sex was moderated by a strict etiquette. Ladies could not ask gentlemen to dance, partners were frequently changed and gloves guarded against skin to skin contact. Although there was seldom such a rigid code of conduct at smaller domestic gatherings, activities were still conducted within a closely monitored social framework. Dancing might quicken the blood and sharpen the libido, but there were rules and conventions to hold its wilder effects in check.

No such controls could be exercised over public dancing. In the streets and parks outbreaks of dancing were disturbing manifestations of an independent working-class culture. At the 'twopenny-hops' attended by costermongers during the 1850s, Henry Mayhew

ILLUSTRATION 18. Girls dancing in Drury Lane, 1872.

observed a lack of 'decorum', adding that the most popular dances were 'jigs, "flash jigs" – hornpipes in fetters – a dance rendered popular by the success of "Jack Sheppard" – polkas, and country-dances, the last-mentioned being generally demanded by the women'.[1] Public holidays during the summer were given over to uninhibited behaviour. Max O'Rell wrote in the early 1880s:

> At eight or nine in the morning, the public houses are ready, the animals are out of leash, the riot begins. The sky-blue, apple-green, blood-red figures appear, shouting and dancing to the strains of concertinas: the penny cigars are lighted, the mob is in motion. The fête opens with drink, continues with drink, and closes with drink […] The people crowd into the open spaces to drink, dance and lie about.[2]

The night houses, clubs and pleasure gardens where dancing took place were frequented by prostitutes to such an extent that in 1857 William Acton could write that 'the union of Terpsichore and Melpomene, long forbidden by Puritanism, has now for some time been sanctioned by the magistracy'.[3] After a visit to Cremorne, the same writer suggested that a passion for dancing had altered the physical appearance of prostitutes:

> I noticed a great prevalence of sunken eyes, drawn features, and thin lips, resulting from that absorption of the cellular tissue which leaves mere threads of muscle stretched upon the skull. Inasmuch as within my recollection women of the town had a well-known tendency to stoutness, and they now live no worse than heretofore, I am inclined to attribute these symptoms not so much (as in the vulgar error) to the practice of prostitution, as to the dancing mania, which has been the only remarkable change of late years in their mode of life.[4]

Subscription balls were often drunken and disorderly, open to anyone with the money to purchase a ticket or, in the case of attractive young women, with free passes issued by the organiser. 'The Masher King' created by music-hall singer Charles Godfrey in 1884 had his own euphemistic appreciation of such events:

> If I went to a soiree, a rout or a ball
> I was sure to be found hanging on the wall,
> And while others were smoking and drinking like fun
> I was wrapping myself round a tart or a bun.[5]

Changes in theatrical fashion meant that watching dance onstage ceased to be an activity followed by both sexes, becoming instead the voyeuristic pursuit of a predominantly male audience. With the demise of the Romantic Ballet at leading theatres during the middle of the nineteenth century, performers migrated to the opulent but raffish music halls that had largely replaced older tavern-based concerts. Motivated by profit rather than artistic taste, proprietors presented grandiose ballets in which attention was constantly directed to the physical attractiveness of the performers. Such a masculine approach and the inevitable presence of large numbers of prostitutes meant that a visit to a central London music hall was not considered to be an appropriate family event. Writing in 1912, J. Crawford Flitch observed:

> Twenty-five or thirty years ago, if one went to the Empire or the Alhambra, the Oxford or the Pavilion, one did not choose to have it known. The music-hall was not a proper subject of conversation at the dinner-table or the tea-party. No respectable British matron would have dreamed of being seen within its walls, much less of taking her daughters there.

Although ballet girls were probably not as scarlet as they were painted, many sought to amplify their poor wages by striking up relationships with members of the audience. Such fraternisation was often condoned and even encouraged by the music hall's management, particularly that of the Alhambra, Leicester Square, where a sub-stage 'canteen' bar provided refreshments for customers and female performers still wearing their costumes of tights or short skirts. Despite widespread disapproval of the permissiveness of the Alhambra canteen, it was an onstage dance featured in an 1870 ballet that led to the temporary closure of the establishment.

For some years theatre managers had been plucking up courage to present an English version of an abandoned French dance that was notorious for its high kicks and suggestive movements. Popularised in low dance halls from the 1830s and later featured in the operettas of Jacques Offenbach, the cancan was seen as a political as well as an erotic demonstration. Offenbach's biographer M. Kracauer wrote:

Revolutionary-minded romantics used the dance to express their derision and contempt for the sanctimonious social conventions of the new regime, and for Louis Philippe and his dynastic ambitions while the young scions of the legitimate aristocracy used it to show their disdain for the court balls and the bankers who attended them.[6]

Eventually, the daring theatrical plunge was taken by E. T. Smith who introduced the Parisian cancan dancer Finette and her troupe into the Lyceum pantomime of 1867/8, *Harlequin Cock Robin and Jenny Wren, or Fortunatus! The Three Bears; Three Gifts; The Three Wishes and the Little Man Who Wooed the Little Maid*. It was a provocative move aimed to produce maximum publicity. Having run Cremorne for seven years the showman Smith was no stranger to controversy, but even he may have been surprised by the hostility of the reviews. Finette's costume, altered from skirts to more business-like shorts, did little to fend off criticism. *Reynolds's Newspaper* was disgusted with the performance and disappointed with the enthusiasm displayed by the audience: 'Persons of depraved taste nightly applaud this obscene dance, which the police in Paris have long ago suppressed in the lascivious balls.'[7] Finette was a genuine French dancer who had frequently performed the cancan at the Bal Manille in Paris. However, the next major demonstration of the infamous dance was performed by the Colonna Quartet, a troupe consisting of British performers.

Headed by Mme Colonna, otherwise Miss Amelia Newham, the quartet had appeared with great success at music halls throughout Britain before featuring in a ballet at the Alhambra in September 1870. Alerted by a lurid newspaper description, the police, represented by Inspector Perry and Sergeant Pope, visited the ballet and subsequently opposed the music hall's entertainment licence when it became due for renewal. A thoroughly observed account of the dance was submitted as evidence to the Middlesex magistrates:

We beg to report having attended the Alhambra Palace Music-hall on the 8th inst., when the ballet 'Les Nations' was performed, in which Mdlle. Colonna and Troup (four in all) appeared and danced the Parisian Quadrille, or ordinary 'Can-can'. Two of them personated men dressed in bodices and trunks to match, or flesh coloured hoses; the others as females, dressed as ordinary ballet girls, except that more of the thigh was visible in consequence of wearing very

ILLUSTRATION 19. Sarah Wright ('Wiry Sal') and cross-dressing dance partner.

scanty drawers. The dance, on the whole, is indecent especially on the part of one dressed as a female, who raised her foot higher than her head several times towards the public, and who was much applauded. There was a loud influx of visitors shortly before the ballet commenced, but which decreased immediately after.[8]

After losing its music-hall licence, the Alhambra was closed for several months before reopening as a theatre regulated by the Lord Chamberlain. The dancer who had made such an impression on Inspector Perry and Sergeant Pope continued to create a sensation when the Colonna Quartet was immediately engaged to appear in a burlesque at the Royal Globe Theatre, Newcastle Street, Strand. Sarah Wright was the daughter of a waiter at the Oxford Music Hall and her ability to kick higher than other dancers and to dust the floor with hair when leaning back resulted in her being known as 'Wiry Sal'. With cancans proliferating under the protection of his licence, the Lord Chamberlain began to show signs of concern. In 1872 complaints had forced him to attend a production of The Forty Thieves at the Gaiety to pronounce on the acceptability of Julian Ryley and Marie Barnum depicting a Quaker couple dancing a cancan. With a few slight modifications, the burlesque representation of the recreational activities of the Society of Friends was deemed fit to continue. Two years later, however, a cancan danced by The Orpheon Troupe in Offenbach's Vert-Vert in June 1874 proved totally unacceptable. When the St James's Theatre sued Vanity Fair for libel ('some of the worst orchestra, some of the flattest singing, and one of the most indecent dances in London') the Lord Chamberlain was called as a witness. His pronouncement that the dance was 'decidedly and professedly indecent'[9] resulted in a verdict for the defendant and a decision about the future of the troublesome dance. The Lord Chamberlain declared that 'all dances of a cancan character' were permanently prohibited.

The interdiction meant that the cancan became consigned to the music halls, with its practitioners always likely to incur the wrath of local licensing authorities. As a 'serio-comic', Lottie Collins belonged to a class of performer whose presentation and material frequently resulted in complaints of impropriety. Most serios dressed provocatively, sang saucy songs and interspersed their acts with uninhibited dancing based on the steps of the common jig and clog-dance. Although Lottie retained the general characteristics of the serio-comic she was not content with such homespun and vulgar material. In the course of her career she refined her songs, investing such potentially solemn figures as 'Quakeress Ruth' and 'The Little Widow' with unexpected piquancy. Rejecting the short, flouncy skirts associated with the serio-comic, she assembled a fashionable wardrobe. And, having become a skilled performer of the sophisticated but superficial skirt dance, she adapted it to encompass the subversive cancan.

Lottie was born Charlotte Louisa Collins, in Stepney, East London, on 16 August 1865. Although her father William Alfred Collins was a lowly woodturner and part-time music-hall performer, he was a member of a respected Jewish family, originally named Kalish. Among Lottie's ancestors and relatives were Hyman Henry Collins (1832–1905), a well-known architect involved with the planning of the Strand Music Hall; Hyman Collins (1780–1835), a picture dealer from Notting Hill; and the Polish émigré Zvi Hirsch Kalish who changed the family name to Collish, later Collins, on his arrival in England. Zvi was son-in-law to Rabbi Dr Hayyim Samuel Falk (1708–82), also known as the Baal Shem of London. As an alchemist and sorcerer, Rabbi Falk (Lottie's great-great-grandfather), was remembered for a number of supernatural feats, including conjuring a small candle to burn for several weeks and employing a timely spell to save the Great Synagogue at Aldgate from destruction by fire.

Receiving an early training from her father, Lottie first appeared as a juvenile singer and dancer at music halls in the Woolwich and Gravesend area of south-east England. During the late 1870s, she and her younger sisters Rose and Lizzie formed an act, featuring with success in pantomimes at the Albion Theatre, Poplar, in the late 1870s and early 1880s. Soon outgrowing the Sisters Collins, Lottie became a serio-comic at the age of 15 in 1881, gradually establishing herself as one of the most popular female performers on the halls. By Christmas 1886 she had become a sufficiently polished artist to be recruited for a burlesque at the Gaiety Theatre. Playing Mariette, 'a lively young person',[10] in Monte Christo Junr., she shared the stage with Gaiety stalwarts Nellie Farren, E. J. Lonnen and Fred Leslie. Lottie was already music hall's leading exponent of the skirt dance; in joining the cast at the Gaiety she had arrived at its spiritual home.

Popularised by Katie Vaughan at the Gaiety during the 1870s and 1880s, the skirt dance originally combined ballet steps with graceful movements of the arms and upper body. Unlike the strict discipline of the ballet, the dance allowed a greater degree of self-expression, with some of its exponents introducing their own variants. The dance was also distinguished from the ballet and the usual serio-comic performance by the use of long skirts and petticoats which

**ILLUSTRATION 20.** Lottie Collins sketched at the London Pavilion Music Hall by Leonard Raven-Hill in 1891.

were manipulated to produce flowing, natural lines. Costumes which deflected the spectator's attention from the performer's technical ability, while also providing an open invitation to self-expression, resulted in the dance becoming immensely popular with both music-hall performers seeking to add novelty to their acts and society ladies in search of a novel experience. Despite its adoption by many inferior practitioners, the skirt dance remained a popular feature of burlesques until the advent of musical comedy in the mid 1890s.

Lottie's fusion of cancan and skirt dance was central to her most famous song. The incomprehensibly named 'Ta-ra-ra-boom-de-ay' was first performed at the Tivoli Theatre of Varieties, 68–70½ Strand, on Saturday, 7 November 1891. Lottie had been a regular performer at the luxurious new hall since its opening 16 months earlier, frequently sharing programmes with such stars as Cockney singer Jenny Hill, the actor-vocalist Charles Godfrey, leading comedian Dan Leno and the singer of 'Knocked 'Em in the Old Kent Road', Albert Chevalier. The Tivoli provided an exotic showcase for such home-grown talent. A heavily ornamented façade combined a row of Plantagenet windows separated by French Empire pilasters and topped by a Romanesque attic storey. Situated at the rear of restaurants decorated in Indian, Flemish and Palm Court styles, the auditorium was equally sumptuous. A gilded and painted relief of Indian gods and goddesses ran round the top of the theatre, with white elephant heads topping the cast-iron ceiling columns. Despite the excess of decoration, an air of warmth and comfort prevailed, with an audience capacity of 1,500 ensuring that acts onstage were relatively close to all areas of the house. A performance such as Lottie's was bound to convey maximum impact.

The origins of 'Ta-ra-ra-boom-de-ay' are obscure and controversial. Lottie explained:

> It has been a popular *Volkslied*, or song of the people, in Europe for years. I did not get it from the Continent, however; it was sent to me from America. I liked the air of the refrain, and thought I would have the thing written up in my own style.[11]

Others explained that it had been a peasant march in Eastern Europe and that it had supplied the tune for the *Danse de Ventre*, 'a cross between the Indian nautch dance and the can-can', performed in Paris in the early 1870s.[12] Lottie had purchased the rights of the song from the American Henry J. Sayers who had heard a version sung by a black performer, Mama Lou, in a St Louis brothel. Impressed by the song, Sayers introduced it with some success into his minstrel show *Tuxedo* in the early 1890s. When the song became a hit for Lottie, at least three composers claimed that they written the melody. The lyrics, however, were generally acknowledged to have been Sayers' laundered version of an obscene original, later adapted by the English writer Richard Morton. Sayers' words still retained a hint of the bordello about them, but, with a few slight changes, Lottie's character was transformed into a respectable young woman who revealed a shockingly impetuous inner-self.

At the commencement of the song, Lottie came quietly onto the stage, nervously fingering a lace handkerchief. Her costume was fashionable, but restrained, consisting of an ankle-length brocaded evening dress, a wide-brimmed 'Gainsborough' hat and long black gloves. Although not powerful, her voice was clear and precise. Each word was carefully articulated, her measured delivery creating an air of tension in the opening verse:

A smart and stylish girl you see,
The Belle of High society;
Fond of fun as fond could be –
When it's on the strict Q.T.
Never forward, never bold, –
Not too young, and not too old,
Not too timid, not too bold,
But the very thing, I'm told,
That in your arms you'd like to hold.

And then, after the slightest pause, cymbals and drums crashed to signal the mayhem of the chorus. The rousing incantation 'Ta-ra-ra-boom-de-ay' was repeated eight times during the course of which Lottie projected herself into a breathtaking display of leaps, lunges and high kicks. 'Sometimes she simply runs headlong round the stage, finishing the lap with perhaps a swift whirl and a kick', wrote an American observer, 'sometimes she simply jumps or bounces, and sometimes she doubles up like a pen-knife with the suddenness of a spring lock to emphasise the "boom"'.[13] Another reviewer commented:

Taken altogether, the performance is like nothing ever heard or seen before 'on any stage'. There is no grace about it, no sentiment, no prettiness of any kind; its merits are simply grotesque extravagance and strength [...] When the slight restraint that is upon the singer is for an instant removed, she flings herself into the chorus and the dance that goes with it, a wild, corybantic, grotesque dance that partakes of the character of the most extravagant dances of East and West; something between the passionate *fandango* that came to Spain from the East, and the grotesque *cancan* that was born in France. It is a dance of the body, as Eastern dances are, and of the feet, as in the Western fashion of dancing. It is a paroxysm of motion and emotion, such a Bacchic frenzy as was known in Ancient Greece, wherein head, and arms, and feet and body participate – a gliding run round the whole stage, a frenzied leap in the air, and then the dancer comes to a sudden pause with the singer fixed in act to move at the ending of the bar.[14]

'Ta-ra-ra-boom-de-ay' took the lace petticoats of the serene skirt dance and provocatively flourished them in the public's face (although it was never true that Lottie exposed bare thighs like the stereotype cancan dancer). For a 'smart and stylish girl' to lose such a degree of poise and self-control was breaking what Edward Carpenter described as an 'unwritten law [...] which forbids natural and spontaneous gestures as unbecoming and suspicious – and indeed in any public place as liable to the attention of a policeman'.[15] It was a song of unsettling contrasts. Extravagant in its movement, it was circumscribed by the theatre's relatively small stage. Its music changed suddenly from quiet to loud; its words from a reasoned exposition of moderation to a shriek of unalloyed self-gratification. In a form of entertainment where dancing had been reduced to dull uniformity, Lottie's performance was unpredictable and shocking. She was a slight and delicate woman who seemed hardly able to sustain such furious outpourings of energy.

The impact of the song was such that other music halls and theatres clamoured to obtain Lottie's services. She had already been booked to play the principal girl in the Christmas pantomime Dick Whittington at the Grand Theatre, Islington; a stroke of good luck for the proprietors who made sure that the song featured in every possible performance. Constant repetition of the song and dance taxed even Lottie's considerable stamina. Her co-star at the Grand, Harry Randall, remembered that 'she would take innumerable encores till she was absolutely exhausted'.[16] On a number of occasions she fainted in the wings. Further exertion was caused by extra matinees that were added and by the production's run being extended into March in an attempt to satisfy the demand for tickets. During the second half of Dick Whittington Lottie had to hurry away to fulfil her engagement at the Tivoli, racing back to the Grand to be present for the show's finale.

Shortly before the close of the pantomime she was engaged at £60 per week to boost a failing burlesque at the Gaiety Theatre. The absence through ill-health of the Gaiety's favourite leading lady, Nellie Farren, had resulted in poor box office receipts for Cinder Ellen Up-Too-Late, a difficult situation made worse by a mood of national mourning caused by the sudden death of the Duke of Clarence. With 'Ta-ra-ra-boom-de-ay' dropped into the plot, the air of gloom evaporated and 'Standing room only' notices were soon placed outside the theatre. The burlesque, which had been on the verge of folding in March, ran until 6 July 1892. As with Lottie's appearance at the Grand Theatre, the Gaiety engagement brought her to the attention of audiences who would never have attended a music hall, however many orders of architecture it might possess.

Lottie's performance was fascinating to many and horrifying to others. Despite relatively inoffensive lyrics, the song was almost immediately taken to be subversive of social and artistic values. At the most immediate level, its repetitive nonsense chorus and accompanying dance represented a radical change to the standard music-hall song. After each verse, audiences were accustomed to join in with a cheerful chorus that summarised the content or meaning of the song. Popular choruses might be repeated several times. 'Three times over at the least – five times with our special fancies', remembered W. R. Titterton, 'the orchestra usually struck at number four, and number five was shouted unaccompanied'.[17] 'Ta-ra-ra-boom-de-ay' seems to have confounded such enthusiastic participation. Frank Rutter described Lottie singing 'as if in a trance to an audience as still and serious as if it had been in church'.[18]

'Ta-ra-ra-boom-de-ay' became conferred with significance far deeper and wider than Lottie might have thought possible when it was first presented. She had certainly sought to create a novelty, something different from the run-of-the-mill music-hall 'number', but creating a song and dance that encapsulated the seething discontent of a generation was probably some way beyond her original vision. Two years after Lottie's death, in 1912, J. E. Crawford Flitch drew parallels between Lottie's high-kicking dance and wider society during the last years of the nineteenth century:

> It is always interesting to observe the interaction of life and art. All art is of its time, the greatest as well as the least. It may be that the dance has too slight a content to express to be under the obligation of borrowing anything from the ideas of the age. But it has always responded not only to the rhythm of personal emotional life, but also to the larger social rhythm of the time [...]
>
> As the century waned, the older formal and unhasting rhythms tended to break up; the pace quickened; the tranquillity which the nineteenth century had carried over from the eighteenth century disappeared in the excitement of the fin-de-siècle spirit. The temperature of the blood was rising towards the fever-point of the 'naughty nineties'.[19]

In his 1913 survey, *The Eighteen Nineties*, Holbrook Jackson remembered the song as an anthem of modernity:

> Our new-found freedom seemed to find just the expression it needed in the abandoned nonsense chorus of 'Ta-ra-ra-boom-de-ay' which, lit at the red skirts of Lottie Collins, spread like a dancing flame through the land, obsessing the minds of young and old, gay and sedate, until it became a veritable song-pest, provoking satires even upon itself in the music-halls of its origin. No other song ever took a people in quite the same way; from 1892 to 1896 it affected the country like an epidemic; and during those years it would seem to have been the absurd *Ça ira* of a generation bent upon kicking over the traces.[20]

For a song that provoked *Punch* to declare, 'great is the might of the meaningless',[21] 'Ta-ra-ra-boom-de-ay' proved itself remarkably well suited to accommodating different interpretations. With hindsight, the song embodied the shock of the new, the whirling wind of change. Though hardly expressive of female emancipation, the hysteria of its dance laid open a Freudian world of repressed sexuality. As a 'Belle of good society' breaking so suddenly with formality and tradition, Lottie's character resembled the anti-heroes of Modernist literature. And, unlike the traditional skirt dance that conjured up the undulating lines of Art Nouveau, the violent, angular actions of her performance anticipated savage, new art movements. Even Dada was suggested by the meaningless Ta-ra-ra.

The popularity of the song and its absorption into the national psyche had many unusual manifestations. With new words by John Martin (author of 'Ballyhooly' in *Faust Up to Date*), the melody was adopted as a campaign song by the Central Conservative Committee. In courts of law 'Ta-ra-ra-boom-de-ay' came to be employed as a victory celebration or as a gesture of defiance. Anticipating a longer sentence for a second conviction for possessing counterfeit coins, Arthur King was so pleased to receive only 18 months' hard labour that he astonished the Old Bailey judge and jury by waving his hat, dancing and shouting 'Ta-ra-ra-boom-de-ay'.[22] In Birmingham Alice Loxley, on receiving a two-month sentence for contempt of court, shouted, 'I don't care what you do with me; you can give me two months if you like'. It was reported that 'she then gave a vigorous exhibition of the 'Ta-ra-ra-boom-de-ay' dance, singing the refrain with great abandon'.[23]

Sensing a subversive element to the song, contemporary critics immediately launched a campaign of denigration and derision. Perhaps the most damaging accusation that could be made in the ordered, mechanistic world of late Victorian Britain was that it was uncivilised. Truth, a radical weekly periodical run by Henry Labouchere, was both racist and condescending, linking Lottie's song and dance with American revivalist gatherings:

> Ta-ra-ra-boom-de-ay. How few there are who really understand the true meaning of what appears to be the idiotic refrain of the most popular song of the day. It is questionable if even the great Lottie Collins herself is aware how this apparent gibberish came into notoriety. The Negro of the west is as fond of religious excitement as the dervish of the East, and expresses it by frenzied dancing and wild gyrations. All who have witnessed that Eastern form of hysterical devotion that by slow degrees rises with chants, howling and frenzy into almost uncontrollable madness, are aware of the interesting effect. It is the same with the Western Negro. He begins at one of his camp meetings with a slow wail, and an imperceptible swaying of the body, moaning to himself 'Ta-ra-ra-boom-de-ay'. Louder and louder becomes the chant; more intense the scream as the music advances. Gradually at every 'boom' he claps his hands louder and louder, until the rhythmic song merges into an idiotic scream that fascinates and half-maddens the spectators. At the end the whole assemblage is dancing, shouting and screaming 'ta-ra-ra-boom-de-ay', till the chorus becomes deafening.[24]

Despite the suggestion that 'Ta-ra-ra-boom-de-ay' represented a return to barbarism, a number of middle- and upper-class women expressed an interest in replicating the dance in the privacy of their own ballrooms. A dance teacher explained:

> Step dancing will, indeed, be all the rage, and I have no doubt that the fashion will not end with the season. To show you the extent of the craze I may tell you that some of my pupils begged me to teach them the dance 'Ta-ra-ra-boom-de-ay', and amongst them were two well-known leaders of society. I told them that it was really impossible for anyone but Lottie Collins to sing and dance that.[25]

Although few women would have had the skill or nerve to dance like Lottie Collins, many were beginning to take their first liberating steps in other areas. Greater involvement in recreations such as swimming and roller-skating – and the consequent necessity for adopting suitable forms of 'rational dress' – were beginning to make unrestrained movement a greater possibility. Cycling became a major pastime during the 1890s, with actresses and music-hall performers keen to pose with their machines in divided skirts or bloomers. The liberation gained by women in the fields of personal comfort and independent travel caused the bicycle to be celebrated in numerous cartoons in the illustrated press and by comic songs such as Marie Lloyd's 'Salute My Bicycle' and Lottie's 'A Bicycle Marriage'. 'Ta-ra-ra-boom-de-ay' could hardly be categorised as a coherent dance, but in demonstrating that a conventionally attired woman might indulge in extreme physical activity, it not only reflected the growing spirit of the time, but anticipated African–American-inspired ragtime dances such as the Cake Walk, the Bunny Hop and the Fox Trot.

There was one special night when the 'uncontrollable madness' of 'Ta-ra-ra-boom-de-ay' appeared to have spilled over onto the streets of London. Despite its imperial might, Britain in 1899 and 1900 had suffered a number of morale-sapping defeats at the hands of a makeshift army of Boer farmers in the South African War. The first good news, that the township of Mafeking had been relieved after an eight-month siege, led to unprecedented scenes of public jubilation. On 18 May 1900 a vast crowd made up of all social classes gathered in the centre of London to revel in the restoration of national pride. Pubs ran dry of alcohol and street vendors and novelty shops exhausted their stocks of flags, toy bugles, tickling sticks, rattles and party-blowers. One of those present, Shaw Desmond, recalled: '[there were] young ladies "doing Lottie Collins" on the pavement and "white-fronted Johnnies", town bucks in capes and canes [...] capering with Donahs from the East End.'[26] Such was the degree of fraternisation among the crowds that the sexually transmitted disease expert, Dr Malcolm Alexander Morris, later wrote that he knew of three women who had contracted syphilis from kissing strangers during the celebration.[27]

After such a triumph the remainder of any performer's career would have been an anti-climax. Lottie remained a top-ranking star of the music hall, but the many subsequent songs that she introduced stood little chance of approaching 'Ta-ra-ra-boom-de-ay's' hold on the public. There were ups and downs in her life. In 1897 she won £25 damages after bringing a libel action against the editor of *Society* who had condemned her song 'The Little Widow' as being in 'gross bad taste which is not redeemed even by the singer's ability and rose-red petticoats'.[28] A year later she was briefly treated in a North London hospital after slashing her throat and wrists with a pocket knife. Her husband Stephen Cooney died in 1901 and she married the songwriter James W. Tate in 1902. Retiring after a career spanning four decades she succumbed to a heart condition at the age of 45 in 1910. In her last years she saw the oldest of her three daughters, José Collins, make rapid progress in music hall and theatre.

The fame and form of 'Ta-ra-ra-boom-de-ay' was spread by word of mouth, written descriptions and artists' impressions. In 1892 the song featured on two of the earliest sound recordings, one a disc solemnly performed by the Gramophone's German inventor Emile Berliner and the other a wax cylinder featuring a Bournemouth brass band. It was perhaps a good thing for the song and dance's long-tem reputation that motion pictures had yet to be introduced, for early cinema's fixed camera position and dependence on natural light meant that most dance films, although extremely popular, were pale reflections of the original subjects. Perhaps the most spectacular representation of 'Ta-ra-ra-boom-de-ay' was also the most ephemeral. In the autumn of 1892 Brock's firework display at the Crystal Palace in Sydenham consisted of a giant set-piece depicting Lottie dancing. A series of extravagant high kicks replicated in blazing silhouette against the city skyline[29] was a trick that might have impressed even the Baal Shem of London.

# 9

# A PEEP INTO THE UNKNOWN

By peering into the narrow aperture it was possible to see a curious and illicit episode unfold: an artist, while painting an apparently nude female model, was interrupted by a lady caller accompanied by her teenage son. Quickly, the artist put up a folding screen to avoid potential embarrassment. But while he chatted to his visitor, the schoolboy looked behind the barrier. Soon he was flirting with the model, tickling her under the chin as she smiled at his youthful impudence. When discovered, he was dragged reluctantly away, still gazing at the 'shameless hussy' who blew him a lingering kiss. It was a shocking scene that provoked outraged letters to the press and a rush of visitors to 138 Strand and to other Mutoscope parlours where this early motion picture was on exhibition. The Mutoscope viewer and the slightly earlier Kinetoscope peepshow provided the first experience of movies to a wide range of people during the 1890s. But it was not an easy birth for the new form of entertainment. Intrigue, controversy and scandal were seldom far away as pioneers sought to gain a lucrative foothold in the developing market.

Views exotic, erotic, historic, spectacular and jocular; scenes educational and exciting had been provided by panoramas, dioramas and magic lanterns for consumption by the populace before the first faltering flickers of motion pictures. In the autumn of 1801 visitors to the Lyceum, a converted art gallery and lecture theatre at 354 Strand, were astounded to witness a display of moving ghosts, monsters and 'apparitions of the absent' conjured up apparently out of thin air. Although containing all the elements of a Gothic horror story, including a howling thunderstorm, Paul de Philipsthal's elaborate magic lantern display, the Phantasmagoria, was advertised as an exposure of 'the Practices of artful imposters and pretended

Exorcists'.[1] Within a short time the show proved so popular that it was transferred to a larger upstairs auditorium leaving the ground level available to an exhibitor of lifelike wax portraits that had just arrived from Paris – Madame Tussauds.

As the Phantasmagoria and Tussauds' waxworks went from strength to strength, a new entertainment opened across the road on a site previously occupied by the ancient Talbot Inn. Thomas Barker's New Panorama opened at 168–9 Strand in 1803, displaying large-scale reproductions of foreign cities and contemporary events, the continuous, all-round paintings being inspected from a central point. Becoming Burford's Panorama in 1817, the exhibition continued with dwindling fortunes until 1828. Two years later the building was reconstructed as the Strand Theatre. A humble relation of such exhibitions was to be found in the streets and at fairs and other public gatherings. Whether a simple box carried on the back of an itinerant showman or a large horse-drawn cabinet with multiple viewing lenses, the peepshow's images demonstrated that there was widespread public demand for devices that provided an individual, rather than a mass viewing experience.

From the advent of photography in the late 1830s inventors had looked for ways in which enhanced reality might be added to the medium. The first photograph of London, a daguerreotype view of Whitehall taken from one end of the Strand in September 1839, amazed viewers with its clarity and exactness when it was displayed at the Adelaide Gallery, close to the Lowther Arcade. It could not, however, be described as true to nature as the process resulted in the reversal of the image. The time taken for the exposure of the Whitehall plate was so slow that the only human visible was a small boy who had rested for several minutes at the foot of the equestrian statue of King Charles I. By the late 1850s, Valentine Blanchard had contrived to add both depth and arrested movement to his series of 'Instantaneous London Views', published as twin photographic prints mounted on cards which were examined through a double-lensed viewer. For the remainder of the century magic lanterns and stereoscopic apparatuses were employed for both the private and public display of photographs. Being used for group exhibition, the magic lantern was generally regarded as an instructive device, disseminating useful and instructive information or harmless family orientated entertainment. The stereo viewer, on the other hand, was a solitary pleasure and, without the regulating effect of an audience, was always likely to be used to present risqué and pornographic scenes.

When American inventor Thomas Alva Edison, 'The Wizard of Menlo Park', set himself the challenge of creating the first 'animated photographs', peepshow presentation seemed to be an attractive proposition. Although the solo viewer carried some unsavoury connotations, its economic viability was not to be argued with. Projected moving pictures had been considered, but 'The Wizard' decided that public displays would soon exhaust the demand for the new medium: 'If we put out a screen machine there will be a use for maybe about ten of them in the whole United States. With that many screen machines you could show the pictures to everybody in the country – and then it would be done.'[2] It was far better to accumulate the steady drip, or drop, of nickels and pennies into the slot of a single viewer. Relying on the inventive genius of his assistant William Kennedy Laurie Dickson, Edison had a viable movie camera ready by 1893 and was able to launch his viewer in the United States in April 1894. Externally, the 'Kinetoscope' resembled the wooden cabinet stereo viewers already familiar in amusement arcades and other public venues. It was electrically driven and illuminated, running a continuous loop of 50 foot-long 35 mm celluloid film. In Europe the Edison publicity machine had heralded the Kinetoscope and its living pictures for several years, creating a widespread curiosity that many showmen were keen to exploit.

The arrival of Kinetoscope and its moving pictures in the United Kingdom in October 1894 caused a temporary sensation which was soon followed by complaints about the American nature of the subjects displayed. Films were exhibited by the Continental Commerce Company, run by Edison's European agents Franck Z. Maguire and Joseph Baucus, in special shops in Oxford Street, the Strand and at several other London sites, but the main objective of the operation was to sell Kinetoscopes to exhibitors who would become dependent on Edison for a supply of films. At a prohibitively high cost of 70 guineas, however, few viewers were sold. Quickly realising that the Kinetoscope was not a particularly complex machine, a number of entrepreneurs decided to undercut the price by commissioning their own copies. In the autumn of 1894, a series of chance meetings in a Strand tobacconist's shop led to the construction of the first replica Kinetoscopes and the birth of the British film industry.

Among the patrons of John Melachrino's tobacco establishment were two Greek businessmen, George Tragides and Demetrius Georgiades and an electrical engineer with an interest in photography, Henry W. Short. When Melachrino heard the Greeks discussing the possibility of copying a genuine Kinetoscope that they had purchased, he suggested they contact Short who had frequently praised the technical abilities of his friend Robert W. Paul. Tragides and Geogiades waited for Short at the shop and then the three conspirators visited Paul with their plan. 'The course of motion picture destiny', wrote cinema historian Terry Ramsaye, 'had now become as thinly fanciful as the curling smoke of a cigarette.'[3] Paul commenced the construction of Kinetoscope machines which the Greeks started to exhibit and to offer for sale. Although Edison had failed to patent the Kinetoscope in Europe, it was still illegal to pass off a replica as an original Edison machine. In January 1895 the Greeks were summonsed by the Continental Commerce Company and an injunction was imposed upon them.

Despite the result of the court case, Paul and others continued to manufacture British Kinetoscopes. With half price, non-Edison machines becoming available, the Continental Commerce Company withdrew the supply of films to non-authorised exhibitors. It was a desperate move, for within a few months the repetitive and unimaginative nature of film subjects was already beginning to disappoint customers. Having been told that the Kinetoscope would eventually be capable of presenting full length plays and operas the British public were increasingly underwhelmed by 30-second snippets of little-known variety acts and simple staged scenes that ended almost before they began. The Continental Commerce Company realised that to maintain public enthusiasm, films with local interest needed to be obtained. From the time of the earliest British shows they pleaded with Edison to send them a movie camera to produce subjects more attractive to the British market. As it was the embargo imposed by Edison's agents, Robert W. Paul was prompted to find a way of producing his own films. Fortunately, the cigarette-smoking Short was on hand to introduce him to a like-minded American photographer and inventor, Birt Acres. By March 1895, Paul and Acres had devised a working movie camera, their first subject being an animated portrayal of their mutual friend Harry Short.

Before their brief and acrimonious partnership ended in July 1895, Paul and Acres produced a number of films that differed substantially from Edison's Kinetoscope subjects. With the benefit of a portable camera, they were able to film real events such as *The University Boat Race* (March 1895); *The Derby* (May 1895); and a *Railway Station Scene* (April 1895). Their first attempt at a dramatic film, *The Arrest of a Pickpocket* (April 1895), featured actors playing a Royal Navy Jack Tar and a London Bobby. And the well-known cartoonist Tom Merry was portrayed sketching the Prime Minister Lord Salisbury and the Grand Old Man of British politics, William Ewart Gladstone. But the partners stuck to one genre that had proved extremely successful in the United States – dancing girls. Edison's first female subject, the Spanish dancer Carmencita (March 1894), was rapidly followed by other films in which attractive young women performed in a variety of styles and costumes. Such dances, and those filmed by Paul and Acres, were only tiny, truncated versions of what might be seen in any music hall or burlesque entertainment, but the solitary nature of their viewing and their constant repeatability caused critics to raise moral objections.

A pattern for Kinetoscope exhibition had already been established in the form of shops and arcades devoted to other mechanical forms of amusement. A further democratisation of entertainment had been provided by ephemeral establishments which provided a selection of coin operated games, automatons, stereoscopes and phonographs for adults of every class and, more controversially, children of any age. Unlike other entertainments, admission was free (although pennies were required for individual machines), and the duration of visits could be as long or short as the patron required. However, there was the discomforting suggestion that those employees not confined in a place of business might drop in while they were meant to be working:

All the fun of the fair! Where can you find this in London? Why, in the Strand, of course. Stop at Wellington-street on the left-hand side going westward, and ask yourself if anywhere, outside London or a very small provincial town, you would discover quite such a singular spectacle as here presents itself to the gaze of the passer by. It is a veritable fair or raree show which has got itself established for the edification of pedestrian London here, in the very heart and centre of one of the very busiest streets of the metropolis. And beyond doubt it is appreciated, as you shall see, by the crowds of patrons which flock to witness it. Here, microcosmically epitomised, the discerning may perceive all London. The clerk, the artisan, the shopkeeper, the lawyer, the actor, the artist, the journalist and many more, whom to catalogue exhaustively would tax the energies of Whitman himself – all may be discovered herein at some time or other throughout the day, whiling away a minute or so of their employer's time, and gaining at the cost of a copper or two an astonishing amount of innocent fun and amusement. And not merely fun and amusement, but instruction withal – for who shall deny the application of this term to an entertainment which includes a speech by Mr Gladstone? [...] Mr Chevalier, too, and many other favourite of the people, is here – the phonograph reproducing the utterances of one and all with a fine impartiality which knows no differences, save those of timbre and tone. And then at the back of the show, for those who lack interest in these victories of peace, there is an excellent shooting-gallery, wherein if you be a marksman, or even if you be not, you may indulge in your passion at any range from 600 yards downwards. The place is not 600 yards long, of course – it is only 90 feet – but it looks as if it were.[4]

By January 1895 a number of exhibition sites for both legitimate and bogus Kinetoscopes had been established in London. A reporter for Fun was enthusiastic:

Thursday, January 10th – London is bristling with Kinetoscopes. One in Bond Street, one in Regent Street, one in Piccadilly, one in Holborn, two in Oxford Street, two in the Strand, and Heaven knows where else. These are the ones I meet in my rounds, and I always pop in and have a peep at 'em. They amuse me very much [...] There are some kinetographs of high-kicking dancing girls. My stars! How high they do kick! How perfectly![5]

An interest in the high-kicking and diaphanously costumed dancers displayed by the Kinetoscope could be represented as a natural appreciation of graceful movement and artistic merit. No such justification could be advanced for many of the subjects presented by the Kinetoscope's peepshow successor, the Mutoscope. With titles such as Should Ladies Wear Bloomers?, A Mouse in a Girl's Bedroom, Through the Keyhole, What She Found in Bed and Trying on her New Bathing Suit, the device could hardly be argued as being aimed at a discerning public.

# ILLUSTRATED·BITS

No. 837.
Week ending March 16th, 1901.     Edited by T. H. ROBERTS.     32 Pages.  Price 1d.

A MODERN EVE.

ILLUSTRATION 21. 'A Modern Eve' peeps into a Mutoscope viewer.

The ornate cast-iron Mutoscope viewer was introduced into Britain in December 1897 by the Mutoscope and Biograph Syndicate, an offshoot of the American Mutoscope Company. Unlike the Kinetoscope, the Mutoscope viewer provided the illusion of movement with a reel of photographs flicked by the turning of a handle. The hundreds of images were printed from original film negatives, meaning that many subjects also featured in displays given by the company's Biograph projector. Although the novelty of motion picture peepshows had been eroded by films projected to mass audiences since February 1896, the Syndicate integrated both solitary and collective viewing experiences into their carefully planned strategy. As in the United States, the company's Biograph projector was used to exhibit views of topical and scenic interest, while the Mutoscope often offered studio-made subjects that relied on broad humour or erotic content for their effect. But, despite a ready market for the Mutoscope's vulgarity and smut, the United Kingdom and Europe provided powerful new subjects for Biograph films – various members of royal families and the head of the Roman Catholic Church. To capture such photogenic subjects, the American company sent their most experienced and diplomatic film-maker, Edison's one-time right-hand man, William Kennedy Laurie Dickson. Having virtually invented Edison's movie camera, Dickson had developed a bigger and better device for the newly founded company. To photograph the less salubrious Mutoscope subjects, Dickson designed an ingenious open-air studio which he arranged to be constructed just off the Strand, on waste ground in front of the Adelphi Arches.

Dickson arrived in London in May 1897 with a stated mission to consolidate the success that the Biograph projected shows had achieved since their first exhibition at the Palace Theatre of Varieties, Charing Cross Road, in the previous March. Less well publicised was his responsibility for providing the technology to launch the company's Mutoscope viewers in public areas throughout the country. His was a triumphant return to a country he had left 18 years earlier. Back in 1879 he described himself in a letter of application to 'The Wizard of Menlo Park' as 'a friendless and fatherless boy'.[6] Young Dickson was well qualified to become a sorcerer's apprentice as he possessed a character imbued with erratic genius. He had inherited artistic and scientific skill from his father, a painter of miniatures, student of dead languages and keen astronomer. His scholarly mother had conferred on him her musical talents and good looks. Both parents passed on a fierce pride in a Scottish and English ancestry which was said to include the Royal Stuarts and the artist, William Hogarth. Dickson was formidable: a perfectly groomed dandy with graceful manners and fluent conversation that made light of his scientific expertise. He was a man of action, a good linguist and a convincing publicist for both his inventions and himself. Perhaps the most striking of many photographic images of Dickson is the experimental Kinetoscope film of 1891 in which, with waxed moustache and piecing gaze, he performs a 'Hey Presto' gesture to his employer Edison and to cinema history.

During the remainder of 1897–8, Dickson roamed Europe, persuading many notable figures to sit, stand and perform for 'animated portraits'; among them were the Prince of Wales (later Edward VII), Queen Wilhelmina of the Netherlands, Kaiser Wilhelm II, the Emperor Franz Joseph I, Queen Margherita of Italy and, above all, the elderly Pope Leo XIII. His views of Queen Victoria's Diamond Jubilee Celebrations in 1897 were shown around the world and he was called upon to give special command performances to the British royal family. And when not travelling with the gigantic movie camera, he occupied rooms at one of the most luxurious hotels in the world. From its opening in 1896, the massive Hotel Cecil, situated at 60 Strand between the Tivoli Music Hall and the Savoy Hotel, had acted as a magnet to wealthy and powerful Americans. They were made to feel at home amid surroundings that most English hoteliers would probably have considered decadent. During his stay it is likely that Dickson encountered many familiar faces from the other side of the Atlantic:

> This middle-aged man, with the kindly face and the grey moustache, stepping into a hansom is a great American railroad king who means to revolutionise railway London; the slight dark figure in the porch is that of a man who is an engineer of monopolies and trusts. These are men who are feared.[7]

Dickson may well have met a fellow guest who had arrived from America to promote another area of the mechanical entertainment industry. In the summer of 1897, William Barry Owen used the hotel as his base as he attempted to interest backers in Emile Berliner's Gramophone. Within a year the Gramophone Company had been set up with a recording studio across the Strand, at 31 Maiden Lane.

Having already devised the original film studio for Edison in 1893 and another for the American Mutoscope Company in 1896, Dickson looked for a site on which to construct the first British film studio.

Like William Barry Owen he did not look far – just out of the terrace windows at the rear of the hotel towards the elegantly proportioned Adelphi Terrace and the rigorously maintained flower beds of the Embankment Gardens. Dickson soon discovered a curiously hidden strip of land that lay between the gardens and the terrace, home to a ramshackle collection of small businesses that made use of the once notorious Adelphi Arches. It was here that a plot was acquired and an open-air studio constructed some time in the latter part of 1897 or the opening months of 1898. Requiring natural light for filming, the studio had a wooden stage, with glass roof and sides, mounted on a turntable that could be revolved to make full use of whatever sun pollution-plagued London might offer. The camera was housed in a separate structure that could be moved towards and away from the stage for close and longer shots.

The Biograph studio was well suited to the mysterious hinterland, which, before the construction of the Embankment and its gardens, had been the foreshore of the Thames. None of the wealthy residents or club members who looked down on the area from the Terrace left a memoir of the studio's activities or even a mention of its existence. Of the many illustrated journals which zealously published accounts of obscure and outlandish scientific developments, none printed a description or picture of the studio. For their part the publicity conscious Mutoscope and Biograph Syndicate were thunderously quiet about their remarkable new facility. It was a sensible policy not to attract an audience when the actors included women in a state of undress and simulated nudity.

In 1900 the Embankment Studio became redundant after the renamed British Mutoscope and Biograph Company opened one of the world's earliest artificially lit movie studios at 107 Regent Street. When in 1946 Rachael Low was gathering information for her seminal work, The History of the British Film, she wrote to Emile Lauste who as a young man had been Dickson's main camera operator during his European activities. Emile responded:

> Thanks for your letter of Feb 28th which reminded me of something long forgotten, the studio which was situated on a plot of ground at the Adelphi Arches. This was a glass affair as many were in the early days dependent on daylight. It was reached by going down alongside the Tivoli Music Hall, through the Arches, across a roadway facing

the Arches Embankment side. Wine was stored under the Arches and horses drawing vans with equipment were frightened to enter this very dark place. Badly lit indeed.

One of the last occasions on which the Embankment studio was used was also the only one to be widely publicised. In September 1899 the acclaimed actor-manager Herbert Beerbohm Tree agreed to bring his theatrical company to the studio to feature in extracts from his forthcoming production of Shakespeare's *King John*. Although the four scenes filmed were extremely brief (less than a minute each), they represented the first attempt to present Shakespeare on film. Paradoxically, while the appearance of a famous actor in a Shakespearian role conferred greater respectability on the new medium, the presence of such a prestige subject in Mutoscope shops drew unwelcome attention to the less salubrious titles that were offered. Throughout the country a wave of prosecutions for indecency resulted in the police seizing objectionable reels and magistrates ordering their immediate destruction.

Two of the titles most frequently complained about were made in London. *Wicked Willie*, otherwise known as *Studio Troubles*, depicted the naughty schoolboy and the 'naked' model (Mutoscope nudes actually wore close-fitting body stockings called fleshings). *Why Marie Blew Out the Light* provided a genuinely voyeuristic experience, revealing a young woman securing her privacy by drawing the bedroom blind. Having removed her outer clothing, she came to the uneasy realisation that some low individual might be peeping and this caused her to inflate her cheeks and purse her lips. The rest was darkness. While still filming and distributing such sexually orientated subjects, the British Mutoscope and Biograph Company contrived to deflect criticism by setting up a network of autonomous regional companies who arranged Mutoscope exhibitions. In turn, the companies blamed the public for demanding 'What the Butler Saw' type subjects. A particularly candid Mutoscope parlour manager was interviewed by the London *Daily News*:

'You see' explained the representative in extenuation of some of the pictures they are showing in London, 'we have to cater for all sorts and personally, I would rather show pictures of high class artistic taste even though just a little bit[...]'

'A little bit risky'?

'Just a little bit risky, rather than show anything merely vulgar. The fact is we must do it if the thing is to be made a commercial success. It may be very deplorable that the public taste should be so low; but then, we don't make the public taste.'

'No, of course not. You only pan [...] you only supply what the public taste requires.'

'We supply what we find the public taste requires, and we should only be too delighted to be able to make our exhibitions displays of nothing but the finest works of art, entirely free from anything objectionable, if we could get the support of the public. At present we can't get that support.'

'That is a wonderful fine thing' said the intelligent young man in charge of these establishments: pointing to an instrument showing the launching of a great ship; 'but it is no good for making money. The one next to it there, is worth a dozen of it.'

It was *The Artists Model*.[8]

The question of obscene peepshow exhibitions was raised in parliament on several occasions by the member for Camborne, Cornwall, W. S. Caine. 'These filthy mutoscopes and similar photographic abominations were everywhere', he reported, 'at sea-side resorts, country fairs, in the main thoroughfares of great towns, and even at places devoted to Sunday-school treats.' He recommended that the Home Secretary should inspect premises in the Strand, a course of action apparently acted upon by Charles Ritchie. In September 1901 he reported back that he had 'paraded up and down the Strand one whole afternoon and detected nothing'.[9]

A more eventful excursion was that taken by a 17-year-old girl in the spring of the same year. Annie Moss had become suspicious of a group of young men who were hanging around the streets of King's Cross and she made it her business to observe their movements over a period of several months. On the Bank Holiday Good Friday she shadowed two of the gang to Westminster where they entered a Mutoscope shop. She watched as they stole the pocket watch of a gentleman who was engrossed with a particularly interesting subject. Wary of attracting attention, but oblivious to their dogged pursuer, they moved on to another Mutoscope shop at 138 Strand. There the resourceful Annie alerted a police constable as they attempted to pick a lady's purse.[10] Annie's presence in a Mutoscope shop would have been unremarkable, even though she was an unaccompanied teenage girl. Children and young adults mixed freely while viewing 'risky' material, their uninhibited comments and interaction causing widespread public concern and condemnation. The location of a Mutoscope shop, in the heart of much reviled Holywell Street, set a final seal of disapproval on the new medium.

The only subject to rival sex in popularity was violence. On the outbreak of the Transvaal War in the autumn of 1899, Dickson abandoned the comfortable and familiar surroundings of the Hotel Cecil to rough it with the British forces in South Africa. Shown as films in music halls and municipal venues, and as Mutoscope reels in shops and exhibitions, his views of military actions brought home the brutal realities of modern warfare to the public for the very first time. His extensive and intrepid coverage of hostilities was the highlight of his career, chronicled in regular newspaper reports and in the 1901 book, The Biograph in Battle. Having nursed film-making through its earliest years, William Kennedy Laurie Dickson decided that it was time to pursue other areas of invention. In 1902 he established an experimental laboratory at 64 Strand where he collaborated with his old friend Eugene Lauste (Emile's father) on a series of sometimes eccentric projects. Although his mind remained as fertile as ever, he never recreated the glory days of the Kinetoscope and the Biograph.

Long before he died, in 1935, Dickson had witnessed cinema becoming the dominant form of public entertainment. By the outbreak of World War I, films exhibited in purpose-built theatres had evolved from short single-shot sequences into extended productions with complex narratives. During the 1920s and 1930s, sound and colour were added to the entrancing medium, with giant picture palaces offering a luxurious experience for a small financial outlay. Having all but mastered the illusion of reality cinema began to reinvent history. In 1940, Dickson's old boss became the subject of a romanticised biopic with Spencer Tracey playing Edison, the Man. The 'Wizard's' gifted apprentice did not feature in the cast.

The social changes brought about by moving pictures were more than just encouraging impressionable folk to waste their time and money in Kinetoscope or Mutoscope shops or, later, kiss and cuddle in the back rows of darkened cinemas. Films combined with sound recording, the telephone and other areas of technology to develop a culture whose principal objective was immediate and sustained personal gratification. Earlier entertainments had demanded less attention, allowing their audiences to come and go as they pleased and to interact with the performers. By 1914 the proliferation of cinemas in London had begun to encroach on music-hall profits and to influence the types of entertainment that they offered. The Tivoli, home of the stand-up comedian and serio-comic, was closed in 1914 in readiness for a scheme to widen the Strand. World War I put the plan on hold, leaving the music hall to stand empty for two years before it was finally demolished. In 1923 a new Tivoli arose on the site, a giant, 2,100-seat cinema exhibiting the latest American blockbuster movies.

# 10

# LOOKING FOR MUGS IN THE STRAND

George Formby Senior, ironically billed on the music halls as 'The Wigan Nightingale', used to perform a song about a northerner coming to London and 'Looking For Mugs in the Strand'. Like much of Formby's repertoire, the humour lay in his gormless 'John Willie' character not appreciating that he was the biggest mug of all. But whether predator or prey, he correctly identified the Strand as London's principal mug-hunting territory. It had always provided a wide variety of mugs to be targeted. Some mugs might be persuaded to give money to people who pretended to be in need. Other mugs surrendered cash for services that they did not require or receive. And some unfortunate mugs were quite literally taken to the cleaners

Rather than walk along the Strand, the comedian Dan Leno found it cheaper to take a cab from one end to the other. On foot his progress would have been constantly impeded by beggars asking for handouts, and out-of-work performers seeking 'loans'. The shabby-genteel professional fallen on hard times, the temporarily embarrassed lady or gentleman and the importuning vagrant ensured that anyone with the slightest appearance of prosperity was constantly dolling out small amounts of money. Although some of the hard luck stories were undoubtedly true, they were often an unimaginative and over rehearsed convention that added a degree of formality to a crude financial appeal. Cadgers or 'ear biters' sometimes operated in well-organised groups. Another famous comedian, Arthur Roberts, recalled:

> I was going in the direction of Charing Cross one day and met Dan, who asked me to have a drink.
> 'But for Heaven's sake, Arthur,' he said, 'don't let us go into any place in the Strand.'
> I told him I was happy to go wherever he wanted to go. So, we walked into the Adelphi Hotel.

Then Dan told me why he was so afraid of the Strand. In those days there was a man called Dodgers who was one of an organised gang working under a master-mind whose business in life was to claim acquaintance with famous actors and Music Hall Singers. The master-mind got a chronological list of your play-bills. He would then tell one of his gang to follow Dan Leno or Arthur Roberts or whoever it was along the street and when you got into a bar or a restaurant, you would find somebody whom you had never seen before in your life saying to you in the most familiar way:

'I was in Manchester, with you, sir, when you played as Dr Syntax, and if I may say so as an old actor and colleague, it was a wonderful performance.'

Your natural vanity made you think that the stranger was speaking the truth and you were glad to give him five shillings.

I afterwards learnt that the money was at once taken back to the master-mind and that the scouts who pestered us were simply paid a weekly wage.[1]

Female cadgers might add sexual allure to their male counterpart's use of flattery. Many were looking for small amounts of money, like the apparently distressed damsel in Reuben Hill's comic song, 'People You Meet in the Strand':

In the Strand – the Strand at night-time
Though it's strange I must confess
You will always meet a maiden
Who appears in great distress.
She's a stranger quite in London,
All alone – no one she knows
And as on one side she draws you
This is how her story goes:

Chorus:
'Pardon me – but you see I'm a stranger and worse
I'm alone – all on my own – And I've just lost my purse.
Feel so bad – should be glad if a hansom you'll stand.'
That's the lost country maiden you meet in the Strand.

Some ways of separating mugs from their money were too indelicate even for the raucous humour of 'the halls'. Patrick Duncan, a carpenter, lost a small fortune after picking up a prostitute in the Strand in June 1891. He had just returned to England from Australia, making his way to London with £95 in £5 notes which he had exchanged for gold at a Plymouth bank. He had perhaps struck lucky in the Antipodean goldfields, but his good fortune was soon to abandon him. Five days after arriving in England and nine hours after reaching the capital he encountered a prostitute who took him to 34 Exeter Street, a road running from the Strand to the rear of Haxell's Hotel and Exeter Hall. They went upstairs to a room on the first floor, minimally furnished with a washstand and a curtained bed. Behind the bed and obscured by its drapes was a closed door in front of which stood a carefully positioned chair. Like a magician's stooge, Duncan placed his clothes, which contained the thick roll of banknotes on the chair, unaware that the prostitute's assistants Helen Schmidt and William Schneider were hidden in the adjoining room. Soon after leaving the house Duncan discovered that his money was missing, but on returning with the police, both rooms, like his pockets, were empty. Although Schneider and Schmidt were soon arrested, most of Duncan's £95 had disappeared without trace.

Another sure way of losing money was provided by the gambling and betting 'clubs' which flourished in the area. Although common gaming houses and betting shops had been made illegal under government legislation during the 1840s and 1850s, the law was widely flouted throughout the Victorian period. Periodically, the police would descend in force on a particular establishment, hoping that the element of surprise and force of numbers would enable them to apprehend gamblers before they had a chance to dispose of cards, dice or other gambling paraphernalia. Such operations were often closely co-ordinated, as in the case of raids on the Agar Club, 50 Strand, and the New Falmouth Club, 164 Strand. At 3.15 p.m. on Tuesday, 8 April 1891, Inspector Steggles, followed by a small army of police constables, forced their way into the two rooms that constituted the Agar Club. Finding about 40 men gathered around a tape machine awaiting the result of the City and Suburban horse race, the Inspector announced: 'Gentlemen, you must consider yourselves in custody by order of Sir Edward Bradford, Chief Commissioner of Police.' When ordered to hand over the club's books, its young proprietor, Ernest Henry Hart, cut a sorrowful figure: 'You can have all; but you won't find much. I have been doing very badly; in fact, the other day I had to pawn my watch. Here is the ticket. It only wanted a raid to finish me off.'[2] Formerly a music-hall comedian, Hart had graduated to book-making and betting-club ownership. The run of bad luck so eloquently described to Inspector Steggles was extended when his club was closed and he received a fine of £50. Subsequently, he opened the Quadrant Club in Regent Street and the El Dorado in the Haymarket, but both failed, leading to his bankruptcy in 1893.[3]

At the same time as the raid on the Agar Club, Chief Inspector Wells, backed up by two other inspectors and twenty constables, stormed through a ground level tobacconist's shop and up to the first floor of 164 Strand. Pushing aside a guard on the door they discovered a group of men placing bets and the usual tape machine chattering out its flow of information (which in a few minutes was to include news of the Agar Club raid). As the arrested patrons of the club were escorted to cabs to deliver them to Bow Street Police Station, each of them was cheered heartily by a large crowd that had gathered in the Strand.[4]

If such things as ley lines of criminal activity existed they would certainly have intersected at 164 Strand. An ancient, timber-framed building, it was one of a row of four that had survived from the seventeenth century. Situated between St Mary le Strand and St Clement Danes, it stood close to the Opera Comique and within a few feet of the Strand Theatre. Across the way, unhallowed Holywell Street lay screened by the north side of the Strand, its hiding place occasionally betrayed by gentlemen exiting Half Moon Passage clutching discretely wrapped parcels of books or prints. With the exception of a single semi-circular pediment, number 164 was architecturally nondescript: four tiers of large windows surveying the passing world rather than inviting inspection. Its anonymity made it well suited for the pursuit of underhand activities. Following the New Falmouth Club incident, the next recorded misdemeanour at the address occurred in 1893 when a theatrical and music-hall agent was charged with deception and fraud.

George Edwin Bishop reduced his business overheads by the simple expedient of vacating offices every time a landlord asked him for rent. Running costs were further trimmed by not informing his clients that he had moved. Premises were plentiful and there seemed an endless queue of young hopefuls desperate to part with their money for a course of simple instructions in how to become a music-hall star. Two sisters, Amy Rose Pigot and Florrie Stevenson, called at Bishop's previous office at 1 Catherine Street, Strand, in

**ILLUSTRATION 22.** A crowded Strand seen in the mid 1890s.

August 1891, having seen an advert attached to the programme
of the Royal Music Hall, Holborn. The agent agreed to teach them
step dancing, elocution, singing, the art of make-up; to provide
each of them with six original songs; and to find them music-
hall engagements. In return they were to pay 10 guineas, in half-
guinea weekly instalments. Despite promises that he would obtain
them work in pantomime at the Theatre Royal, Drury Lane, Bishop
did little to prepare them for a theatrical career. Some desultory
lessons were given by his assistants at Catherine Street and then at
86 Waterloo Road where he moved after a year, owing £17 rent. He
did not inform the sisters when he relocated to 289 Kennington
Road (an address occupied five years later by Charles Chaplin Senior
and his young son, Charlie), but they were able to track him down
in October 1892. Asking them to return to the address in three
weeks, he moved the following week to new offices at 164 Strand.

Other clients received similar treatment. Elizabeth Ann Davis
reported that all the songs he supplied had the same tune and that
the dance steps she was taught were 'not worth twopence'.[5] With the
repossession of the piano from Kennington Road, Harold Augustus
Weld had the disconcerting experience of having to practise singing
to the accompaniment of Bishop's humming. Clara Watt was told

that her demeanour made her well suited for stage tragedy, but her acting lessons were abruptly cancelled after she declined to lend the agent sums of money. Even a performer with some theatrical experience was exploited when he approached Bishop to find him a pantomime engagement. William Wyatt was recruited to act as the agency's manager, his first task being to help Bishop abscond from 289 Kennington Road where he not only owed rent, but had been illegally subletting rooms. Moving to 164 Strand on 13 November 1892, Wyatt took only eight days before deciding to leave his new employer. Much of the time Bishop was out of the office drinking and the tuition provided by his stepdaughter and stepson fell far short of professional standards. Following complaints, Bishop was charged with fraud at Bow Street Police Court in February 1893, subsequently appearing at the Old Bailey where he was sentenced to twelve months' hard labour.[6]

A year later, 164 Strand provided the location for a string of curious cases of extortion practised by a German barber and his staff. The constant flow of visitors to the Strand meant that there were many opportunities for one-off frauds, some of which were perpetrated by apparently legitimate businesses. Undermining one particular staple of masculine existence – the opportunity to enjoy a cheap haircut or shave in a convivial and confidential environment – was the scam practiced by hairdressing saloons at 47 and 164 Strand. From the beginning of 1895 the police had begun to receive complaints about extortionate charges being made for cosmetic dental treatment at the two establishments. Paul Baron, 'a tall, fair man of common German appearance',[7] trained his staff to target customers from outside London, hoping that the shortness of their stay in the capital and their unfamiliarity with its customs would make them easier to swindle. Likely victims were selected by checking the makers' addresses in their hats or by asking seemingly innocent questions about the weather in their part of the world. The modus operandi was always the same. While shaving or cutting a customer's hair, the assistant would comment on the poor condition of their teeth, offering to whiten them with a precious fluid imported from California (in reality the cleaner was the very cheaply procured spirits of salt). Sometimes teeth would be removed or an electric shock 'friction' treatment for the hair offered. Having undertaken very little and generally ineffective work, the assistant would ask for a large amount of money; usually

£3 to £4 for teeth whitening. If payment was refused, Baron and his wife threatened legal action or attempted to hold customers captive until they settled their bill. Others who had insufficient funds were escorted to local banks or told to take their watches and watch chains to a pawn shop close to Villiers Street.

The customers treated in this atrocious manner usually came from abroad or distant parts of the United Kingdom. Among them were Benjamin Prince, timber merchant from Canada; Chengalath Krishna Menon, lecturer in the Madras College of Agriculture; the Revd William Coleman Williams of Ebbw Vale, Wales; Duncan Crerar and James Neish, two friends from Glasgow, Scotland; Ernest Gallichat from Jersey; and Frederick Ratcliffe from the Isle of Man. When informed by the shop's manager that it was not uncommon to receive £10 for the whitening treatment, a gentleman from Leicester evoked the name of England's most highly paid barrister: 'Why, what are you? Why do you keep a barber's shop if you can do all this? You are attempting to earn money faster than Sir Charles Russell did over the way!'[8] After two warnings from the police, Baron and his manager Browett were tried and found guilty of deception at the Old Bailey on 20 November 1895, the owner of the shop receiving a sentence of 15 months' hard labour and his assistant a year.

Paul Baron's corruption of the traditional English barber shop was a cause of much popular resentment. The veteran music-hall singer Herbert Campbell likened his activities to the 'Demon Barber of Fleet Street', the arch villain of stage melodrama and 'penny dreadfuls' who cut his customers' throats and turned their bodies into the filling for meat pies. In the 'The Modern Sweeney Todd' Herbert sang:

When a foreigner comes you can bet ten quid,
He'll pinch your trade like this one did
In the Strand. In the Strand. In the Strand. In the Strand.
Then after a while the Joker begins
To scrape our 'Oof' and scrape our chins
In the Strand. In the Strand. In the Strand. In the Strand.

Chorus:
This Foreign Todd the Barber – has shown – you'll own
That when a Briton wants a crop,
He ought to go to a British shop.

In the Strand. In the Strand. In the Strand. In the Strand,
And not to a Foreign Barber.

The song expressed a widespread xenophobia that was regularly
enflamed by accounts of crimes commented on by foreign nationals.
CID officer turned private detective Maurice Moser expressed
little doubt that, on the whole, crime was an un-English pursuit.
Discussing the sale of pornographic images, he concluded:

> in the scores of cases of this kind in which I have been engaged or
> interceded I have never found – be it to his everlasting credit – an
> Englishman engaged in this abdominal traffic for it has always – in
> the range of my own experience of course – been some outcast
> member of some foreign country or other.[9]

Inspector Moser seldom missed an opportunity to assert that
foreigners were involved in crime at all levels, often being associated
in conspiratorial organisations or in evil microcosms of wider
society. In one case, the arrest of a French waiter for petty pilfering
was presented as proof of his assertions when it led to the capture
of a wanted murderess, also from France. In 1884 the detective was
enjoying lunch at his favourite Strand restaurant when his attention
was drawn to a flashily dressed young woman and an older admirer.
On leaving, the 'auburn-haired divinity' (actually a member of the
corps de ballet at the Alhambra or Empire) left an expensive umbrella
behind. Eagle-eyed Moser watched as Alphonse, the devious foreign
waiter, secreted the forgotten item. Soon after, Alphonse finished
his morning's work, forcing Moser to sit in the restaurant for a
further three hours until he returned for his next shift. When finally
challenged, the waiter agreed to take the patient and presumably
replete inspector to retrieve the umbrella from his lodgings. It was
'one of those suspicious sort of places – part club, part gaming-
house, part hotel, part anything-you-please, which abound in the
neighbourhood of the Haymarket'.[10] While there, Moser recognised
one of the servants as Suzanne Ricord, a young woman wanted in
France for murdering and dismembering her 3-year-old child. Moser
escorted the murderess back to her native country where she received
a suspended sentence. The disappointed detective reflected that the
French were 'sentimental'. Back in London a magistrate demonstrated
British resolve by sending Alphonse to prison for 14 days.

Given the fact that George John Binet hailed from an offshore location (the Channel Islands), it is surprising that he managed to find employment in Maurice Moser's detective agency. Having worked for Moser for 18 months, Binet proved himself a perfidious foreigner by setting up a rival firm and establishing a fraudulent scheme in which members of the public paid to become detectives. In 1890 he took rooms at New Inn Chambers, Wych Street, Strand, where he established the National Detective Agency, shamelessly borrowing the name from the famous Pinkerton organisation in the United States. Though not as extensive as its celebrated American counterpart, the London-based National Detective Agency could boast the services of 'Chief Inspector' Godfrey, a one-time lieutenant in the Jersey Militia; Mrs J. Gray 'celebrated Lady Detective'; and Binet himself, an ex-coal merchant, ex-corn dealer and, by his own account, ex-head of the Jersey police force. It was not long before the triumvirate sought to amplify their numbers – and their bank balances – by selling commissions in their detective army. Toward the end of 1891 a series of adverts began to appear in the regional press:

DETECTIVES! – Wanted in every locality, persons of both sexes in all ranks of Society, to act as Private Detectives under own instruction. Age no object, and present occupation, if any, no hindrance. Good pay. Send photo and stamped envelope for particulars to the National Detective Agency, New Inn Chambers, Strand, London. Manager, G. J. Binet, ex-Chief of Police.[11]

In anticipation of a flood of applicants, Binet ordered 640 parchment certificates from a local printer, despatching them to his newly recruited staff on the receipt of a 10s 6d postal order. Sadly, the certificates were all that the aspiring detectives received, for the promised work in their neighbourhoods did not materialise. 'We are sorry not to have sent you anything yet; we gave not had a single case in your district', wrote Binet to Annabella Jones of Billinghurst in Sussex. Eventually, on 27 April 1893, he found himself summonsed for fraud and conspiracy. Lieutenant Godfrey and Mrs J. Gray had already demonstrated their detective skills by vanishing from the New Chambers office, leaving Binet to plan his own escape. Although ingenious, he did not prove as successful as his colleagues. Having failed to appear at Bow Street Police Court, he was arrested on 18 May at Victoria District Line station, disguised as a sea captain. On 24 July 1893 Binet was sentenced at the Old Bailey to 12 months' hard labour for 'unlawfully obtaining postal orders by false pretences with intent to defraud'.[12]

The supply of receptive mugs in the Strand was unending, as were the dishonest schemes for relieving them of their cash and property. But novelty was seldom the swindler's forte. Usually the same old frauds were repeated, sometimes in the same old premises. In 1901 a barber Laurence Cohen and his assistant John Pou were charged with conspiring to obtain money by false pretences by telling customers that their infected scalps required a special steam treatment. The address from which they operated their pseudo-scientific scam was 164 Strand.[13]

# 11

# THE CASEBOOK OF
# MAURICE MOSER

'The Strange Disappearance of Mabel Love', 'The Affair of the Duchess of Sermoneta's Pearls', 'The Great Russian Rouble Forgery', 'The Battersea Lunacy Mystery' and 'The Blue Cross of Austria Scandal' were just a few of Moser's better known cases. As a renowned private investigator, he had a steady stream of clients visiting his Strand consulting rooms, trusting that he could resolve their problems in a discreet and efficient manner. Unlike many in his profession he was cultured and formidably intelligent, mixing easily with all ranks of society. A polyglot and a talented musician, he was once honoured by the future king of England. His adventures were chronicled in a series of magazine articles and in two popular books. But, unlike his fictional counterpart Sherlock Holmes, Maurice Moser was sometimes hot-blooded and impetuous. A passionate affair with his associate in detection led to humiliating court appearances and to public ridicule and opprobrium.

Befitting a famous sleuth, Moser's origins are obscure. Born, possibly in Yorkshire, in about 1852–3, he was the son of Gustav Moser, a silk merchant. That his family were once prosperous can be inferred from Moser's later comment:

> I found myself early in life – through the untoward act of a defaulting trustee – financially crippled and thrown suddenly and entirely on my own resources. I had not received the benefit of any commercial training whatsoever, as it had been hoped that my means would prove sufficiently adequate to enable me to live, if necessary, without work.[1]

With no means of studying for a career in one of the traditional professions, Moser drifted between jobs, mainly those of a clerical nature. At one time he considered enlisting in the army, but not being tall enough to join the relatively well rewarded Brigade of Guards, he declined to serve his country for 'a miserable, microscopic remuneration ironically termed pay'.[2] When he married in 1874, he described his professional role as 'manager of a chocolate factory'. Finally, in 1877, he joined the Metropolitan Police, commencing his career as Constable B 392 based at Walton Street Police Station, Brompton, in the Royal Borough of Kensington. His recollections of police life conform to the comic stereotypes perpetuated by humorous magazines and music-hall songs:

> An officer on night duty gets quite a 'connection' in the range of his beat. A friendly land-lord of a public-house here and another one there often supply what is greatly appreciated – a cheery, hot glass of grog to the almost half-starved mortal. The servants, the female ones, of the houses in the neighbourhood are generally open for a gossip (although all this is expressly against the regulations), between the area railings in the evening, after the dinner things are cleared away, when sundry dainty tid-bits find their way to the palate of 'Mr. Policeman'. Should he be single, good-looking, and amiable, our police-officer needs never go short of a supper, that is, I take it, if he knows his duty properly.[3]

After nine months chatting to servants, tipping his helmet to publicans and patrolling the ghostly avenues of Brompton Cemetery, Moser was called to Scotland Yard where he received the exciting news that he was to be transferred to another country. With few, if any, police constables possessing the ability to speak five languages, Moser was considered an ideal candidate to accompany the Prince of Wales and the Royal Commission to the Exposition Universelle in Paris. Sharing security duties with a superintendent and another PC, he remained in Paris for the run of an international exhibition that was intended to demonstrate the revival of France's national pride and self-confidence following the demoralising defeat by Germany in the Franco-Prussian War. New inventions that Moser may have marvelled at included the telephone, Thomas Edison's Phonograph and the electric light. On finishing his duties in Paris in the autumn of 1878, Moser was presented with a gold and platinum scarf pin by the Prince (the president of the Commission) and a purse of money from British exhibitors. More valuable still, Sir Philip Cunliffe

Owen, Director of the South Kensington Museum and Secretary to the Commission, recommended that he should be drafted into the newly established Criminal Investigations Department of the Metropolitan Police.

Entering the department as a detective constable third class, Moser rapidly progressed to first class, repeating the process as he became a detective sergeant. He was not particularly impressed by the effectiveness of his fellow officers whose formal training, he felt, had undermined their ability to function in a clandestine fashion. Despite wearing plain clothes, they suffered 'from all the peculiarities of carriage, gait, and dress which unmistakably mark the ordinary preserver of the peace'.[4] In much of his early CID work Moser was able to demonstrate the absence of such 'peculiarities', operating undercover to pose as a would-be purchaser of indecent photographs.

Photography, an earlier scientific marvel than the telephone and phonograph, had been utilised by pornographers from its inception. Many shops exhibited photographic prints depicting actresses and dancers in brief costumes and reproductions of cartoons with suggestive subjects. Often a quiet word with the shopkeeper resulted in an invitation to step into a back room where more extreme material was stored. Moser's mission was the entrapment of shopkeepers offering to sell him photographs that might be regarded by a magistrate as obscene. One such occasion took place on the afternoon of 23 June 1880 when Moser, by then a sergeant, called at a bookseller's shop at 21 White Hart Street, Drury Lane. After purchasing an item from the window, he asked the bookseller, William Williams, if he could see an assortment of other photos. A visit to an upstairs room failed to provide any indecent images, but Williams' wife Ellen suggested that Moser be shown an album which, it transpired, contained pornographic photos. Having secured seven items, Moser reported back to Chief Inspector Shore who agreed to apply for an arrest warrant. Ellen and William Williams must have harboured some suspicions regarding the detective's carriage or gait for they abandoned their shop the day following his visit. Unfortunately for Williams, he was spotted by a uniformed police constable in Villiers Street, Strand, and arrested. Later in the summer, Moser contrived to purchase eight photos from Caroline Thoreste, a French governess and bookseller, of 19 Leicester Square. When searched, her shop was found to contain a further 500 indecent photos which had been imported from Paris. Claiming ignorance of the British legal system, she was spared prison, but fined £50.

In 1881 Moser again found himself in Paris, apparently ordered to monitor the movements of an Irish Republican leader. James Stephens had been on the run from the British authorities since 1848 when he escaped to France following the abortive Young Ireland uprising. Throughout the intervening years he had devoted himself to the cause of overthrowing British rule in Ireland, founding the Irish Republican Brotherhood in 1858 during an unauthorised return to his home country. A fellow Young Ireland insurgent, John O'Mahony, left Europe for the United States in 1856, establishing the Fenian Brotherhood, a society dedicated to creating an Irish republic by armed force. Members of both organisations and fellow sympathisers were all referred to as Fenians during a bombing campaign that rocked Britain from 1880 to 1885. In the United States a 'Skirmishing Fund' to pay for the attacks had been set up by Jeremiah O'Donovan Rossa, an exiled Republican who had frequently called for the 'scientific' destruction of London.

Moser was quickly drawn into the struggle to combat the bombers. While shadowing Stephens, he received news from London of an attempt to ignite a box packed with 40 lbs of gunpowder against a wall of the Lord Mayor's residence, the Mansion House, on 15 March 1881. When one of the suspects, Thomas Mooney, was located in Paris, Moser adopted the disguise of a bricklayer to call at his hotel room. He was able to lure the supposed bomber into the street where a delegation of English police detectives was waiting to confront him. Strained political relations between France and the United Kingdom meant that extradition was not possible, but Chief Superintendent Williamson warned Mooney that he had been identified and would immediately be arrested if he entered any area under Britain's jurisdiction. On his return from Paris, Moser later claimed to have discovered a number of 'infernal machines' after a long investigation conducted in the Liverpool docks. Newspaper reports from July 1881 confirm that 24 bombs were discovered hidden in barrels of concrete shipped from the United States, but fail to confirm Moser's involvement.

Early in 1883 Moser was back in Paris with Chief Superintendent Williamson, investigating one of the most significant murders in British political history. A previously unknown organisation, 'The Invincibles', had assassinated the newly appointed Chief Secretary for Ireland, Lord Henry Cavendish and the Permanent under Secretary, Thomas Henry Burke, in Phoenix Park, Dublin, on 6 May 1882. Although several members of the group were identified by an informer and subsequently executed, the alleged organiser of the plot, Frank Byrne, managed to escape to Paris in mid-February 1883, hotly pursued by Williamson and Moser. After liaising with the French police authorities and keeping Byrne and his associate John Walsh under close surveillance for two weeks, the detectives were frustrated when they were refused permission to arrest their suspects.[5]

Soon afterwards, London was shocked by bombings in Whitehall and at the offices of The Times, and by the discovery of an explosives factory in Ladywell, Birmingham. Four conspirators were arrested on 5 April 1883. Their organiser, a United States citizen, Dr Thomas Gallagher, had taken a room at the Midland Hotel, Charing Cross Station, also using the nearby American Exchange (a bank with reading and writing rooms) at 449 Strand as a convenient base. A fellow American, 21-year-old Joseph William Lynch masquerading as William J. Norman, was despatched to Birmingham to collect a large supply of highly explosive nitroglycerine. Transporting the 170 lb chest back to Euston Station, Lynch caught a cab to the Beaufort Hotel, 2 Wellington Street, Strand. It was hardly worth hauling the deadly container up to the third floor as two hours later, at 12.30 a.m., the police who had tracked him from Birmingham moved in to make an arrest.

With the prospect of an extended bombing campaign, Moser was directed to report on Fenian activity in Paris. His assessment that the Irish expatriates based there posed little threat was not shared by a correspondent writing under the byline, 'Old Irish Colonist'. In an article published in The Westminster Gazette, he expressed the view that that there were many Irish 'dynamiters' in the French capital who were not known to the British police. He continued:

Inspector Moser of Scotland Yard made a searching investigation of the dynamite conspiracy in Paris some weeks ago; but failed to

## DAYS WITH CELEBRITIES (187).
### A DETECTIVE.

ILLUSTRATION 23. Maurice Moser caricatured by Alfred Bryan in 1883.

discover anything of a startling character, simply because he had
opponents to meet who knew from childhood the ins and outs
of secret movements in Ireland, America, and, above all, on the
Continent of Europe where they studied profoundly in past years
the working of the Carbonari and other such formidable societies.

Inspector Moser had to leave Paris almost as much at sea as when he left London to unravel the mystery that surrounded the doings of these desperate men. He had been foiled in his efforts at every step; and all he could say on his return to home was that he only found some fourteen or sixteen dynamiters in Paris and firmly believed that the continent did not number more. The Inspector has committed a very grave mistake there.[6]

Whether or not Parisian plotters were potentially dangerous, American-funded bombings continued with an audacious attack on the headquarters of the CID and the recently created Special Irish Branch at Scotland Yard. On 30 May 1884 Moser narrowly avoided serious injury when he left his office shortly before it was destroyed in the explosion.

Although much of Moser's professional career is recorded in newspaper accounts and court reports, little is known of his private life. In August 1874 he married Harriet Ellen Quinton at St Mary's Church, Lambeth, their address given as Albert Square, Lambeth, an elegant development of mid-Victorian terraced houses. In addition to his linguistic skills he appears to have been an accomplished musician. In February 1884 his composition, the ironically named 'Captivity Waltz', was performed at a star-studded entertainment presented at the Oxford Music Hall on behalf of the Police Orphanage.[7] At the end of the year, his waltz arrangement of Arthur Briscoe's 'Love's Evensong' was dedicated to the wife of his old benefactor, Sir Cunliffe Owen. Within four years Moser had reached the rank of inspector, answerable only to three chief inspectors and a superintendent. Unlike his fellow inspectors (about nine in number), his cases often involved foreign criminals and necessitated frequent excursions to continental Europe.

In the summer of 1887, his comprehensive knowledge of Irish revolutionary politics resulted in him leaving the CID to become a private detective. Earlier in the year The Times had published a series of articles in which it was alleged that the leader of the Irish Parliamentary Party, Charles Stewart Parnell, had condoned crimes committed by Irish Nationalists, including the Phoenix Park murders. Proof of the 'Parnellite conspiracy'[8] was provided by facsimiles of a number of letters allegedly written by the Irish leader. In an attempt to unearth further incriminating letters that Parnell might have sent to Fenian leaders, Joseph Soames, the solicitor to *The Times*, despatched Moser to the United States. Having resigned from his police post, Moser adopted the pseudonym H. L. Walters to negotiate with a number of Irish Nationalists. Authorised to offer large amounts of money, he was able to acquire some apparently compromising correspondence, although his doubts about its authenticity were soon confirmed. American sources claimed that he had made a dishonest profit by overcharging *The Times* for the letters, but the newspaper appears to have been satisfied with his efforts, continuing to employ him on what was eventually to prove a futile mission.

Moser's trip to the United States was discussed during the Parnell Commission, a parliamentary inquiry set up in September 1888 to investigate the allegations made against the Nationalist leader. Once again Soames called upon Moser, entrusting him to shadow three central figures in the case: Parnell, who was alleged to have written the original letters; Richard Pigott, who had indirectly supplied them to *The Times*; and Henry Labouchere (the proprietor of *Truth*), who was attempting to expose them as fakes. Moser discovered that Labouchere had been paying Pigott sums of money and that he had offered the disgruntled Nationalist £1,000 to admit that he had forged the letters. Before the detective could uncover any additional information, Pigott's guilt became obvious when he was discredited at the Commission hearing of 21 February 1889. Confessing his crime to Labouchere, Pigott fled to Spain where he committed suicide a week later. *The Times* eventually paid Parnell the substantial sum of £5000 in damages, while Moser received £1,400 for his undercover work.

The large financial inducement offered by *The Times* was not the only reason for Moser leaving the police and setting up his own detective agency with offices at 31 Southampton Street, Strand. He had become frustrated by 'rampant red-tapeism'[9] and lack of adequately trained staff. And it appears that he had been hatching plans for a future that combined both his professional and personal life. He had met Charlotte Antonia Williamson, a strikingly tall, athletic and intelligent woman who harboured a burning desire to become a detective. Unfortunately, Charlotte's husband, Edward James Clarendon Williamson, was not enthusiastic about her pursuing her dream, let alone suspects. Ten years earlier, the death of her father had resulted in her joining the household of her uncle Philip, a Baptist minister residing at Belle View Lodge in Fulham.

She married his son, her cousin Edward, in 1882 when he just turned 21 and she was 26. Although young, Edward appears to have followed a profitable trade, manufacturing engravers' blocks for the printing industry. Despite becoming a mother, Charlotte was reluctant to remain in her comfortable Bloomsbury home. It is not clear whether she developed her investigatory passion before or after she met Moser, but their intense relationship quickly resulted in the break-up of both their marriages. Edward Williamson had been deeply troubled when, in 1888, his wife announced that she was to work for Moser as a 'lady detective'. His concern turned to dismay as she started to spend periods of time away from home. His suspicions were confirmed when she attempted to hang a portrait of Moser in their bedroom, also requesting that she might be allowed to accompany him on a trip to Constantinople. A rival agency, Slater's, was engaged and soon reported that Charlotte and Moser were frequently seen in bed together in an apartment in Garrick Street, Covent Garden. By 1890 the couple were living together at 4 Sussex Mansions, Maiden Lane.

Moser expanded his business in 1889 by establishing Charlotte as manager of Moser's Ladies Detective Agency, 'conducted entirely by ladies' with offices at 156 Regent Street. The unsavoury nature of much private detective work meant that female members of the profession were not highly regarded. When, in 1889, it was suggested that it was hard to understand why any woman would undertake such work unless she had fallen to a low social status, a female 'expert' in the field (perhaps Charlotte) responded:

> That is as unjust and as wrong to think as was the assertion the other day that all ballet girls are immoral. Most people run away with the idea that all the work done by women detectives must be of the dirtiest and basest nature. But it is not necessarily so. Suppose an innocent woman has been slandered. Well is it not pleasant work to vindicate her character? Not infrequently, some wealthy lady is appealed to for charity. She would willingly bestow it, if she thought the object was worthy; so she obtains the services of a female detective to make enquiry for her.[10]

Years later Charlotte explained that her methods were quite different from those of her partner:

[I]t was only when he left Scotland Yard, in order to become a private detective on his own account, that the combination of circumstances enabled me to join him in his work, which I confess is exceedingly interesting. One thing is very curious, that we both attack the same case in entirely different ways, and arrive at our results sometimes from opposite poles.[11]

Well versed as witnesses in divorce proceedings, Charlotte and Moser soon found themselves appearing as defendants in a case heard at the High Court of Justice in July 1890. In the face of overwhelming proof of their relationship, the judge dismissed Charlotte's counter charge that her husband had committed adultery with an Ada Williamson (possibly Charlotte's own sister). The divorce was granted in Edward Williamson's favour, leaving the two detectives a heavy bill for costs and damages.[12]

Another drain on their financial resources occurred in September 1890 when Moser was summoned to court and ordered to pay weekly maintenance of £2 to his wife Harriet and their two children. In an extraordinary attempt to have their marriage dissolved, Moser accused Harriet of adultery with John George Dalzell in Brixton and at Clements Inn, Strand, and with numerous men at a brothel at 89 Loughborough Road, Brixton.[13] His petition was dismissed on 14 June 1892 and in the face of mounting legal costs Charlotte was forced to sell her jewels. Back in the 1880s Moser had built a reputation as a fearless and implacable adversary to elements who threatened the fabric of British society; by the beginning of the 1890s he was seen as an adulterous private eye struggling to avoid contributing to the upkeep of his wronged family. It was not the sort of behaviour expected of an English gentleman.

Moser was able to present a more positive image of himself in a series of newspaper articles and two popular books published in Britain and the United States. A selection of Moser's cases were written up by a colleague, journalist Charles F. Rideal, although Rideal appears to have been a somewhat less scrupulous chronicler than Dr John Watson who detailed the exploits of Sherlock Holmes, the fictional character who was introduced to the reading public in 1887. In *Stories from Scotland Yard* (1890) and *True Detective Stories* (1891), not only names, but facts were frequently altered. What dramatic effect such revisionism might have achieved was soon dissipated by verbose passages concerning the dastardly machinations of the Irish Nationalists, the criminal proclivities of foreigners and the debilitating effects of pornography. Moser held similarly strong, but more enlightened views about the future of the CID which he felt was poorly funded, badly organised and understaffed. Training, he concluded, was a major problem, as was the non-employment of female detectives. Both Moser and Charlotte were quick to promote their respective inquiry agencies in interviews with the popular press. Moser even made a brief appearance in the *Strand Magazine*, contributing an erudite, illustrated article on the history of handcuffs.

Charlotte's passion for detective work appears to have outlived her fondness for her partner. By the early 1900s the couple had separated, although both continued to run their respective agencies. Charlotte's 25-year-old daughter, Margaret Williamson, joined her in January 1908, taking over the firm after a few months when her mother was declared bankrupt. The crisis had been precipitated by crippling debts that Charlotte had incurred in an unsuccessful legal action to prove that her sister, A. Williamson, had falsified their father's will. Charlotte died at the age of 63 in 1919.

As with Moser's early life, details of his later days are limited. Investigations into matrimonial disputes and white-collar crimes were not as well reported as battles with revolutionaries and the apprehension of murderers. In 1893 he moved his base from Southampton Street to 'more commodious offices' in the newly built Effingham House, situated on the corner of Arundel Street and the Strand. His 24-hour, seven-day–a-week service was described as 'Prompt', 'Secret' and 'Reliable', with agents in every city of the world and a 'staff of detectives (including ladies) in every station of life'.[14] Fifteen years later in 1908 Moser's Detective Agency became a limited company, Morris Moser Ltd, with a nominal capital of £1,000. The now incorporated Moser continued to frequently visit the continent to pursue covert activities, but he was alleged to be taking time off when he died in Boulogne in June 1913.

# 12

# ALIAS JACK THE RIPPER

Elizabeth Mary Baldock read the letter with horrified amazement. Even allowing for the crimson ink and capital letters, it was not the sort of communication that an elderly invalid expected to receive. Its threat of assassination by dynamite with detailed references to how such an act might be engineered seemed very real when considered against the recent bombings in London. The writer was clearly as desperate as any terrorist. He stood in want of £500 and was determined to obtain it 'or perish in the attempt'. Had Mrs Baldock's impoverished tormentor chosen to sign a name to the letter he would have had a wide selection to choose from: Christian Briscony, Charles Grandy, Captain Armstrong, Mr Anderson, Mr Ohlsen, George Jackson or 'The French Colonel'. Many knew him as Charles Le Grand, a private detective with offices at 283 Strand. In recent years it has been suggested that the list of aliases should be extended to include the most famous pseudonym in criminal history – 'Jack the Ripper'.

While few things were as they seemed in the life of Charles Le Grand, it appears that his real name was Christian Neilson and that he was born in Denmark in about 1853. By the mid 1870s he had started his British criminal career by committing a series of opportunist thefts. Like his criminal predecessors, Jack Sheppard and Jack Hall, Le Grand started in a small way by purloining knives, razors and pocket books. Such misdemeanours were largely inconsequential, but, in 1877, the number of repeated offences resulted in him being sentenced to seven years' imprisonment. On his release in 1884 he adopted a new nationality, a new criminal activity and at least two new names. Masquerading as Charles Grandy or Charles Le Grand, he pretended to be from France, a claim given dubious credibility by the French prostitutes with whom he began to associate. His wildly equivocal attitude towards prostitution was an early manifestation of an increasingly psychotic personality. While living off the 'immoral earnings' of Amelia Marie Pourquoi Demay at 243 Elgin Avenue, Maida Vale, he made numerous complaints concerning the conduct of women of the streets. A compulsion to write long, overdramatic letters found expression in diatribes about the lack of police action against prostitutes sent to the Chief Constable and the Home Secretary.

Early in 1887 he initiated a campaign of intimidation against Henriette Pasquier, a prostitute who had lived at his Maida Vale address. His persecution of Henriette appears to have been an attempt to drive her from the area where Amelia Demay also made her (and his) living. In March 1887 he was fined £5 for a 'violent and cruel' assault on Henriette after which he recruited thugs to molest her as she went about her trade. A police constable was also approached and offered a bribe to take her and other prostitutes into custody. When John Tysell, one of Henriette's assailants, was sentenced to two months' imprisonment Le Grand (or Grandy) reacted violently. On the afternoon of Saturday, 19 March 1887 he stormed up to the persecuted prostitute in Great Portland Street. After calling her an offensive name, he threatened: 'You got the man two months hard for assault. I'll kill you.' As well as striking her twice he also attacked Ellen Perin, 'a cook out of place',[1] who tried to intervene.

Considering his previous conviction and the sustained nature of the harassment inflicted on Henriette, Le Grand seems to have been treated leniently by the magistrate. He was sentenced to keep the peace on two sureties of £50. In an account of the case, The London Standard stated that he was also known as 'The French Colonel', printing a description which accorded with the martial sobriquet: 'a tall, military-looking man, wearing a fashionable overcoat with a sealskin collar'.[2] Five months later. Le Grand again came to the notice of the police – or rather he brought himself to the notice of the police – by writing a long letter complaining about the conduct of PC William Hughes. A distinctive feature of the letter was that it was written in both black and red ink.

Le Grand's hatred of the police found a degree of expression in his next venture, the setting up of a private detective agency. His offices at 283 Strand were located close to St Clement Danes and only two

doors from the premises of *The Illustrated Police News*, a publication that
was to devote considerable column inches to his subsequent career.
An assistant was procured in the miserable form of James Hall, a
destitute clerk whom he had found wandering in the Strand. In 1888
Le Grand aligned himself with two of the most sensational cases of
the day, one involving a series of horrifying murders and the other
the murky intrigues of Irish revolutionary politics. While the Parnell
Commission steadily sifted through a mountain of evidence relating
to the Irish leader's involvement with Fenian crimes, Le Grand started
to investigate a number of its principal participants, including Richard
Pigott; the MP Henry Labouchere; and the Irish Parliamentary Party
MP Justin McCarthy. He was to claim that, like Maurice Moser, he had
been acting on behalf of Joseph Soames, solicitor for TheTimes, although
it is more likely that such activity was an uninvited attempt to unearth
material to sell to the press or use for blackmailing purposes. On one
occasion he and an ex-policeman named Scanlan arrived at the Ely
Place office of the well-known solicitor George Lewis (also deeply
immersed in the Parnell case), seeking employment as detectives.
Le Grand was wearing a fur coat, perhaps not the best apparel for
undercover work. Undeterred by Lewis' negative response, Le Grand
made a return visit, claiming that if engaged he could supply 'very
wonderful information'.[3]

Details of Le Grand's role in the investigation of the 'Whitechapel
Murders' are similarly sparse. Somehow, the abuser of prostitutes
and vehement critic of the police managed to persuade a group of
local residents and businessmen to employ him in their hunt for a
serial killer who had just commenced a short, but sensational reign
of terror. Although brutal assaults and murders were commonplace
in the densely populated streets of East London, the murder of a
number of prostitutes, which took place in Whitechapel during
the summer and autumn of 1888, had sufficient common factors
for them to be considered the work of a single person or small
group. The possibility that a blood-crazed maniac or a sadistic gang
were running amok fixed the attention of London and the wider
world on an area of the capital that had long been ignored. Time
spent in prison and as part of the criminal underworld may have
equipped Le Grand with a better knowledge of the locality and its
inhabitants than most. With a colleague, J. H. Batchelor (of whom
nothing appears to be known), he was recruited by the Whitechapel

Vigilance Committee, a group that organised street patrols and offered a £500 reward (around £40,000 in current reckoning) for the apprehension of the murderer. The two detectives also appear to have been retained by The Evening News, feeding the newspaper an account of an important discovery they had made – or fabricated.

At 12.30 a.m. on Sunday, 30 September 1888, a steady stream of people had left the International Working Men's Educational Club at 40 Berner Street, close to the Commercial Road. They had been present to debate 'The Necessity of Socialism amongst Jews' and to participate in a community sing-song, both no mean feats for an assemblage made up of diverse nationalities. The last of the group had drifted away by 12.45 a.m. when Israel Schwartz saw Elizabeth Stride, a prostitute, being pushed to the ground by a man close to the gates of Dutfield's Yard, alongside the club. The assailant was short and stocky and was watched from the opposite side of Berner Street by another man. This other individual, who may or may not have been connected with the assault, was described as about 35 years old, five feet eleven inches in height with a fair complexion and light brown hair. He was wearing a dark overcoat. Fifteen minutes later Louis Diemshitz, the club manager, returned after a day selling cheap jewellery at a South East market. As he drove his pony and cart into Dutfield's Yard, he stumbled over Stride's still-warm body. Her throat had been cut. Soon the narrow street was reverberating with cries of 'Murder' and 'Police', and, according to a report in The Evening News, someone shouted 'Come out quick, there's a poor woman with ten inches of cold steel in her'.[4]

Elizabeth Stride is usually numbered as the Whitechapel murderer's third victim, the fourth, Catherine Eddowes being killed just an hour later. The sensational news of the two murders was compounded on 1 October when The Daily Telegraph published a transcript of a letter that had been received by the Central News Agency four days earlier. Written in red ink and purporting to be the work of the killer of the first two victims, it was signed 'Jack the Ripper', the first time the infamous nickname had been used. A second communication from the same writer was received by the Central News Agency on 1 October in the form of a postcard, also penned in red ink, which made reference to the 'double event'. Although legend-forming, at the time both letter and postcard were considered by the police to be concocted by a journalist intent on creating new copy.

Le Grand's and Batchelor's 'breakthrough' in the investigation of Stride's murder was reported in *The Evening News* on 4 October:

> We are enabled to present our readers this morning in the columns of *The Evening News* with the most startling information that has yet been made public in relation the Whitechapel murderer, and the first real clue that has been obtained to his identity. The chain of evidence that has been pieced together by two gentlemen connected with the business of private enquiries, who, starting on the track of the assassin without any 'pet' theory to substantiate and contenting themselves with ascertaining and connecting a series of the simplest facts, have succeeded in arriving at a result of the greatest importance. What they go to establish is that the perpetrator of the Berner Street crimes was seen and spoken to whilst in the company of his victim, within forty minutes of the commission of the crime and only passed from the sight of a witness ten minutes before the murder and within ten yards of the scene of the awful deed. We proceed to give hereunder the story of the two detectives, Messrs. Grand and J. H. Batchelor, of 283 Strand.[5]

Following the discovery of Elizabeth Stride's body, a routine police interview with an elderly greengrocer, Matthew Packer, had failed to elicit any useful information. Undeterred by Packer's zero recall, Le Grand and Batchelor arrived at his small shop and home in Berner Street, adjacent to the murder scene. Although two days had elapsed since first questioned by the police, Packer's memory had greatly improved and he was able to tell the detectives that shortly before the murder he had sold some black grapes to a man and to a woman who fitted the description of the victim. Mrs Rosenfield from further along the street added that she had seen a grape stalk on the ground shortly after Stride's body had been removed. A visit to Dutfield's Yard and an examination of the 'heterogeneous filth' in a drain revealed the vital stalk. On 4 October Le Grand and Batchelor took Packer to the morgue where he identified Stride, known locally as 'Long Liz', the woman with a liking for grapes. On escorting Packer back to Berner Street they were met by Sergeant Stephen White who asked them on whose authority they were acting. Reluctantly they admitted that they were private detectives. Later the same day they returned in a Hansom cab and persuaded Packer to come with them to make a statement at Scotland Yard.

Unfortunately for the sleuths, an examination of the contents of Stride's stomach failed to reveal the remains of any grapes, black, red or white. There were no further newspaper reports, suggesting that the police might have become aware of Le Grand's unsavoury past or that *The Evening News* decided to drop his self-congratulatory contributions. The detectives' partnership soon foundered. Some time before June 1889 Batchelor summonsed Le Grand for assaulting him in the Strand.[6]

Finding that the detection of crime didn't pay, Le Grande added blackmail to the enquiry work undertaken from his new office at 10 Agar Street, Strand. Drawing on his comprehensive knowledge of prostitutes, he sent letters to married men who had been observed with 'fast' women in the vicinity: 'Dear Sir, Please give me a call at your earliest convenience, otherwise an action of a serious nature will be commenced against you.'[7] In 1889 Le Grand enlisted Amelia Demay in a reckless and ill-conceived plot to extort money from a prominent Harley Street surgeon. Her allegations that Malcolm Alexander Morris (1849–1924) had reneged on a promise to marry her appeared somewhat unlikely when set against the existence of his wife of nearly twenty years and four children. Morris was a distinguished doctor with an extensive private practice; a Fellow of the Royal College of Surgeons of Edinburgh; head of a department and lecturer at St Mary's Hospital, Paddington; and a member of eight learned societies connected with medicine. Demay was also well known – as a prostitute often to be found touting for business in Regent Street. The decision to select Morris as a victim may have been prompted by an incident in November 1887 when he had attended a male patient at 35 Charlotte Street, Portland Place, an address also occupied by Demay and Le Grand. Morris claimed that he had not previously met either of his accusers, although a *La Ronde*-like set of circumstances may have provided a tenuous link between them. One of Morris' areas of expertise was the treatment of sexually transmitted diseases.

It seems that Demay and Le Grand hoped that Morris would pay them to prevent the embarrassment of legal proceedings. They had discussed the plan late in 1888 and in February of the following year Demay sent the doctor a letter demanding money. She claimed that he had visited her at her lodgings at 85 Bolsover Street twice weekly for five months and proposed marriage in the first floor sitting room on 21 March 1886. It was also alleged that he had presented her with 'a fancy performing dog'. Apparently Morris had no recollection of the trips to Bolsover Street or of the talented canine. When he ignored her letter, she took out a writ against him in the Queen's Bench Division of the High Court for breach of promise of marriage and slander, claiming £2,000 damages. In an attempt to break Morris' resolve, Le Grand began to spend long periods of time outside his Harley Street home, also pursuing him, his wife and servants both on foot and by cab. After following him on a professional visit to Sir George Campbell, Le Grand waited in Bryanston Square, Westminster, menacing him with a cane when he emerged from the house. When Morris' solicitor complained to Demay's solicitor about the harassment, Le Grand brought an action against him for libel.

At Demay's and Le Grand's subsequent trial for extortion, two witnesses testified that they had been offered bribes to supply false evidence in the original breach of promise case. Over a drink in Short's Wine Lodge in the Strand, Le Grand had offered Alfred Walking, an East End porter, £10 to say that he had seen Morris and Demay walking arm in arm. Le Grand had told him, 'as soon as you get into court I will put £10 into your hands and you will bunk or slope as soon as you like'.[8] Demay sought out Elene Williams, a French prostitute she had known for several years, offering her £10 to testify that she had seen Morris in Bolsover Street and heard his promise of marriage. Another prostitute, Vallet Brown, testified that Demay and Le Grand lived together as man and wife, but when other men came to visit her 'sometimes he went into the kitchen, sometimes he went away, and sometimes he waited'.[9] The case for the prosecution could hardly have been stronger. On 28 June 1889 both were found guilty, Demay being sentenced to eighteen months' hard labour and Le Grand to two years.

As soon as he was released from prison Le Grand resumed his criminal activities with a vengeance. From the top back room of a Kennington Road boarding house he began to send letters to a number of wealthy women demanding large sums of money. Elizabeth Baldock, Baroness Bolsover and Lady Jessell, the widow of the late Master of the Rolls were among those who received rambling demands written in capitals with red ink. The message was always the same – unless they expressed their willingness to pay £500 they would have their brains dashed out. Mrs Baldock received her first communication at her home in Grosvenor Place on 17 July 1891. Her irritation on seeing that there was two pence excess postage to pay on the letter soon turned to terror as she read its content:

Madam, Take notice that if you do not pay me the sum of £500, I dash your brains out as soon as you read this note, by a Dynamiet [sic] explosion. I stand in want of the said sum, and I must have it, or perish in the attempt. Remember, madam, that desperate men, or rather a man brought to despair by the villainy of a woman, will do desperate things, and indeed a woman shall pay for it. Be careful how you proceed in this case, You may be advised to apply to the police for protection, but if you do you will find that their protection is not much better than that of your lapdog, if the English detectives cannot even apprehend the man who killed on the open streets in Whitechapel seven or eight women, then indeed their detective qualities must be limited; in fact, skill should not protect you from my hand. If I do not get the sum I have demanded, understand, I am firmly determined to have it or your life as the value for it. If you estimate your life so low that you would not pay £500 for, then I must leave you to your own reflections. Do not believe that it is my intention to dash your brains out with a revolver, that, indeed, would be a madman's work. No, madam: a thin cake of dynamite placed between some mounted fulminate of silver, and the whole placed between the door and mat on the floor upon which you have to pass, or under your seat in the church, or even under the cushion of your carriage, will immediately explode the moment the weight of your body comes upon it, and dash you to pieces. I intend to do what I say; I have been ruined by a woman, and a woman shall pay for it. I have sent a letter like this to nine other ladies for the purpose, that if you do not pay I will dash your brains out, and you will then serve to the others of us an example of what they have to expect if they do not pay up. If you feel disposed to comply with my request, please then to insert in the Daily Telegraph the following advertisement: 'A. M. M. will comply,' and an address will be forwarded to you where to address the money, or it may be that it may be called for, only mark well that treachery on your part will be punished with instant death, as I am well prepared for such an emergency. I am sorry to trouble you in this way, but I must have the money.

Hoping you will be sensible enough to give the required reply, I remain, Madam, yours truly, A. M. M.

On discovering that Mrs Baldock was communicating with the police, Le Grand sent an indignant second letter in which he accused her of 'treachery'. He offered an alternative way in which he might take her life and demonstrated a sardonic sense of humour:

> And if I cannot get you with explosive material I may do it by poisoning your bread, your milk, etc., with arsenic or cyanide [...] You had better act a la preciptice [sic] as to your testament and not at all surprised if you find yourself comfortably located in one of His Imperial Majesty's drawing rooms for you cannot expect to go to Heaven having exposed yourself to what must fairly be called voluntary suicide while in a sound state of mind. Hoping you will excuse my jest, which is as rude as my demands for money.[10]

His communication to Lady Jessell concluded with an appeal for sympathy:

> I hope you will consider my request. It may be that one day I may be able to repay it back to you, only I must have it now. If you knew who I am I feel sure you would pity me – to see that I am come to an act like this, which is highly criminal and void of all human feeling. I knew you once. But enough.[11]

Le Grand's obsessive letter writing of previous years rebounded on him when his handwriting was recognised by the police. His whereabouts were quickly established and detectives began to keep watch on his lodgings. Realising that he was under surveillance, Le Grand left 83 Kennington Road on 12 August, later writing to tell his landlady that he had gone to Paris and would no longer require the room. Although he may have gone to Paris for a few days he was soon established at another boarding house in Shirley Road, West Kilburn. There he and an accomplice, Edwin Smith, hatched a scheme to obtain money with forged cheques.

Towards the end of August, Le Grand discovered that the police were once more on his track. His response was extraordinary, even by his execrable standards. He sent a letter to Sir Edward Bradford, the Commissioner of Police, warning that if efforts to apprehend him were not abandoned he would begin to set fire to public buildings with a solution of phosphorous. On 3 September a letter arrived at Tottenham Court Road Police Station addressed to Sergeant William James, an officer who had given evidence leading to Le Grand's previous conviction

Hyde Park Scoundrel, do not let me see you in my way again. I could see you yesterday, although your detective Smart could permit perjury when well bribed; you dog, you could not see me. Be careful, and do not come in my way; for, sure as this is written by me, the man whom you have injured by your crime of perjury, I dash your brains out the moment you come near me. I will see your heart blood before they get me again by your perjury. My hand is used to firearms, and by heaven I shall not miss you when I get you in my sight.[12]

For some reason the police chose not to arrest Le Grand immediately, but watched as he moved into a house with Smith and his wife at 1 The Oaklands, Acacia Road, Maldon, South London. Three days after the move, on 26 September, Sergeant James and Detective Holder intercepted Le Grand and Smith at Maldon railway station. Smith 'did a bunk' leaving his partner in crime in the hands of the police. On their way to the local police station Le Grand snarled:

You dirty scoundrel, this is your work, you who have received £50 from Morris to put me away before; if I had seen you I would have blown your brains out. You dirty dog! You are good at perjury when you are bribed. I shall soon be back out of this, and then look out; I will not shoot you, I will put about six inches of steel into your back.[13]

Le Grand's threats were not hollow. The bag he carried was found to contain a revolver and a heavy duty knuckleduster. And at the house in the Oaklands, Sergeant James discovered two bottles of acid and a prototype brain-dasher in the form of a cigar box fitted with springs and a patch of gunpowder. Even without the assistance of weapons or infernal machines he was a dangerous and unpredictable prisoner. While waiting at Maldon Station to return to central London, he attempted to push his old adversary in front of the incoming train. On the journey to Waterloo, he harangued James:

It was my intention to push you under the train. I would not mind doing it. You, as a clever detective, could not catch me. I have seen you many a time when I sent a boy from the Messenger Company to the bank in Victoria Street. I saw you, I was in the churchyard, and you, the gentleman detective, you bloody fool, you could have seen me; I saw you in Hyde Park following the poor little boy, you bloody fool, and you could not see me.[14]

Le Grand repeatedly told police that they had been lucky to catch him when they did for he had been intending to leave for New York within the next few days. The large amount of cash in British and foreign currency found on him suggested that, for once, he might have been telling the truth.

After an initial hearing at Westminster Police Court on 6 October 1891, Le Grand appeared at the Central Criminal Court on 16 November charged with extortion and possessing a forged cheque. He was found guilty and sentenced to 20 years' imprisonment on the first count and seven years on the second. After completing 15 years at Portland and Parkhurst prisons he was released on license on 5 January 1907.

Most criminals from the past are remembered, if at all, in a generalised way, their sordid careers reduced to a few sensational features or reconstructed to form allegories of good and evil, or of protest and repression. Not so with Charles Le Grand. In recent years his life has been subjected to minute examination, with contemporary records scoured for any mention of his various pseudonyms. For Le Grand has become a posthumous prime suspect in the ongoing hunt for the perpetrator of the Whitechapel murders. It is a far-flung investigation carried on by hundred of internet-linked sleuths around the world.[15]

Over the past century, 'Jack the Ripper's' anonymity has led to his character (or lack of it) becoming an emblem of the dark, threatening side of Victorian London. Shrouded in fog and mystery, he is an ethereal bogeyman dissociated from the human viscera that he left in stinking piles. Such a melodramatic image is possibly powerful enough to survive a definite identification, but the London Tourist Board might harbour some concerns as tenacious computer 'tecs' attempt to add flesh and blood to Jack's alluringly shadowy figure. Without prejudicing any further lines of enquiry it may be of interest to summarise Le Grande's qualifications to fill the position of London's most famous criminal.

He was a calculating and desperate criminal with convictions before and after the murders. He had many underworld contacts and a close knowledge of police procedures. He had spent much time with prostitutes, but is also known to have persecuted and physically assaulted them. He despised the police force, taunting them with their failure to find 'Jack the Ripper'. He attempted to push Sergeant James under a train and, in an echo of Elizabeth Stride's murder, threatened to bury six inches of steel into him.

Like the sender of the 'Jack the Ripper' communications, he was an inveterate letter and postcard writer, both anonymous and signed. As with the letters purporting to come from 'Jack the Ripper', his were sometimes written in red ink. He also used working-class slang as did the 'Ripper' letter writer. He is known to have been in Whitechapel at the time of the murders and was involved with investigations into the crimes. Most significantly, he appears to have suffered from an extreme personality disorder with a need to manipulate events and to create intricate mysteries.

When released in 1907, Le Grand went straight – straight back to crime. Adopting the alias George Jackson, he became involved with a gang attempting to cash forged cheques, only to be apprehended in 1908 and sent back to prison for a further four years. He explained to the court that during his brief period of freedom he made a living by escorting sightseeing parties around London. Along with the dangers implicit in following such a violent and unpredictable courier, Le Grand tours might well have taken in much that was off-beat and curious. As he once informed solicitor George Lewis, he had some very wonderful information.

# 13

# CRYSTALS OF MORPHINE

The scene was a back bedroom on the third floor of the Craven Hotel, Craven Street, overlooking Charing Cross Station. A fire was burning brightly in the cast-iron grate. It had not been lit for warmth or cheer, but to help dissolve the crystals of morphine with which Alexander Woodburn Heron intended to end his life. Swallowing a dose of the mixture he took up a pencil and started to chronicle his own, slow suicide. His notes were rambling and sporadic, addressed to his dead mistress's best friend:

Dear Dolly, impress on all our friends how strictly I avoid all spirituous liquor. Goodbye, dear. Good-bye, Dolly. Ruby and I shall soon meet now, Dolly, if people do meet there.

1.10 am. Have just mixed another 10 grains to take directly, I don't feel any drowsiness. My God, how dreadful for it to be disclosed that I gave my darling anything. If my grief is not real, nothing in the world is real. I must guard against getting dozy; it should never do to fail. I have now laid on the floor so that no fall shall rouse the house.

1.25 am. I am feeling quite foolish. My pulse is very slow.

1.40 am. I feel death coming fast. I made up my mind to die when I was giving my evidence, long before I finished. Oh, for a man to have such power over a girl as I had over my darling.

Fancy – fancy; actually half-past two – 2.30 am! Good-bye. I feel comfortable. Good-bye.

2.38 am. It seems very slow. However, there is more left for I bought, for I bought 30 grains. I have now fully taken fully 18 grains now. I feel perfectly healthy and well. I feel as you know most beautifully warm and comfortable, as people always do after morphia.

With death seeming to approach at a snail's pace Heron took a bone-handled razor and drew it across his throat, having first taken the precaution of positioning a bowl beneath the cut to catch the flow of blood. His body was discovered twelve hours later when hotel workers forced open the door.

Alexander Woodburn Heron was a product of the British Empire. The first legitimate son of a wealthy plantation owner in the West Indies, he spent the latter part of his life as a doctor and administrator in the central African colonies. When Alexander was born in 1857 the Herons were well established in Manchester, Jamaica, having emigrated from Scotland in the eighteenth century to similarly mountainous terrain in the county of Middlesex. His father, also Alexander Woodburn Heron, was known locally as 'The Captain', probably because he commanded most of the plantations and workers in the district. On his death in 1901 Alexander Woodburn Heron Senior was provided with a suitably elevated burial place, his tomb on Shooter's Hill overlooking many of the properties that he bequeathed to his family.

Alexander Woodburn Heron Junior came to England during the mid 1870s with the intention of becoming an officer in the army. Tall, clean-cut and brimming with confidence, he would have suited a uniform, but after rejecting a military career he began studying medicine in Glasgow. At the age of 18 he met Rose Anna Redding, 'a very amiable, pretty and accomplished young lady', marrying her against the wishes of her parents. Although talented and popular, he possessed an air of superiority that verged on condescension, not helped by a violent temper which once led to an embarrassing court appearance. During a hotly contested argument after a lecture he struck one Rawlinson Potts on the nose. Appearing before Sheriff Spens in a court crowded with fellow students, he was found guilty of assault 'to the effusion of blood and serious injury' and fined £5 or 14 days' imprisonment.[1]

The Herons had two children and lived on 'very affectionate terms', although it was said that Rose was extremely jealous and had uncontrollable fits of temper.[2] On qualifying as a surgeon, Heron took his family back to Jamaica where he was appointed district medical officer. Rose apparently contracted a long-term illness and to ease her pain and sleeplessness Heron prescribed morphine which he himself administered. It is possible that, like many doctors' wives, Rose was actually suffering from 'morphinism' or morphine addiction. Having become increasingly weak, Rose died on 13 August 1881. Despite the inability of a post-mortem to establish the cause of her death, a close colleague of Heron's, Dr George Rogers, was of the opinion that she died from the effects of prussic acid or a morphine overdose. At the inquest a local chemist who had dispensed the prescription agreed that the bottles containing prussic acid and morphine stood next to each other on his shelf, but insisted that they were clearly labelled, presumably indicating that he felt that he had not made a dispensing error. Heron did not help his own case by claiming that he had thrown the medicine bottle away. Considerable public suspicion surrounded the mysterious death, giving the inquest the feeling of a trial for manslaughter or even murder. Aided by a solicitor, Heron mounted a vigorous 'defence' of his position and, with only one dissenter, the jury decided that the death was due to natural causes. But with the majority of his patients deserting him it was not surprising that Heron left the island soon after.

He returned to England with the story that his wife had died in childbirth. Initially, he appears to have worked in Brighton, Sussex, after which he acted as an assistant to a doctor with an extensive practice in Plaistow, East London. For a time he had a medical practice in the dock area of West Ham where his children and their black nurse aroused considerable interest. In 1884 he made the major decision to join the Colonial Medical Service and leave Britain. Sending his two young children back to live with his family in Jamaica, Heron set off for the Gold Coast (now Ghana) in central Africa. Stationed in Quittah (now Keta) and Axim, he at first acted as a doctor, later adding the responsibilities of a district commissioner to his medical duties. The quaint colonial towns with their old forts, palm trees and fishing boats must have been reminiscent of his West Indian homeland. After a while he started a relationship with a pretty young local girl who bore him two children. Despite the attractions of his new life, Heron sometimes startled colleagues by sudden acts of violence. Once, while hearing a case, he became annoyed by a native policeman who was chatting in the background. When the man ignored a stern warning not to resume his conversation, Heron sentenced him to a month's imprisonment and repeatedly knocked his head against a wall.[3]

Heron eventually became Chief Medical Officer in the Gambia with an official salary of £500 a year, increased by a further £500 to £600 from private patients. With time and money to spare it was not long before he found someone with which to share both.

On a visit to London early in 1891 he met Marion Fanny Sharpe, an attractive teenage actress whose stage name was Ruby Russell. At the time the description 'actress' was more flexible than elastic, stretching from the profession often claimed by arrested prostitutes through to the respected grand dames of Victorian theatre. On the scale of things Marion was clearly closer to the former than the latter. At the age of 17 she had run away from her parents' pub in central London and after some provincial engagements was appearing as a chorus girl in the 1890–1 pantomime at the Theatre Royal, Drury Lane. Heron introduced himself to her behind the scenes, amid the exotic clutter of props required for staging the fairy tale *Beauty and the Beast*. The production's stars, Dan Leno, Herbert Campbell, Vesta Tilley and, particularly, Belle Bilton may well have looked on with weary recognition as the situation unfolded. It was not unusual for gentlemen to seek intimate acquaintanceship with performers of lower social rank. Two years previously beautiful Belle, the daughter of an Aldershot canteen sergeant, had been ardently pursued by young Lord Dunlo, only for their marriage to be cynically contested in the divorce court. On hearing that Heron was a doctor, Marion declined his invitation to a post-performance rendezvous. She was afraid of medical men and decided to have nothing to do with him. But Heron had become obsessed with the young actress and next day sent a large box of crystallised fruit to her lodgings, which he had established to be at 34 Studland Street, Hammersmith.

Marion's landlord, Mr Clayden, expressed concern as she began to weaken in response to Heron's repeated gifts, telegrams and messages. Since first arriving in Hammersmith from an engagement in Coventry, she had become popular with her host and his family. She and another girl, who she claimed was a cousin, had come to London in November 1889 to appear with the great P. T. Barnum's circus which was the Christmas attraction at the gigantic entertainment venue Olympia. With friendship blossoming between Marion and their daughter Dolly, the Claydens adopted a parental concern regarding Heron's approaches. But despite their ban on him visiting the house he contrived to meet her in the street when she left for the theatre. Soon she was regularly visiting him at his apartments in Vernon Chamber, Southampton Row. They continued to meet until August 1891 when he returned to his post in the

Gambia and she remained in London where she was suffering from an undisclosed illness. Whether her ailment was real or feigned, she continued to pursue her theatrical career, appearing as one of more than 50 peasants and courtiers who packed the stage in the comic opera La Cigale at the Lyric Theatre, Shaftesbury Avenue. Some degree of advancement was demonstrated when she was chosen to act as understudy to Mabel Love.

In January 1892 Marion took on her most challenging role, that of the spouse of an important official in the colonial service. Arriving in the Gambian capital Bathurst, 'Mrs Woodburn Heron' was introduced at the Governor's House and on the admiral's yacht. Although making progress as an actress it was manifestly clear that she came from a less elevated class than her 'husband'. At first she struggled with the temperature and the etiquette of colonial life, but she eventually made friends and busied herself by helping Heron dispense medicines. Like Rose Heron, she began to take morphine to combat what was said to be a feverish condition. Outwardly they were an ideal couple – Woodburn Heron was handsome with fair skin and wavy hair and moustache while Marion had once been described as 'one of the most beautiful women on the stage'. Their relationship was troubled, however, with both exhibiting signs of morbidness and jealousy. 'If anything were to happen to her I believe I should go mad. One cannot help remembering that there is always the chance of the brightest happiness being blown away,'[4] Heron wrote to a friend. After their 'little quarrels' both had threatened to commit suicide.

Heron was granted three months' sick leave in August 1892. On the voyage back to England Marion also appears to have been unwell, confined to their cabin with supposed malarial fever. Her continuing poor health forced an unplanned stay in Liverpool for four days and was still in evidence when they arrived in London on 7 September. It seems that they were planning to marry during their stay, and to return to Africa with their relationship legitimised. Marion was certainly in high spirits when she resumed her acquaintanceship with the Claydens. Dolly remembered her drinking tea with the family and dancing happily around their Hammersmith home. Heron and Marion had taken furnished rooms within walking distance of Studland Street at 32 Lillie Road, West Brompton, where their landlady, Mrs Ellen Williams, welcomed them as a respectable married couple. She must have been particularly reassured that

Mr Heron was a medical man for her late husband had been a deputy inspector of hospitals. Within a fortnight Mrs Williams was dismayed to find herself, her home and her neighbourhood at the centre of shocking and sensational newspaper coverage.

On Tuesday 21 September, Mrs Williams provided dinner for her guests. Heron had ham and Marion rashers of pork accompanied by a glass of stout. At 8.15 p.m. the landlady cleared the dishes and left the house to purchase some shopping. A few minutes after she had left, Heron came to the front door frantically shouting: 'Help! Help! Police! Police!' PC Turner was soon on hand and, running upstairs to the drawing room floor, discovered Marion lying unconscious and semi-naked in the bedroom. An elderly locum, Dr Harris, was summoned, but when he expressed uncertainty at her condition the recently returned Mrs Williams was despatched to the Jubilee Hospital to fetch another doctor and a stomach pump. From 10 p.m. Dr Fitzroy Benham battled to revive the unresponsive woman, administering numerous injections of ether and strychnine. In an attempt to counteract a possible morphine overdose Heron also injected her with belladonna. Dolly Clayden was sent for. She was present to see her old friend take her final breath at 5 o'clock in the morning.

The inquest into Marion's death commenced at Fulham Mortuary three days later. With an autopsy still in progress, there was understandable speculation that she had died from poisoning. Heron was distraught as he described the events preceding Marion's death. They had argued during the afternoon, apparently over his failure to inform a female relative that they had arrived in England. Somehow the omission had brought Marion's simmering jealousy to boiling point and she became tearfully hysterical. After dinner she had said that she was going to lie down, only for Heron to find her unconscious a few minutes later. A bottle of morphine found on a mantelpiece was his own mixture, he explained. On finishing his evidence he went into a corridor where he leaned wearily against the wall.

The coroner had shocked Heron by mentioning the inquest held on his wife in Jamaica. Taken with the circumstances of Marion's death, this could only mean that he would become the subject of fevered discussion in the press. Although he was not to read them he could imagine next day's headlines screaming:

WEST BROMPTON MYSTERY
SUDDEN DEATH OF A BEAUTIFUL ACTRESS
IMMORALITY, JEALOUSY AND THREATENED SUICIDE[5]

Leaving the inquest at 3.15 p.m. Heron travelled to Victoria where he attempted to change his appearance by buying a razor and shaving off his moustache in a public lavatory. In memory of his dead mistress he went for dinner at the Hotel Continental, a favourite Regent Street restaurant. At about 11.15 p.m. he arrived at the Craven Hotel asking for a bedroom for one night. Miss White, the receptionist, charged him 5s, thinking that he looked tired and pale. Seated in the hotel's smoking room he wrote a number of letters – one to Dolly bequeathing her two of Marion's rings and all her clothes, and another to the Fulham coroner attempting to explain his state of mind:

> Now that it appears that death must have been due to poisoning it comes to me that had I noted more carefully not what was said, but the manner of saying it, my poor darling might have been alive now. I presume the case will be carried on to a conclusion in the usual way, and that there is thus every hope that all suspicions against the writer will be shown to have been unfounded. As before stated, however, now I am alone it is out of the question I should go through any horrors for the paltry privilege of continued existence. I shall, therefore, take an overdose of morphia as soon as some other matters have been satisfactorily settled.[6]

After leaving the hotel briefly he returned at about midnight, commenting to the porter that 'it was a lovely night for a walk'.[7] He explained that he had no luggage to be taken up to his room. His only requirements were carried in his pockets – the newly purchased bone-handled razor and his old nemesis, a bottle containing morphine crystals.

# 14

# AN ADELPHI DRAMA

The blade flashed and the golden harvest fell to the ground. By the side of the hayfield a baby lay in its cradle. It was a warm, sunny day. Too warm and too sunny, for his mother found that young Richard's face had turned an unnatural colour and that his eyes were screwed up and watering. As he grew into a non-communicative, querulous child, Margaret Archer often thought that the prolonged exposure to the sun had damaged his brain. In later years Richard retreated into a delusional world in which he imagined that he had risen from his humble origins to become a great actor, singer, poet and author. He was, he thought, a genius whose ultimate triumph was only thwarted by a small group of mean-minded fellow performers and theatre managers. One man became the focus of his paranoia and after years of resentment Richard's attempt to break the power of his tormentor shocked the entire Victorian nation.

Richard Millar Archer, known to his family as Dick, was born in 1858 at Balmydown, a farm on the Baldovan Estate, near Dundee, Scotland. His father was a ploughman whose two marriages had resulted in nine children, at least three of whom suffered from mental illness. After a time, the large family moved to the city of Dundee where they appear to have lived in poverty. Like many young adults Archer sought to escape the deprivations of working-class life by becoming a performer. In similar circumstances many chose the egalitarian world of music hall as a route out of poverty, content that their standard of living would improve while their social status remained much the same. But Archer rejected the vulgarity of the variety profession, seeing the theatre as a portal to a new life in which he would become 'a gentleman' respected for his handsome features, impeccable style and histrionic abilities. It was a plan that contained at least three major flaws. Leaving school at the age of 14, he compensated for the dull routine of manual employment at the Gourlay Brothers' shipbuilding works by haunting the theatres in Dundee, picking up odd jobs and sometimes being allowed to 'walk on' in crowd scenes.

An older half-sister, whose name is unknown, decided on a different exit strategy from the Dundee slums. She headed for London where she almost certainly became a prostitute. It was a career move which does not appear to have unduly scandalised her family for, in about 1875, Mr and Mrs Archer came to stay with their daughter in the capital. They were later joined by young Archer who managed to find fairly regular, if poorly paid, theatre work. Although he claimed to have acted at the Gaiety, the Prince of Wales, Her Majesty's Theatre, Covent Garden, Crystal Palace and the Theatre Royal, Drury Lane, his most frequent employment occurred at the Adelphi Theatre, 399 Strand. Archer did not consider himself as a 'super', i.e., a supernumerary or theatre extra, but as a 'utility gentleman', a fine distinction that many performers from the lower ranks of the acting profession might also have made. Whether 'super' or 'utility', his lowly, usually non-speaking, appearances alongside some of the West End theatre's leading actors provided him with a cachet that he was to use and embroider for many years to come. Whenever applying for a new engagement he more often than not described himself as 'late of the Adelphi Theatre'.

Fortunately for Archer, Adelphi productions were spectacular in nature, often requiring large numbers of supers – and utility gentlemen. The theatre had opened as the Sans Pareil in 1806, but in 1819 it changed its name to reflect the close proximity to the Adams' riverside terrace. Early successes at the theatre included a dramatisation of Pierce Egan's *Tom and Jerry; or, Life in London* (1821), an epic account of high and low life in Regency London; and *A Flight to America* (1836), a vehicle enabling the American blackface performer Thomas Dartmouth Rice to perform his sensational song and dance 'Jim Crow'. Early in its existence the theatre became particularly linked with melodramas, an association that would continue from the Gothic plots of the first half of the century to exciting tales often set in the far flung, late Victorian Empire. The formulaic plots in which the hero and heroine survived a succession of perilous situations to triumph over a seemingly invulnerable villain found able delineators in three actors during the 1880s and 1890s. W. L. Abingdon had an unrivalled reputation 'for depicting the acme of scoundrelism';[1] Jessie Millward was, despite her dark looks, a typical English rose; and William 'Breezy Bill' Terriss seemed blessed with eternal youthfulness and was equal to any challenge, both on and off the stage.

Born the son of a barrister in 1847, William Lewin — later to become William Terriss — entered the Royal Navy as a midshipman at the age of 14. On leaving the service he became a tea planter in Chittagong, India, where a voyage to Calcutta ended in shipwreck and 'ten days of terrible exposure to the broiling sun, on the inhospitable shore of the Holy Gunga'.[2] After two successful years on the London stage in 1871 he travelled to the Falkland Islands to establish a sheep farm. Tiring of this occupation within a few months, he set sail for Britain on a Swedish whaling vessel only to spend two storm-tossed days in a lifeboat following a second shipwreck. Another short period of acting ended when he decided to breed racehorses in Kentucky. His daughter, Ellaline, later to become a star of musical comedy, also remembered silver mining in Colorado and farming in Australia. Eventually Terriss managed to contain his wanderlust, becoming a permanent fixture of the London stage from the late 1870s.

Setting up home with his wife and three children in the newly established artistic suburb of Bedford Park in West London, Terriss largely shunned clannish theatrical society to mix in wider intellectual circles. 'Breezy Bill' had one very special theatrical friend, however, his leading lady whom he affectionately nicknamed 'Sis' — Jessie Millward. He and Jessie were devoted to each other, their long-term love affair finding tolerant acceptance from the Terriss family. Strikingly handsome, amazingly athletic and possessing infinite charm, Terriss was the first and possibly greatest matinee idol. Of his many good qualities, bravery and modesty were exemplified in one anecdote related by the actress, Ellen Terry. A stagehand at the Lyceum Theatre asked the soaking actor whether it had been raining, unaware that he had just rescued a drowning boy from the River Thames. His biographer, Arthur J. Smythe, wrote: 'he was the embodiment of health, life, sparkle and manly vigour.'[3]

While the dashing Terriss drew large audiences to the Adelphi, Richard Archer appeared as a face in the crowd, playing anonymous

soldiers, servants, courtiers and villagers. Occasionally he was allowed
to play named roles such as Sligo Dan in O'Dowd (1880); Rattlesnake
in a revival of the old Adelphi favourite The Green Bushes (1880/1); the
first traveller in Michael Strogoff (1881); a groom in It's Never Too Late to
Mend (1881); O'Flanigan in In the Ranks (1883/4): Lanty in Arrah-na-
Pogue (1885); and Diego in The Silver Falls (1888/9). The actor Charles
East remembered sharing a dressing room with his brother, John
East, G. P. Huntley (later to achieve fame as a comedian) and Archer
during the run of one of the Adelphi's greatest hits The Harbour Lights
(December 1885).[4] Archer's close-hand observation of leading actors
was not as beneficial as might be expected; rather he developed a
grotesque caricature of their acting styles and offstage behaviour. As
early as March 1883 when Robert Beverage from the Dundee Theatre
met him in the Strand, he was boasting about the progress that he was
making at the Adelphi. To confer added distinction upon himself he
took to wearing a long 'Inverness' cape and a wide-brimmed felt hat,
a costume that made him look more like an archetypal conspirator
than an off-duty actor. His deficiency of talent was not helped by an
unprepossessing appearance – unruly dark hair, a shaggy moustache,
pallid complexion and squinting eyes. A broad Scottish brogue was
gradually replaced by an indeterminate, slightly sinister accent.
Occasional French phrases were randomly thrown into conversation,
with Shakespearian quotations delivered whenever the slightest
opportunity arose. Onstage he annoyed performers and managers by
striking histrionic poses and drawing attention away from the main
players.

Archer's flighty sister sometimes visited the backstage of the
Adelphi, not to see her brother, but to meet the actor W. L. Abingdon
with whom she had started a relationship. She was remembered by
Terriss' son-in-law Seymour Hicks as 'a woman well known to be a
frequenter of the then notorious Empire promenade [...] she was by
no means an unattractive specimen of her class'.[5] Hicks also claimed
that through his jealousy of Terriss, Abingdon played a cruel practical
joke on his lady-friend's brother. The sister was frequently entertained
by Abingdon in his dressing room and after the performance Archer
was also invited for refreshments. During their conversations Abingdon
became aware of Archer's ambition to become a leading actor and in

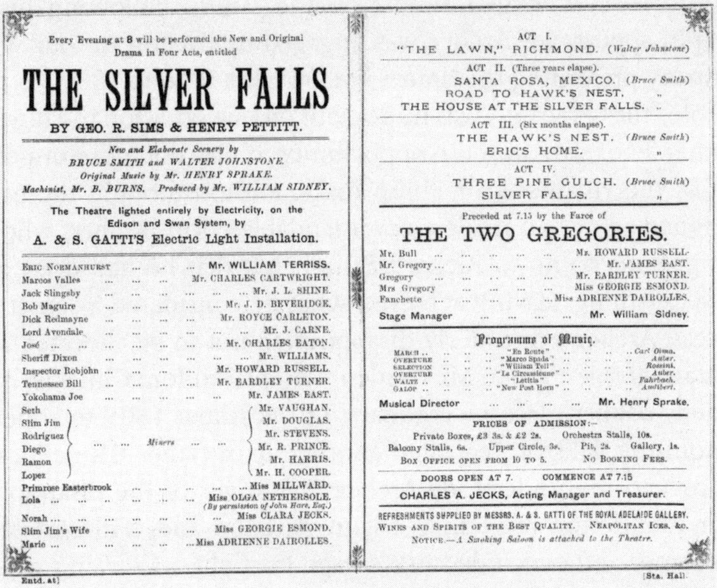

Every Evening at 8 will be performed the New and Original Drama in Four Acts, entitled

THE SILVER FALLS

BY GEO. R. SIMS & HENRY PETTITT.

*New and Elaborate Scenery by*
*BRUCE SMITH and WALTER JOHNSTONE.*
*Original Music by Mr. HENRY SPRAKE.*
*Machinist, Mr. B. BURNS. Produced by Mr. WILLIAM SIDNEY.*

The Theatre lighted entirely by Electricity, on the Edison and Swan System, by
A. & S. GATTI'S Electric Light Installation.

| | |
|---|---|
| Eric Normanhurst | Mr. WILLIAM TERRISS. |
| Marcos Valles | Mr. CHARLES CARTWRIGHT. |
| Jack Slingsby | Mr. J. L. SHINE. |
| Bob Maguire | Mr. J. D. BEVERIDGE. |
| Dick Redmayne | Mr. ROYCE CARLETON. |
| Lord Avondale | Mr. J. CARNE. |
| José | Mr. CHARLES EATON. |
| Sheriff Dixon | Mr. WILLIAMS. |
| Inspector Robjohn | Mr. HOWARD RUSSELL. |
| Tennessee Bill | Mr. EARDLEY TURNER. |
| Yokohama Joe | Mr. JAMES EAST. |
| Seth (Miners) | Mr. VAUGHAN. |
| Slim Jim (Miners) | Mr. DOUGLAS. |
| Rodriguez (Miners) | Mr. STEVENS. |
| Diego (Miners) | Mr. R. PRINCE. |
| Ramon (Miners) | Mr. HARRIS. |
| Lopez (Miners) | Mr. H. COOPER. |
| Primrose Easterbrook | Miss MILLWARD. |
| Lola | Miss OLGA NETHERSOLE. *(By permission of John Hare, Esq.)* |
| Norah | Miss CLARA JECKS. |
| Slim Jim's Wife | Miss GEORGIE ESMOND. |
| Marie | Miss ADRIENNE DAIROLLES. |

Entd. at]

ACT I.
"THE LAWN," RICHMOND. *(Walter Johnstone)*

ACT II. (Three years elapse).
SANTA ROSA, MEXICO. *(Bruce Smith)*
ROAD TO HAWK'S NEST. "
THE HOUSE AT THE SILVER FALLS. "

ACT III. (Six months elapse).
THE HAWK'S NEST. *(Bruce Smith)*
ERIC'S HOME. "

ACT IV.
THREE PINE GULCH. *(Bruce Smith)*
SILVER FALLS. "

Preceded at 7.15 by the Farce of

THE TWO GREGORIES.

| | |
|---|---|
| Mr. Bull | Mr. HOWARD RUSSELL. |
| Mr. Gregory | Mr. JAMES EAST. |
| Gregory | Mr. EARDLEY TURNER. |
| Mrs Gregory | Miss GEORGIE ESMOND. |
| Fanchette | Miss ADRIENNE DAIROLLES. |
| Stage Manager | Mr. William Sidney. |

Programme of Music.

| | | |
|---|---|---|
| MARCH | "En Route" | *Carl Oima.* |
| OVERTURE | "Marco Spada" | *Auber.* |
| SELECTION | "William Tell" | *Rossini.* |
| OVERTURE | "La Circassienne" | *Auber.* |
| WALTZ | "Letitia" | *Fahrbach.* |
| GALOP | "New Post Horn" | *Audibert.* |

Musical Director ... Mr. Henry Sprake.

PRICES OF ADMISSION:—
Private Boxes, £3 3s. & £2 2s. Orchestra Stalls, 10s.
Balcony Stalls, 6s. Upper Circle, 3s. Pit, 2s. Gallery, 1s.
Box Office open from 10 to 5. No Booking Fees.

DOORS OPEN AT 7. COMMENCE AT 7.15

CHARLES A. JECKS, Acting Manager and Treasurer.

REFRESHMENTS SUPPLIED BY MESSRS. A. & S. GATTI OF THE ROYAL ADELAIDE GALLERY.
Wines and Spirits of the Best Quality. Neapolitan Ices, &c.
Notice.—*A Smoking Saloon is attached to the Theatre.*

[Sta. Hall.

**ILLUSTRATION 24.** Programme for *The Silver Falls*, the last Adelphi theatre production in which Richard Archer Prince and William Terriss appeared together.

a spirit of mischief not far removed from his own villainous stage characters, he encouraged the utility gentleman to think that he might eventually outshine Terriss. Extending the joke, Abingdon presented Archer with a typescript of the hero's part, organising a mock rehearsal where all those participating were party to the deception. Archer was unaware that his pathetic posturing in the central role made him a laughing stock in the theatre. Remembering only Abingdon's praise, he felt that a subsequent drying-up of Adelphi engagements resulted from Terriss' fear of competition.[6]

Whether Hick's account was accurate or not, 'Mad' Archer was frequently baited and ridiculed by his fellow performers. There were, though, a few acts of kindness which he hardly seems to have noticed. He was frequently allowed free admission to theatres on presentation of a card that stated him to be an actor from the Adelphi. That he was allowed to appear in so many of that theatre's productions suggests a management remarkably tolerant of his idiosyncratic behaviour. Later, the patience of J. F. Elliston with the disruptive actor verged almost on the saintly. Following his last Adelphi appearance Archer was engaged by Elliston to tour with a company presenting the drama The Union Jack in June 1889. As usual his role, 'the Sergeant', was minor, but on one occasion the illness of another actor gave him the opportunity to play the more important part of the villainous Sir Philip Yorke. Elliston thought the much-maligned actor had made a commendable effort. Archer, who had changed his name to Richard Prince, felt that he had done a far, far better thing. Having achieved what he considered a sensational success, Archer was bitterly disappointed not to be allocated more substantial roles. When Mr Warden who played Tom Chuckle, 'a low comedy soldier', left the company in December 1889 to appear in pantomime, Elliston recruited another actor rather than allocating the part to the understudy Archer. The anger of the disappointed actor manifested itself in constant derision and criticism of the newcomer and concluded in a savage fist fight on a train travelling between Aberdeen and Leicester.[7]

After putting up with Archer's inflated ideas of his own worth for three years, Elliston refused to employ him in any further acting positions. He had not, however, completely abandoned the troublesome actor, allowing him to carry baggage during a Scottish tour of Alone in London (January to April 1895). Eventually, Elliston was forced to discharge him for insubordination. Thereafter, Archer bombarded his generous former employer with abusive and threatening correspondence. On 25 September 1895 he wrote:

> You hell hound, you Judas, you told me in a note you would give me a manager's or an actor's reference. A gentleman has written for a reference and I now know why I have not obtained an engagement, you cur. This is my thanks for saving you pounds in 'Alone in London,' and saving it from being a disgrace; I have suffered worse than death. I now know why I did not get engagements. When I left the 'Union Jack' tours you never spoke the truth about me to any manager, blackmailing me to get yourself on. The next time I ask for a reference will be at Bow Street police-station, where my lawyers will make you tell the world in Court why you have dared to blackmail a Highlander. I am not a woman, you hound. I shall

expose you and others; they have no mercy on me, and if I die at Newgate, after you have not given me a reference, the world shall judge between us. I would advise you to take this note to Scotland Yard this time, and when they cannot find any thing against me I shall write to every newspaper in London. We shall see who will come out best in the end. I, poor Prince, or a cad with a bank at his back and the Pope's Bulls. Victory or Death is my motto, and the fear of God.

With no further engagements available, Archer was forced to move back to his family in Dundee. Between May 1895 and March 1897 he returned to Gourlay Brothers where his work record was considered good, despite the antagonism of other workers who nicknamed him 'Tripe'. His deteriorating mental condition often resulted in tirades against managers whom he claimed were conspiring against him. He claimed that, not content with undermining his career, William Terriss and Robert Arthur (the owner of the Theatre Royal, Dundee) were in league to blacken his reputation by sending individuals of dubious character from Dundee to London to corrupt his sister. There were times at home when he would sing continuously for several hours and moments of suspicion when he feared that his family were poisoning his tea. He was the second Jesus Christ he declared, while his mother was the Virgin Mary. His brother Harry was heading straight for hell, a process that he attempted to accelerate by attacking him with a knife and a poker.

His behaviour in public was no less alarming. Like many other residents of Dundee, Archer liked to spend Sundays on a pleasure steamer cruising on the River Tay. A captive audience proved irresistible and his declamatory effusions on the scenery, often accompanied by discordant singing, led to attempts to stifle his enthusiasm. When restrained, he would adopt a dramatic stance: 'Avaunt. Dare you lay your hands on a Prince? I command ye as I do the sparkling waves below and the clear blue sky above, avaunt.'[8] A similarly hostile reception to his singing during a Masonic outing on a steamboat precipitated a violent fit which necessitated him being locked up for the duration of the trip. The most serious episode of violent behaviour occurred at one of his old haunts – Her Majesty's Theatre, Dundee. Announcing himself as a professional player, he had frequently been issued with free passes, a privilege that he abused by applauding at inappropriate moments and shouting advice to the performers. During the run of For the Crown in April 1897 his threats to shoot the lead actor, Otto Stewart, understandably resulted in him being refused admission. A few days later he paid for a seat in the stalls and again created a scene. When forcibly removed, he pointed a revolver at theatre staff, discharging the weapon twice in the street outside.

In his constant quest for approval and recognition, Archer sent many communications to famous figures. Queen Victoria received an effusion on her Diamond Jubilee; the Duke and Duchess of York were congratulated on the birth of their son, later to become King Edward VIII; William Ewart Gladstone was sent a complimentary poem; and Princess Henry of Battenberg acknowledged his touching lines on the death of her husband. A play, Countess Otto, arrived for the actor Fred Terry to read, but after a short while Archer decided that Terry had retained his masterpiece for too long a period. Two incoherent postcards were despatched from Dundee on 23 November 1896:

> Sir – Please return play 'Countess Otto' at once. If you are hard up for the money I will send it. Terriss, the Pope, and Scotland Yard. I will answer in a week. Richard A. Prince.

> Sir – Favour to hand this morning at 10 o'clock. The old story about King Charles and the two hundred thousand pounds they sold him for a king. 'I only a Prince.' But a woman. Mon Dieu, a woman. Richard A. Prince.[9]

When Archer approved of a fellow performer, his appreciation was unbounded. After attending a concert by the famous Scottish tenor Durward Lely he swept into a Dundee bar and addressed the puzzled customers:

> 'Oh! It was magnificent, glorious! In front of him, to the right of him, and to the left of him, the audience volleyed and thundered. Oh! He's a great man.'

When a waiter asked him who he was talking about, he snapped:

'Who am I talking about? Who should I be talking about, but the great man, Durward Lely? Give me a glass of beer.'[10]

Such manifestations of mental illness did not prevent Archer from participating in another touring production of *The Union Jack*. Early in October 1897 a casting problem at the Grand Theatre, Glasgow, led Arthur Carlton to offer him the plum role of Sir Philip Yorke, the part that he had played briefly on Elliston's 1889 tour of the melodrama. A highlight of the play was the scene in which the blaggardly Sir Philip stabbed his enemy, Captain Morton. Despite the appearance of a villain and proclivities towards violence, Archer failed to shine in the role. His final appearance with the company took place in South Shields after which he was dismissed.

Surprisingly, Archer found another engagement during the same month. On 23 October 1897 Archer was employed by Ralph Croydon to play the minor roles of Sir Lester Lightfoot in *Nurse Charity* and Sir Geoffrey Dashwood in *Parson Thorn* on tour for 25s a week. If Croydon had not already heard of his new actor's reputation, he must soon have soon realised that Archer would cause him problems. When asked about previous experience he claimed that he had played leading parts at the Adelphi and that he was suited to far better roles than Croydon was offering him. He would have been at the London theatre still, he added, 'but for one man'. Next day at Sunday tea, members of the cast were bemused to see Archer recoil in horror at the sight of a knife being used to open a sardine tin. Some time later he examined a prop dagger and mused: 'A man would not want that stuck in many times.'[11] Rehearsals on the opening Monday morning went extremely badly, his inability to recall the few lines being emphasised by his ridiculously dramatic manner. His suggestion that the opening of the play should be delayed for a day was not well received and he was dismissed without receiving payment. On leaving his last theatrical engagement, Archer cursed the 'dirty dog' Terriss as the main reason for the failure of his career. When Croydon said that he 'must be mad to talk like that', he responded, 'the world will ring with my madness before long'.[12]

The sensible decision would have been to return to his family in Dundee. Instead, Archer chose to come to the lair of that dirty dog, William Terriss. London was where he had first performed before fashionable and sophisticated audiences; where he had been praised by the peerless villain, W. L. Abingdon; and where he had been transformed from a humble Archer to a noble Prince. London was where he would have risen to fame had it not been for the machinations of the terrible Terriss. Croydon's refusal to pay his salary had left him so low on funds that on arriving at Trader's Wharf, Wapping, on 28 October 1897, he was forced to leave his luggage as security for the unpaid fare. Carrying just a brown paper parcel (probably containing his play), he made his way to Eaton Court, Eaton Lane, close to Victoria Station, where he rented a room from Mrs Charlotte Darby. He was only able to provide 3s of the 4s weekly rent, but his landlady agreed to wait a few days for her extra money. With the theatre district close at hand, Archer's chances of raising a little capital were promising.

A meeting remembered by Charles East seemed to date from soon after Archer's arrival in London. East, with another actor and William Terriss were walking along the Strand when they were approached by Archer who humbly asked his arch-enemy for the price of a meal.[13] Having accepted 2s from Terriss, Archer next approached the actor at the Adelphi where he left a letter requesting a written recommendation to present to the Actor's Benevolent Fund. Although they did not meet, Terriss wrote a note: 'I have known the bearer, Mr Richard Archer Prince, as a hard working actor for many years.' On 10 November Archer attended the offices of the Fund in Adam Street where he was awarded a payment of £1. Subsequently, he made further visits to Adam Street, receiving 10s on 27 November, £1 on 2 December and 10s on 9 December. A visit to his sister, whom he had not seen for six years, brought in another £1. The money was sufficient to pay his rent and to buy a little food and a 9d bread-knife, but with no sign of work he was forced to start pawning his clothes.

By the middle of December Archer's very existence was in hock. Mrs Darby had allowed him a few more days to pay two weeks' rent arrears, while the entire contents of his wardrobe now resided in a local pawnshop. He was surviving on a little milk and slices of bread cut increasingly thinly with his 9d knife. With no positive answers to his letters seeking employment and no engagements secured by his agent, Charles St John Denton, Archer decided that the only person to extricate him from his dire situation was the person who had placed him in it. He called at the Adelphi where Jessie Millward heard him shouting at Terriss in his dressing room. As they met in the narrow corridor, the usually charming Terriss exclaimed to her, 'this man is becoming a nuisance'. On 15 December the comedian Harry Nichols found Archer loitering near the Royal entrance, a private door to the theatre in Maiden Lane. Archer demanded: 'Where's Mr Terriss?' to which Nichols responded, 'I don't know; be off, clear out of this place!'

At about 3.45 on the afternoon of 16 December, Archer knocked on Mrs Darby's door:

'Can I speak to you?'
'Yes.'
'I am sorry I have not got any money for you. What shall I do?'
'I don't know Mr Prince. I am very sorry for you.'[14]

Mrs Darby's decision to seek her husband's advice on the problem caused Archer to suppose that he would be asked to leave the lodging house. Stowing a few precious belongings in his pockets, he left Eaton Court not expecting to be re-admitted. Shortly after 4 p.m. he appeared at the office of the Actor's Benevolent Fund. A clerk explained that the Emergency Committee could not meet that day to consider his application for further relief. Crossing the Strand, Archer made his daily call on his agent at 34 Maiden Lane where he received the usual answer that there was nothing for him. At about 6.30 he appears to have met his sister who refused to loan him 10s to return to Dundee. 'I would rather see you dead in the gutter than give you a farthing', she is reported to have said. According to Archer, he made two further attempts to obtain money. A jeweller (possibly in the Burlington Arcade) who had sold many items to his sister was approached for a shilling, only to laugh at the request. Two clergymen who were asked if they knew of anyone who might supply financial assistance were unforthcoming, either in advice or support.

While Archer was wandering in the vicinity of the Adelphi Theatre, William Terriss and an old friend Harry Graves were enjoying an early dinner with Jessie Millward at her Hanover Square apartment. Jessie departed for the theatre first, leaving the two men to finish a game of chess. She liked to allow herself plenty of time to prepare for her role opposite Terriss in an American drama *Secret Service*. The time was approaching 7.30 p.m. when Graves and Terriss arrived at the theatre. Given the narrowness of Maiden Lane they left their cab at one end and walked the short distance to an arched street door surmounted by the Royal Coat of Arms. Terriss said to his friend, 'Wait a minute Harry till I get my keys', and as he removed them from his pocket a cloaked figure approached rapidly and struck him twice on the back. It was an over-hearty greeting, thought Graves. A moment later the appalling truth became apparent. Turning, Terriss received a third blow from Archer's 9d knife which sunk deep into his chest. Collapsing against the wall he gasped, 'My God! I am stabbed.' As he slumped into the arms of Jessie's dresser who had hurried to the door, he asked her to take his keys and to make sure his assailant was detained. A number of passers-by who witnessed the attack were immediately joined by diners from nearby Rule's Restaurant and staff from the stage door situated a few feet away in Bull Inn Court. Archer stood calmly watching events unfold. He had given a masterly performance as the assassin, but he probably felt that Terriss could have made more of his final death scene.

While accompanying Archer and a police constable to Bow Street Police Station, Graves asked: 'What could have induced you to do such a cruel thing?' Archer was certain in response: 'In revenge; he blackmailed me for ten years.'[15] At the police station he produced the blood-stained knife from under his cape:

> 'That is what I stabbed him with. He had due warning, and if he is dead he knows what he had to expect from me; he prevented me from getting assistance from the Actor's Benevolent Fund today and I have stopped him.'[16]

Returning quickly to the theatre, Graves found his friend close to death. He had been carried, half-conscious, into a narrow passage

within the theatre where after about 30 minutes he expired in
Jessie's arms. The body was taken upstairs to his dressing room and
placed on a couch. As the play was about to start, the stage manager
was compelled to announce to the audience that owing to a terrible
accident to Mr Terriss the performance was cancelled. There was
no chance of an understudy playing his part and all ticket money
would be refunded. As the confused theatregoers exited into the
Strand rumours of Terriss' murder began to circulate. Soon a large
crowd had assembled waiting for further information. Garbled
accounts of the incident passed quickly from one theatre to another
with many actors taking the stage in a state of shock. Terriss'
daughter, Ellaline, would normally have been performing in the
long-running The Circus Girl at the Gaiety, but was convalescing at
Eastbourne following the death of her newborn son. Her husband,
Seymour Hicks, who had just rejoined the show, was just about
to go on stage when he was stopped by the manager. Through the
'nosy chorus of a comic song' he was told 'Old man, Bill Terriss
has been killed'.[17]

By 9.30 p.m. newsboys were on the streets shouting themselves
hoarse, as passers-by queued to purchase special editions of the
evening papers. The theatre-going public was incredulous. With
youthful good looks that belied his quarter of a century on the
stage, 'Breezy Bill' had seemed immortal. He had survived so many
near fatal scrapes in life and in melodrama that for him to fall victim
to an insignificant actor seemed impossible to accept.

Archer's appearance at Bow Street Police Court the next day
was a distressing event for all but the accused. On entering the
dock he smiled slightly as he surveyed the full house. In response
to Graves' evidence he denied that he had stabbed Terriss in the
back, but claimed that he had met him 'face to face'. He had not
rushed up to his victim, but had initially tried to talk to him.
When told by the magistrate that he was making a statement and
not questioning the evidence the witness he replied: 'What use
are questions?' Throughout the hearing he scribbled notes which
he handed to his legal adviser. One was seen to read 'That's a
lie!' another 'They all made up their mind to blackmail that

day. They knew I was starving.'[18] On being remanded until the following week he returned to his cell amid a barrage of hisses and booing.

By the time Archer was brought to trial at the Central Criminal Court William Terriss had been laid to rest for nearly three weeks. His funeral had been one of those emotionally charged events by which London measures its history: streets crowded with mourners and an immense column of carriages carrying the elite of the theatre world. Jessie Millward's equivocal status was recognised by Henry Irving who insisted on accompanying her to the ceremony. He was sanguine about the chance of his departed colleague receiving the full penalty of the law. Archer, he declared, would never be executed: 'You see, dear Will Terriss was only an actor.'[19] Of course Archer was also an actor, the most despicable member of an often despised profession. His vaunting ambition, which had so ludicrously exceeded his ability, had led to a real life tragedy played out in a theatrical context. As William Archer Prince, late of the Adelphi Theatre, Dick Archer had come to believe in make-believe.

On the day of the Old Bailey hearing, 13 January 1898, London was in the grip of a heavy 'pea souper'. The 'ghastly brown fog'[20] that drifted within the court provided an eerily melodramatic setting for Archer's last public appearance. Although his plea of not guilty on the grounds of insanity was supported by the overwhelming evidence of family, colleagues and doctors, the jury struggled to deliver a verdict. After half an hour's deliberation, they came to the decision that the prisoner was fully aware of his actions when committing the murder and was therefore guilty. However, taking medical opinion into account they found that he was insane and not responsible for his actions. Archer was consequently sentenced to be detained as a criminal lunatic at Holloway Prison until Her Majesty's pleasure was known. Later he was transferred to Broadmoor Criminal Lunatic Asylum.

William Terriss's widow, Amy, died within months of the trial's conclusion. After suffering a breakdown, his mistress, Jessie Millward, was coaxed back onto the stage by Henry Irving, although she played out the remainder of her career in the United States. The scoundrel Abingdon also went to America where he committed suicide in 1918. The killing of her father remained such a painful memory to Ellaline Terriss that she and her husband Seymour Hicks could not bring themselves to talk about it for many years. Their moment of release came only when they received news of the death of Archer in Broadmoor – 40 years after the murder of 'Breezy Bill'.

# 15

# MADAME ST JOHN

The opening of *Faust Up to Date* at the Gaiety Theatre was delayed because of an injury to its leading lady. Florence St John, 'Jack' to her friends, had not suffered an unfortunate accident, but had been assaulted by her drunken husband when she refused to lend him £100 to retrieve items that he had pawned. It was a sordid affair that would not have reflected well on a theatre that was continually criticised for the loose moral character of its burlesques. Doubts about the pernicious influences exerted on young performers such as Mabel Love would have increased even further if accusations of adultery against Florence had been made public or if the murky background of one of her best friends, Lady Euston, had been examined. Detective Maurice Moser had once been commissioned to verify Mabel's continuing purity; in Florence's case he was called upon to prove exactly the opposite.

Two couples who were considered long-term shining examples to the acting profession in late Victorian Britain were Sir Squire and Lady Bancroft and Mr and Mrs Kendall. They were paragons of propriety and good taste, with happy marriages lasting for a combined 102 years. However, during the 1880s only one partnership dominated the confluent worlds of burlesque and opéra bouffe – that of Florence St John and her French husband, Claude Marius. Unlike the Bancrofts and the Kendalls, the couple did not contribute to the growing respectability of their profession – quite the reverse. They had only wed after their long-term affair had resulted in the break-up of both their marriages and although their relationship was stable for a time, their lifestyle was excessive and extravagant.

A precocious child, Florence grew into an impetuous adult. Born Margaret Florence Grieg in Devon on 4 March 1855, her musical talents were so much in evidence that she began to sing at local charity concerts at the age of 8. She was a headstrong student and after she had caused her private tutor to resign, her father, a keen amateur musician, took over her education. Although her parents were, at best, lower middle-class (running a Plymouth boarding house and keeping a small shop), they found the money needed to send her to study music and voice under Madame Marie Karger at a Kensington boarding school. By the age of 14 she began to appear with touring variety troupes, two of which had a strong visual component. For some time she performed ballads to accompany a Diorama (a painted backdrop in a three-dimensional setting) and with another company she played the piano and also sang in phantom form, her image being projected from offstage onto a sheet of glass by a 'Pepper's Ghost' apparatus.

In all her interviews and even on oath Florence claimed to have run away from her parents and married a young naval officer named St John at the early age of 14 years and 7 months. She may well have left home and had a relationship at this period, but her marriage to Alfred St John did not take place until the winter of 1871 when she was 17. The circumstances were no less romantic than her own version of events for her husband was a gifted pianist and conductor who frequently accompanied her singing. According to Florence's account, she struggled to support a tubercular husband, often going without food to provide him with comforts during a slow and painful decline. The reality of the situation appears to be that both performers were increasingly successful from the time of their marriage. For some months Alfred acted as accompanist to one of music-hall's top stars, 'The Great Vance', while his young wife, billed as Florence Leslie, was widely praised for her versatile singing, graceful dancing and striking good looks.

When Alfred died in September 1875 Florence had just concluded a three-month engagement as a ballad singer at one of London's most prestigious music halls, the Oxford, in Oxford Street. In just over a year she married another performer, the operatic baritone James Lithgow Smith, although she now employed her late husband's name to appear as Florence St John.

**ILLUSTRATION 25.** Florence St John.

For the remainder of the 1870s she was closely involved with the world of opera, playing many principal parts in companies which performed extensive repertoires in English. Long periods of touring were interspersed with occasional London appearances, ten operas alone being presented by the Rose Hersee Company at the Crystal Palace in August 1877. Florence's vocal skills were severely taxed, with her natural mezzo soprano sometimes abandoned as she was required to tackle contralto roles.

In 1878 the impresario James Henderson engaged her to appear in the touring version of his highly successful light opera *Le Cloches de Corneville*, composed by Robert Planquette with an English libretto by H. B. Farnie. Henderson and Farnie were the leading English exponents of opéra bouffe, an entertainment that hovered between the unremitting comedy of burlesque and the heightened drama of opera. Already well known, Florence finally established herself as a star of the London stage when she appeared in Farnie's English version of Jacques Offenbach's *Madame Favart* at the Strand Theatre on 12 April 1879. She was ideally cast as a vivacious eighteenth-century French actress, sharing the top billing with the charismatic French actor and singer, Claude Marius, often abbreviated to 'Mons' Marius. Florence's performance was one of the highlights of Victorian theatre:

> What a night for author, composer, artists – that night which first saw 'Favart' in London. It was wonderful. Who will forget the fairy-like figure of Florence St John, as she floated through the evening, trilling like a nightingale? It was one of the great nights of the stage, though one is not supposed so to dub anything that is not tragedy.[1]

Critics of the theatre's bad moral influence must have felt thoroughly justified when the onstage husband and wife deserted their respective offstage partners. Knowing Florence's temperament, James Lithgow Smith had been reluctant for her to be exposed to the temptations of the London theatre world. He was proved totally correct in his assessment for within a few months she had deserted him. Marius' young wife Laura Gerrish, a dancer who had performed the cancan alongside Sarah Wright in 'The Parisian Quadrille', fought desperately to keep her husband, creating angry scenes at the theatre and on an excursion to Richmond in Surrey. But, with little regard for public opinion, Florence and Marius set up home together in Sion Road, Twickenham, Surrey, and later in New Bond Street, London. Although their relationship had started by June 1879, the couple were not free to marry until their highly publicised divorce cases had been heard in 1882 and 1883. As it was, Florence wed Marius, whose full name was Claude Marius Duplany, on Christmas Day 1885, when she was already pregnant with their son Reginald.

The personal chemistry of the two stars was a major contributory factor to Madame Favart's extraordinary success. After 502 performances, the production was replaced at the Strand Theatre on 18 September 1880 by Olivette, with music by Edmond Audran and libretto by Farnie. Again staring Florence and Marius, the tale of love and piracy in the south of France was only slightly less successful than its predecessor, running for more than a year. With two major hits behind him Marius took possession of a brand new theatre which had been built in Northumberland Avenue, adjacent to Charing Cross Station. The decision to open the Avenue Theatre with a revival of Madame Favart did not prove to be a wise one. Despite the presence of the Prince of Wales at the opening night on 11 March 1882, public interest in the opera had become exhausted. With poor box office receipts, the management was not able to pay the costumiers and, after the new costumes had been repossessed, members of the cast were forced to wear the dilapidated outfits from the original production. It was an exigency made worse by the weight gain of some of the principal protagonists. Florence remembered:

> None of us fitted our old clothes [...] My dress was of pretty stout material, though ancient, and as I was careful not to overstrain their strength, the things behaved very well. But in the last act, when I was dressed as a pedlar, I had to stoop to sell my wares, and there was a crash, and everybody about me knew what had happened. Fortunately I was able to keep my face to the audience, but I was in agony at the thought of my exit, for which I should be compelled to turn round. But Fred [Fred Leslie] rose to the emergency, and, taking off his cloak, threw it rompishly over me, and I was able to make my retreat with honour.[2]

Costume malfunctions aside, the remainder of the 1880s were years of continual success for Mr and Mrs Duplany. Marius became an accomplished stage manager as well as a popular performer, while Florence created a string of characterisations which lingered in the memory of the theatre-going public. Several of her roles reflected her own profession. As well as playing Marie Justine Duronceray, otherwise known as Madame Favart, she also, in 1884, gave a vivid portrayal of the actress and courtesan, Nell Gwynn. There were times when her theatrical daring shocked critics and fellow cast members alike. In The Grand Mogul by Audran and Farnie she took the part of Djemma, a 'frank, vulgar, English girl, who has gone into the snake-charming business "all for love"'.[3] Audiences were horrified to see Florence dancing with two live boa constrictors wrapped around her arms and throat.

Florence became one of the stage's most popular pin-ups – particularly when dressed in close-fitting trousers or tights – and a heart-throb who cast a spell over both young and old alike. She herself poked fun at the allure she exercised over some men, referring to a meeting she once had with a starry-eyed admirer:

> The young fellow was very bad indeed. 'Do I,' he said, with languishing eyes, 'indeed stand face to face with the incomparable,' etc.; I forget the speech. 'Indeed you do,' said I, 'if she is all that.' 'Oh,' he exclaimed, with a deep sigh, 'May I kiss your hand?' 'You may kiss my cheek if you like,' I said, and I held it out to him.[4]

'Mons' Marius was also a charismatic performer. On stage he was a talented singer and actor, while offstage he was debonair, charming and a droll raconteur. His business acumen may have been questionable, but Florence made up for his deficiencies by careful investment, buying two large houses – 55 and 57 Wellington Road – in the homeland of the demimondaine, St John's Wood. Perhaps Florence and Marius should have occupied a house each, for their egos were too massive to exist comfortably beneath a single roof.

There had been an argument after Marius 'sat up' until four in the morning with the actress Maude Williamson on the night of Queen Victoria's Golden Jubilee (21 June 1887). A few months later Florence developed a serious lung complaint and spent some time at Brighton, a seaside convalescence which was to spell doom for her marriage. While there she was nursed by a Miss Isaacson who introduced her to her extended family, the Cohens. Jacob Cohen, a local teacher, had several sons and daughters, one of whom took a particular interest in the charming London star. Somewhat implausibly 20-year-old Arthur Cohen's employment as a sub-editor on The Financial News appears to have provided him with an excess of time and money to lavish on his new, older friend. Although they only met briefly in Brighton, when she travelled to the Riviera he was soon in evidence. And when she returned to London, he was again present to escort her around the town.

Florence travelled to Monte Carlo in December 1887 to stay with her friends Kate Walsh Fitzroy, better known as Lady Euston, and Mr George Haughton, a racehorse owner. To the casual observer her hosts might have seemed eminently respectable. Haughton, however, made his living as a flamboyant book-maker and Kate was none other than the prostitute who had avoided paying Madame Ochse a large sum of money for lace-trimmed drawers and exorbitantly priced parasols. In 1884 Kate (and George) had been involved in one of the most extraordinary and unpredictable cases heard in the divorce court. As Kate Cooke, she was making her living as a minor stage performer and well-known courtesan when she met Captain Henry James Fitzroy of the Rifle Brigade in 1870. As the Earl of Euston and heir to the Seventh Duke of Grafton, he was no ordinary junior officer, and as one of the most celebrated courtesans in London she was no run of the mill whore. Captain Fitzroy soon became besotted with the beautiful blonde 'Cyprian', visiting her frequently at her home in Montpelier Terrace, Knightsbridge. Against the concerted opposition of friends and family Fitzroy married Kate at St Michael's Church, Worcester, on 29 May 1871. She was about six years older than her 22-year-old husband and claimed to be the widow of George Manley Smith, drowned with 269 others in the wreck of the *London* in the Bay of Biscay in January 1866.

Distancing themselves from London society, Kate and Henry lived first at Richmond, Surrey, and later at Rose Cottage, in neighbouring Teddington. As Captain Crosstree from *Caste* might have predicted, the marriage soon ran into difficulties. Although she was a lowly performer marrying a member of the aristocracy, Kate possessed none of the modesty and charm of Esther Eccles. She was bold, brash and bawdy, soon driving away any of Fitzroy's friends and relatives who had remained in contact with him after the ill-advised marriage. Following several separations Fitzroy finally deserted Kate in 1875, travelling to Australia to take up a minor government appointment. When he returned in 1881 he received information that Kate's first husband had not perished at sea, but might still be alive and living in New Zealand. The George M. Smith drowned in the sinking of the *London* was not the George M. Smith who had married Kate. In April 1884 Fitzroy petitioned for a decree of nullity of marriage on the grounds that his wife was already wed when he married her, backing up the accusation by producing a very much alive George M. Smith. Although her continuing grasp on the title Lady Euston seemed to be rapidly loosening, Kate struck spectators in the divorce court as supremely confident. She possessed an unimagined, almost unimaginable trump card – proof that when Smith married her in 1863 he was already married. As her first marriage was invalid, the judge had no option but to find that she was still married to Lord Euston. An exasperated Fitzroy initiated a second petition on the grounds of her adultery with George Haughton, but in the face of his desertion of Kate and alleged adultery with Mesdames Ellen Snow and Georgina Sheridan he decided it was prudent to let proceedings drop.

Despite attempts to buy her off, Kate insisted on her right to be called Lady Euston. She shrugged off the loss of Fitzroy's £10,000 marriage settlement which had been embezzled by a solicitor, throwing in her lack of fortune with the wealthy George Haughton. For several years the couple were conspicuously affluent at major race meetings and at fashionable resorts such as Monte Carlo. Having featured in one of the nineteenth century's most sensational divorce cases, Henry Fitzroy, Earl of Euston, became involved in an equally notorious homosexual scandal. In 1889 he brought a libel action against a journalist, Ernest Parke, who alleged that he had attended the male brothel at 19 Cleveland Street. Fitzroy claimed that he had only visited the establishment once, believing that there would be a display of female nudity in the form of poses plastiques. The famous advocate Sir Charles Russell efficiently discredited the evidence of four rent boys who stated that Fitzroy was a regular visitor, including Jack Saul who claimed to have committed sexual acts with Euston in 1887.

Back in Monte Carlo in 1888 Arthur Cohen joined the Euston–Haughton party at the beginning of February, remaining with them for nine days. Later to become associated with George Edwardes at the Gaiety Theatre, Cohen was described by the actress Jessie Millward as 'one of the best dressed men in London'.[5] While at Monte Carlo he often met Florence at the gaming tables in the famous Casino, also joining her and several others attending the Battle of Flowers and the Carnival Ball in nearby Nice. Marius claimed to have harboured no suspicions about his second wife's behaviour until he visited Maurice Moser about another matter – the suspicions he harboured about his first wife's behaviour. He already knew the detective well and was seeking his help in demonstrating that his former wife was an unfit mother for their 11-year-old daughter. During the course of the meeting their conversation turned to Florence. Moser remarked:

> 'I suppose you have heard what is going on at Monte Carlo?'
> 'I have heard she is enjoying herself immensely.'
> 'I don't mean that; but you have heard that she is going about with a lot of people, and among others with Arthur Cohen. Take my advice; have your wife watched, and if you will give me £30 I will undertake to do the job.'[6]

With the account of his wife's movements confirmed by recent visitors to Monte Carlo, Marius decided to accept Moser's proposal. A not unusual state of financial embarrassment caused him to propose paying for his services by instalments. He wrote:

> My Dear Moser – In looking over my matters I find that I cannot let you have the money to-morrow, but if you will help me in this business I can promise you £10 next Saturday, March 3rd, £10 on March 10th, and £10 on March 17th, without fail. Whoever you have to send out must go at once. For two reasons that I hear they are going to start next week for Naples and Rome. The second is to waste time. Tell whoever you are going to send that I want nothing but the truth and the whole truth. If we all happen to be mistaken, so much the better, and life will go on smoothly as before. But if we have not been mistaken I must have the truth, because it is a big thing to break up a home […] If she has dishonoured my name, tell your agent not to be afraid to tell me.[7]

Having agreed to Moser's plan, Marius then proceeded to jeopardise the whole investigation by writing to tell Florence that she had been observed driving with Cohen. 'Every woman is at heart a whore', he observed, claiming to quote Voltaire.[8] It appears that Marius decided not to go through with Moser's plan, but to use what money he could muster to head off for Monte Carlo himself. After some argument with Florence he persuaded her to return home.

Undeterred by Marius' jealousy and annoyance, Florence continued to meet Cohen while in London. Sometimes the three dined uncomfortably together or attended the theatre; on other occasions Arthur and Florence would go out alone or with Lady Euston and George Haughton. Once in their Wellington Road home,

Marius remonstrated with Arthur saying that a gentleman would not take another man's wife to dinner. Florence flew into a temper and turning to her mother said, 'See how he treats me; making me appear to be a prostitute'.[9] Then, ignoring Marius' wishes, she left for dinner with her admirer. Arthur added fuel to a highly combustible situation by presenting Florence with expensive gifts – a gold purse; a diamond and pearl bracelet; a diamond brooch; an emerald ring; a fan; even a dog.

With London about to be gripped by 'Jack the Ripper' paranoia, Lady Euston, George Haughton and the Duplanys set off for the tranquil German spa town Baden-Baden. They carried with them some of their own favourite neuroses; Marius was apprehensive that Arthur Cohen might decide to take the waters while Florence was piqued by her husband's uncontrolled behaviour and constant requests for money. Their incessant squabbling came to a head when they argued over the ownership of a watch that Marius took from Florence's safe. She accused him of being a thief and when he replied that he could not be accused of stealing his own property she taunted, 'Give a thing and take a thing, Cohen would not do such a thing'. He called Cohen a 'damned Jew' to which she retorted: 'Cohen is a gentleman and you are a damned French pauper!' Marius smashed the disputed watch against the wall and said that if Florence would only give him some money he 'would go out and get some other woman'.[10]

On their return to London, Florence and Marius both faced new professional challenges. Florence had been engaged by George Edwardes to appear in a burlesque at the Gaiety Theatre from September 1888 to Easter 1889. Having abandoned acting for a short while, Marius had become a director of a company set up to establish the Tivoli Music Hall in the Strand. Despite his move into theatrical property development, Marius still had severe cash-flow problems. On 26 September he appeared at the rehearsals for *Faust Up to Date* asking Florence to lend him £100 so that he could redeem his jewels from the pawnbroker. She refused, suggesting that he had spent previous loans on other women. Throughout the day the couple bickered – during rehearsals, at dinner; while attending a play; and at supper. As Marius consumed more alcohol his mood changed from tipsily flirtatious with the Gaiety's chorus girls to drunkenly aggressive towards his wife. On arriving back at

St John's Wood, Marius decided to make a stand – seldom a sensible thing for an intoxicated man to attempt. He prevented Florence from retiring to her room and in front of her cousin said that he must 'insist upon his rights as a husband'.[11] As his scornful wife tried to push past him, Marius struck her several times on the chest and pushed her to the floor. In the act of falling she struck her back painfully against a table. Hearing the commotion, Florence's brother, Donald, burst into the room and threatened Marius with a small brass poker picked up from the fireplace. Marius blustered and, perhaps inspired by Donald's diminutive weapon, invited him to Belgium to fight a duel. Florence and her brother immediately left the house leaving Marius alone with a bottle of brandy.

The next day Marius was abject, writing to Florence:

> My Darling Wife – When I woke up this morning I did not see you by my side [...] I confess I was very drunk last night. Whatever I said I beg your pardon. I don't remember. Your affectionate and loving husband, Marius.[12]

Florence's response to her affectionate and loving husband was to demand that he leave her house without delay. Next evening she attended a dinner party given by Lady Euston at which Cohen was present. The situation with Marius was discussed and after the meal the party went to a performance at the Gaiety. Her injuries were such that she could not attend rehearsals for a week, causing the production to be postponed until the end of October. When the burlesque finally opened, Florence was inundated with gifts and flowers, including a bouquet from her husband – 'With all my heart, wishing you a very great success'. She gave it away.

Despite Mrs Fawcett's complaints about 'the latest nastiness of the Divorce Case', *Faust Up to Date* was a major success, running until August 1889. Florence's marital problems were probably not known to the general public, with the exception of those who saw her riding or dining with Arthur Cohen.

Florence was the star of a Gaiety Theatre company which set out to tour the United States with *Faust Up to Date* in November 1889. Cohen was at the docks to wave her off just as, seven months later he was present to welcome her back. While she had been in America, he had sent her letters and telegraphic communications via the submarine cable. On her return she made another triumphant appearance at the

Gaiety, playing the title role in *Carmen Up to Data* by the same authors as *Faust Up to Date*, Henry Pettitt and George R. Sims. Although performed with her usual aplomb, Florence's portrayal of the sensual femme fatale was probably not best suited to enhance her offstage reputation.

Florence and Cohen quickly slipped back into their old round of parties, balls, dinners and visits to the theatre, although they no longer had Marius' tantrums to contend with. He had not given up on the case, however, and had decided to engage a detective agency, Shrives and Lawson, to monitor Florence's and Cohen's movements. Late on the evening of 20 May 1891 agent Rodney Loxton trailed the couple from the stage door of the Gaiety to nearby Gow's Supper Rooms at 357 Strand and then on to Florence's apartment at 111 Oxford Street where they remained for 20 minutes. Behind the scenes at the Gaiety Cohen often called at Florence's dressing room, but he was only one of a host of other friends and admirers. Although Marius was employing detectives to check for any improprieties in his wife's lifestyle, he does not seem to have worried that she might have engaged similar tactics against him. A year after their separation he had become attached to a young married actress named Marie Luella, making few efforts to hide their affair. On 5 December 1890, Florence wrote to him:

> I hear you have been and are still having me watched. Pray go on doing it; it cannot harm me. As you are so flush of money perhaps you will pay me some of the money you borrowed under false pretences? After the document you received to-day you will have it in your power to make that woman, your mistress, happy. That is, if her unfortunate husband takes the same steps to divorce her, and get rid of such cattle.[13]

Florence instituted divorce proceedings at the end of 1888. She accused Marius of cruelty and adultery, while he made a counter charge of adultery with Arthur Cohen. The hearing (5 to 11 December 1891), during which Florence was represented by the legal heavyweights Sir Charles Russell and Frederick Inderwick, generated massive press coverage. On the first morning she made an early appearance at the Royal Courts of Justice, in the Strand, wearing a 'chocolate brown dress, very low in the neck, with a tartan silk front, and a small fashionable hat'.[14] She was portrayed by Marius' defence lawyer as a 'vindictive and unscrupulous' woman and, worse still, one who was more successful in her financial dealings than her husband. Her way of life was unladylike. She sang and danced on stage (sometimes with snakes) and not only did she expose her emotions in public, but also sundry parts of her body. It was suggested that she swore and uttered blasphemies, although she only owned up to sometimes using 'a big, big d'. Marius was perhaps more difficult to defend. He was a cuckold, a philanderer, a sponger, a wife-beater and, worse of all, a Frenchman, burdened by the comic stereotype that he had helped to create. The co-respondent Arthur Cohen was already judged. As a Jew in a racially intolerant Victorian Britain he was considered even more despicable than a Frenchman.

After five days of bravura performances watched and sometimes applauded by a fashionable audience, the jury found Marius guilty of adultery, but not guilty of cruelty. Although Florence was cleared of adultery, the judge declined to grant a divorce. Instead, a judicial separation was imposed with both parties responsible for their own costs. Florence burst into tears at the close of proceedings, while Marius was cheered by a large crowd when he left the court.

When the original Tivoli Music Hall company collapsed Marius returned to the theatre, concentrating on acting roles rather than comic opera. Following tours of the United States and Australia, he began to suffer from a lung condition which forced him into temporary retirement. Although desperately ill he accepted an engagement to appear in South Africa with a Gaiety Theatre company hoping that a change of climate would be beneficial to his health. But these were to be his farewell performances for immediately after his return to England in January 1896 he died from cancer. The reconciliation between the Duplanys predicted by many of their friends did not occur. Freed once more from marital ties, Florence married Arthur Cohen on 13 February 1897, a short and unhappy union that ended in the divorce courts in 1902.

The complications of her private life did not prevent Florence from remaining one of the most popular figures on the London stage. She continued to break fresh ground during the 1890s, appearing with the D'Oyly Carte Opera Company at the Savoy Theatre and in several of the first musical comedies. In 1900 she even recorded a song from Leslie Stuart's *Floradora* for the Gramophone Company in Maiden Lane. In the same year she was considered to be one of the most versatile of actresses:

Miss Florence St John, is in her own sphere, a great artist. She has won for herself a position which is absolutely unchallenged. There have been light opera singers who have sung as delightfully as she, light opera actresses whose acting has been as fascinating as hers; but there has been none other in our time uniting in herself all the charms and all the gifts of Miss Florence St John. With a voice of velvet quality, so much sympathy, so much pathos, so much fun and so much devilment; a manner insouciant, saucy, sweet, and womanly; a comedian without rival in her own particular style; so bright and sensitive and humorous and pathetic in her acting. That even had she not been a singer, as an actress she would have been in the very front rank—Miss St John has had so many triumphs in so many different spheres, that one wonders if there remains any worlds left for her to conquer.[15]

During the 1900s Florence alternated concert appearances and straight acting roles, appearing for a second time as the seventeenth-century actress Nell Gwynn in English Nell. The highlight of her later career occurred on 4 July 1903 when she headed a star-studded performance of a specially written vehicle to mark the closure of the Gaiety Theatre. A short distance along the Strand a new Gaiety was almost ready to open as the cast of The Linkman recreated memorable moments from the old theatre's 35-year history. Several artists closely involved with the theatre had passed away and were represented by other performers, but Florence appeared briefly in her own role, Marguerite, in Faust Up to Date. At the close of the emotional evening she joined Hayden Coffin to sing 'Auld Lang Syne', the final song heard at the theatre.

Having seen the demolition of the Gaiety, Florence lost another reminder of the past later in the year when Kate Cooke, still clinging to the title Lady Euston, died of bronchitis. She had become a confused and lonely invalid, prone to giving away items from her dwindling stock of fancy goods. From 1906 Florence appeared with her own sketch company at music halls around the country, eventually retiring two years before her death in 1912. Although only 56, she had outlived most of her bohemian friends.

# 16

# THE BACKSIDE OF ST CLEMENT'S

As a centre for publishing and entertainment the Strand was well placed to tell its own story. It was an oblique and rambling narrative laboured over by penny-a-line hacks, jobbing dramatists, trumpeting showmen, bohemian journalists and unprincipled publishers. Despite their frequently intimate acquaintanceship with the Strand, the chroniclers were seldom honest, accurate or consistent. Some had a vested interest in describing the district as an adult playground where the gay women were always stunners, the smutty ditties were slap-up and the cribs the lushest of the lush. Others took an apparently opposite stance, issuing cautionary guides whose lingering detail failed to convince people that they were meant as real warnings to the unwary visitor. Throughout the Victorian period, reformers and social commentators attacked the iniquity and squalor of the area, but by the early days of the twentieth century changes to the physical and social character of the Strand meant that there was very little left to complain about or even to champion.

Before an act of parliament introduced compulsory state education in 1870, a large proportion of the urban working class had already acquired rudimentary reading skills from ragged schools, charitable missions and self-help groups. A demand for mass-produced literature was met by a rapid expansion of small publishers who, from the 1820s, were able to unite the cheapness of machine-made paper with the efficiency of steam printing presses. In London a growing number of booksellers began to establish themselves in an insalubrious locality known in the eighteenth century as 'the Backside of St Clement's', but more specifically defined by the brooding, decaying houses of Wych Street and Holywell Street. Coming into existence at the time of the 1832 Reform

**ILLUSTRATION 26.** Holywell Street, Strand.

Act and the Chartism agitation of the 1840s, many booksellers, newsagents and publishers (the three were frequently synonymous) were often responsible for the production of clandestine political works. Such secrecy in the supply of books and periodicals became habit-forming, leading to the marketing of new and reprinted works of pornography and melodramatic fiction in which criminal protagonists were depicted cheerfully subverting the authority of a morally bankrupt establishment. Of the 90 publishers of cheap fiction operating between 1830 and 1850 listed by Louis James in *Fiction For theWorking Man*, nine were recorded as occupying premises in Holywell Street with a further 30 in the Strand or adjacent streets.

Whatever forces impelled the publisher William Dugdale to pursue a career in pornography they were strong enough to sustain him through several terms of imprisonment and to inspire his extended family to follow the same calling. During the course of nearly 50 years, he became the country's chief supplier of 'curiosa', his prolific output of 'dirty' or 'filthy' books and prints being largely responsible for the passing of a major act of parliament. In his study of Victorian sexuality *The Other Victorians*, Steven Marcus asserts that Dugdale possessed

> a mania for print combined with a mania for concealment [...] He published anything he could get his hands on, from bawdy songsters at 6d or 1s to the gaudiest volumes for as much as he could wheedle. He reprinted the pornography of other pornographic publishers, sometimes changing the title, sometimes not bothering to; and he reprinted his own in as many sizes, shapes, and forms as he could invent – a true pirate, he even tried to steal from himself.[1]

Originally from Stockport in Lancashire, Dugdale came to London as a young man. He was a political radical and is said to have been on the outer fringes of the 1820 Cato Street Conspiracy to murder Lord Liverpool and his cabinet. Such revolutionary zeal gave way to bibliographic obsession as he became an independent publisher in 1822. Within a short time he fell foul of the Society for the Suppression of Vice, an organisation that instigated actions against booksellers marketing pornographic publications. Under the new Vagrancy Act of 1824, which prohibited the display of obscene books and prints, he was reported to the Middlesex magistrates, receiving a four-month sentence in 1825. Many subsequent prosecutions followed, most carrying with them terms of imprisonment up to a maximum of two years. When not in prison he was often in court pursuing counter actions against the Society for the Suppression of Vice, alleging illegal entry, theft and blackmail.

Once described as having a 'sodden and sensual countenance',[2] Dugdale grew old and grotesque amid the old and grotesque buildings of Holywell Street. Running parallel to the north side of Strand, between the churches of St Mary le Strand and St Clement Danes, the street was named after one of London's secret springs, a well that was said to be situated behind the Spotted Dog tavern. During the seventeenth and eighteenth centuries, its narrow pavements and cobbled road were lined by premises belonging to respectable cloth merchants. The street had fallen steeply in social status by the start of the Victorian era, with many prostitutes in evidence and old clothes, second-hand goods and, increasingly, indecent books being offered for sale in the shops. From 1839 to 1854 Dugdale leased number 37 Holywell Street, a tall, possibly Elizabethan house with a pointed gable, overhanging storeys and a carved wooden lion that was incorporated into the shop wall. Next door at number 38, a painted signboard 'The Indian Queen' had once denoted a mercer's shop. At number 36 hung a gilded crescent moon, its features smiling phlegmatically at the squalor that had overtaken it. Hardly noticeable between 37 and 36 was a narrow passage that ran through to the Strand. In later years it was known as Half Moon Alley, but earlier it had been called Pissing Alley.

In 1851 over six million visitors were drawn to London by the 'Great Exhibition of the Works of Industry of all Nations' held in Hyde Park. Not all of them confined their interest to the instructive and artistic exhibits displayed in the gleaming glass Crystal Palace. No doubt a number found their way to Dugdale's far from transparent premises, an influx of out of towners perhaps inspiring his prurient guide book, *The Yokel's Preceptor; or, More Sprees in London; Being a regular and Curious Show-up of All the Rigs and Doings of the Flash Cribs in the Great Metropolis*. Late in the afternoon of 2 September 1851, Dugdale received an unwelcome visitation when the police, directed by officers from the Society for the Suppression of Vice, mounted raids on his two shops. There had been increasing public criticism of Holywell Street's principal trade and the Society had finally lost patience with the chief culprit who at his last prosecution had promised to abstain from publishing pornography. The police gained access to number 16, but, directly across the road at 37, Dugdale's assistant, Sharp, lived up to his name by quickly raising the alarm. With the door slammed shut and bolted, the police were forced to wait outside until Dugdale appeared from a conveniently situated side door in the indelicately named alley. Having disposed of what he considered to be the most incriminating material, the shop owner addressed the police inspector: 'Now Chadwick, you may come in.' He should have kept Inspector Chadwick and his men waiting a little longer for, in a fireplace located in the shop's back parlour, they found a mass of smouldering books and papers.

As the police conducted a search of Dudgale's premises, other booksellers along the street cleared their windows of any literature or advertising that might attract attention. The large crowd that gathered may have been supportive or antagonistic towards the raid – having campaigned against the pornographers of Holywell Street, *Lloyd's Weekly Newspaper* reported that the public's 'hearty wishes were with the police in this attempt to exterminate a batch of reptiles so injurious to society, and whose unblushing offensiveness has been patent for many years in this plague spot of the metropolis, under the eyes of our principal police-office'.[3] But as the Society's porters loaded two large carts with confiscated material (including 882 books; 3870 prints; and 16 cwt of unsewn letterpress), a bookseller's assistant named Henry May was arrested for obstruction and assault.

At Bow Street Police Court and subsequently the Middlesex Sessions, Dugdale made a spirited defence of his position. There was no legal authority to enter the premises while the books and prints found in the back room had not been exposed to public view. Many of the books seized had been regularly advertised in the press and one of the works taken – *The Confessions of Harriet Wilson* – had been cleared at a previous trial. Engravings of the nude figure could hardly be considered indecent or the proprietors of *The Illustrated London News* and the 'fashionable print-sellers of the West-end'[4] would be indicted for printing copies of 'The Grecian Slave' currently on display at the Great Exhibition. Such considerations were swept aside. Judge Adams sentenced Dugdale to two years' imprisonment with hard labour, also criticising the parish of St Clement Danes for not taking action against such a 'great abomination'.

While Dugdale was incarcerated his businesses were efficiently maintained by his family; brothers Thomas and John, son William and daughters Jessie and Frances. Like Marie Elliot who (in 1857) had reputedly sold indecent books at 14 Holywell Street since the 1820s, Frances Thornhill, née Dugdale, had no qualms about her unusual occupation. Giving evidence in an action brought by her father against the agent for the Society for the Suppression of Vice she stated:

> I am married. I have three children. I certainly do sell what 'you' call obscene books. I have sold a book called Fanny Hill. My father has been five times convicted for selling obscene books and pictures. I do not call Fanny Hill obscene. Coloured pictures of naked men and women are in that book, but you can also see them at the Crystal Palace.[5]

Although the authorities were unable to remove the Dugdale clan from their strongholds in Holywell Street, extreme weather conditions forced a temporary vacation of number 37. In the early hours of 27 December 1852 a hurricane hit central London, its violent epicentre apparently located immediately above Dugdale's shop. The high winds propelled a double chimney stack through the roof, destroying the building's lathe and plaster gable and displacing several floors.[6]

On a number of occasions during the winter of 1856/7 Henry Dodgson, an ivory bone brush-maker, and J. G. Eaton, an artist, visited Dugdale's shop at 5 Holywell Street where they purchased several prints and a single book. The items were not for personal edification, but to provide evidence to the Society for the Suppression of Vice who was paying both men 5s an hour for their services. As a result information was laid before the police, Dugdale's shop was raided yet again and the publisher was remanded in Coldbath Fields Prison for 14 weeks. On Saturday, 9 May 1857 a distraught Dugdale appeared at the Court of Queen's Bench before Lord Chief Justice Campbell. He was soon found guilty, but instructed to wait until another case was heard before receiving judgement. William Strange, a newsagent of 183 Fleet Street, was charged with 'publishing and selling an indecent weekly publication called Paul Pry, and another of a similar description entitled The Women of London'. In his summing up to the jury the Lord Chief Justice expressed his horror that Paul Pry was so widely available:

> They had heard of shops being open in Holywell Street, where by some artifice or contrivance persons could purchase immoral books; but here was a periodical regularly published and openly sold in the public streets, and in shops which pretended to be respectable, for the sum of a penny, not containing by accident, as suggested, an immoral paragraph,

ILLUSTRATION 27. Old houses in the Strand, 413-17 depicted in a drawing of 1898.

> but systematically filled with writing of a most obscene and disgusting nature [...] Hitherto there had been some check to the circulation of demoralising publications in the high price which was exacted for them, one of the books sold by the other defendant, Dugdale, having, for instance, cost one guinea; but here this poison, for so he must call it, was sold, and could readily be procured, for a penny.[7]

Before sentence was passed Dugdale requested permission to 'say a few words'. A few turned to a great many as he paced around the court, haranguing the judge, jury and a large crowd of onlookers. It was performance lifted from the pages of cheap melodrama, delivered with declamatory gestures and containing accusations of conspiracy and injustice. Reaching a pinnacle of impassioned indignation, he declared that his life was no longer bearable. He produced a penknife, presumably to bring the oration to a dramatic close, but he was quickly disarmed. Calling for a glass of water he switched to the sentimental side of his repertoire, begging for mercy if only for the sake of 'two beautiful and innocent beings', presumably his daughters then engaged in running his porn empire.

While the prisoner strutted and fretted Lord Campbell sat dispassionately, comparing the nature of both cases. He knew Dugdale as an unreformed and probably unreformable miscreant, a repeat offender who was apparently impervious to the limited sentences that might be imposed upon him. But the younger man, Strange, brought with him a new challenge, that of pornography becoming available to a wider and supposedly more corruptible public. Disposing of the matter in hand – one year with hard labour for Dugdale and three months without for Strange – Lord Campbell considered what might be done to check a traffic which was 'more pernicious to society than poison'.[8] Two days later he spoke in the House of Lords, warning of the dangers of pornography and demanding legislation against its publishers. Over the course of the summer Campbell steered a bill through parliament, which in September 1857 became the first Obscene Publications Act. Although it controversially left the definition of obscenity to magistrates and judges, it made the sale of pornography a statutory crime rather than a common law offence, empowering the police to search suspicious premises and ultimately destroy offending material. In practice it was a slight adjustment to the situation that prevailed before the act, providing only a partial antidote to the 'poison' of pornography. Shortly after the act was passed Dugdale made another court appearance, brought from Coldbath Fields Prison during a prosecution of Frances Thornhill and her husband who were running his shop at 5 Holywell Street. As always he was in combative mood, attempting to read long passages from his publications and asking the magistrate to point out the sections that were considered to be obscene. According to a contemporary account, 'he showed a determination to protract the case as much as possible, declaring that "he did not often get a day out"'.[9]

Towards the end of his life Dugdale moved his operations to Wych Street. He died in Clerkenwell Gaol on 11 November 1868 while serving an 18-month sentence imposed upon him under the act that he had done so much to provoke. His daughter attributed his demise to lack of mental stimulation: 'I believe that if he had had books on history and geography his life would have been saved. He only had a bible, and tracts to read, which he knew all by heart.'

During the 1840s Dugdale's close neighbour at 28 Holywell Street, George Vickers Senior, was another supporter of the radical movement. Although not an outright pornographer, Vickers had published immoderate and indelicate literature for the masses for some years. After his death in 1848 his widow Anne ran the business, handing it over, in 1851, to her son George Vickers, Junior, who continued to peddle a mixture of general literature, serious medical works, smut and sensation from various addresses in the vicinity of the Strand. From Holywell Street he migrated to 334 Strand, and by 1860 his premises were located in Angel Court, a narrow and dingy passage that ran parallel to Catherine Street.

In 1846 Vickers' bestseller was George W. M. Reynold's *Mysteries of London*, an epic part-issue work that sold in 1d weekly issues. One of the Victorian era's most popular and prolific authors, Reynolds (1825–79) abandoned a military career to pursue journalism in Paris. While living in France he became infused with Republican ideals, later introducing attacks on the British monarchy and aristocracy into many of his novels. His labyrinthine plots and ornate prose were often accompanied by pages of facts and statistics included to highlight social injustice and to incite 'the industrial classes' against a self-serving establishment. As a committed Chartist he presided over an illegal, mass demonstration in Trafalgar Square on March 1848, leading his supporters along the Strand to address them from the balcony of his house in Wellington Street. Although often espousing radical sentiments, Reynolds' books were perhaps more popular with a mass readership because of their melodramatic storylines, gratuitous violence and lurid accounts of sexual liaisons. Often condemned as a political agitator, Reynolds was also criticised for glamorising an immoral lifestyle:

> The art which makes the life of a courtesan, or an actress, a life of ease, pleasure and gay delight is an art which can only be exercised with the extremest caution [...] In too many instances this clever

writer has, we regret to say, administered the poison and forgotten the remedy.[10]

Reynolds' novels sometimes featured well-known public figures such as Renton Nicholson and W. G. Ross, alongside descriptions of London slums and night houses. A highly sanitised picture of Holywell Street may have owed something to the presence there of his publishers:

> Time has, however, included Holywell Street in the clauses of its Reform Bill. Several highly respected booksellers and publishers have located themselves in the place that once deserved no better denomination than Rag Fair. The unprincipled venues of demoralizing books and pictures have, with few exceptions, migrated into Wych Street or Drury Lane; and even the two or three that pertinaciously cling to their old templar of infamy in Holywell Street, seem to be aware of the incursion of respectability into that once notorious thoroughfare, and cease to outrage decency by the display of vile obscenities in their windows.

The fusion of fact and fiction that became a standard feature of works issued by Vickers and other publishers of cheap literature was often promoted as possessing a documentary function. In 1860, Vickers' publication, *The Career of an Artful Dodger; His Art and Artfulness*, was advertised as being 'full of startling dodgeries, showing one-half of the world how the other half lives', while a companion volume *Tom Fox; or, The Revelations of a Detective*, provided coverage of 'Adventures, Disguises, Perils, Escapes, Captures, Intrigues, Gamblers, Turfites, Burglars, Homicides, Abductions' and scores of other illegal activities.[11]

During the mid-1860s, George Vickers pushed at the boundaries of acceptability by issuing a series of novels about prostitutes and prostitution. Although short on detail and long on innuendo, works such as *The Soiled Dove; a Biography of a Fast Young Lady Formerly Known as 'the Kitten'* shocked many contemporary critics by a non-judgemental, even light-hearted approach to their subject. To promote the books, the names of well-known courtesans were appropriated for some titles. Three novels – *Anonyma; Skittles* and *Skittles in Paris* – were inspired by one of the most famous demimondaines, Catherine Walters. Although the author of the trilogy (probably William Stephens

Hayward) did not feel obliged to confine himself to anything like an accurate representation of Skittles' career, his long passages of dialogue convincingly evoked 'flash' conversation:

> I once knew a man who wrote for a beastly penny paper that circulates amongst the bargees and omnibus cads, and because I didn't choose to be seen with him in the Park – it wasn't likely, you know – he went home and wrote some ferocious articles, perfect blood and thunder in their nature. He said I should die miserably, and be buried in the *fosse commune*, and a lot of rot of that description; and all because I didn't mind chaffing him, and drinking his wine in a nighthouse, but I did not choose to exactly Siamese with him in the Park. I didn't see it; one must be select or up goes the donkey. Good men don't like to be seen with cads, and if a woman wants to be in a good set, why she must study the primary rules of society.[12]

Vickers' most notorious publication appeared in 1865, a reissue of a work originally produced by the United Kingdom Press of 28 Brydges Street five years earlier. *Charley Wag, the New Jack Sheppard; a New and Intensely Exciting Real Life Romance* was anonymously written by Charles H. Ross, later responsible for the London-life stage melodrama *Clam* (a character called 'Clam' appears in *Charley Wag*). The part-issue work which was advertised as 'rendered in stern, truthful language by one who has studied, in all its blackest enormity, the doings of secret crime' set a thoroughly bad example to its many juvenile readers. Young Charley drank, smoked, dallied with prostitutes and committed a catalogue of crimes before getting away with murder. Authority figures such as magistrates, clergymen and even an ex-prime minister were portrayed as licentious and corrupt, while police were bungling and no match for the quick-witted Charley. The opening of the novel was set not far from Brydges Street and Angel Court, in Villiers Street, which in pre-Embankment days ran directly to the Thames:

> A woman ran wildly down one of the several steep flights of steps leading from Hungerford Market to the Quay below, and creeping along upon the slippery stonework, overhanging the water, paused for a moment at the extreme point, cast one fearful, shuddering glance around, and FLUNG HER CHILD INTO THE RIVER.[13]

Baby Charley, the son of a ravished duchess, was fished out of the water by a disreputable old soak, Mr Toddleboy, and raised to become an inspiration to all London's aspiring criminals. His initial misdemeanour, the theft of a goose and a bottle of rum, involved the first of many thrilling chases:

> [H]is strength began to fail him. He could not hold on for ever. His only chance lay in the hope that that he might be able to get out of sight somewhere, and let them pass him.
> Ah, a happy thought.
> The dark arches!
> He was now in the Strand, rushing across the road suddenly, under horses' heads and before galloping omnibuses, he ran down Durham-street and plunged into the gaping aperture.[14]

When not residing in the brothels of Clements Lane, Charley had a spirited mistress who sometimes adopted male costume to accompany him on his exploits. Julia Jenkins had seen a lot of life and life had seen a lot of Julia Jenkins. She provided Charley with a short autobiography:

> I began life as a shirt-maker: and I used to earn threepence a day, if I stuck hard at it. Then I took to mantle-making, and made about ninepence a day [...] Then I thought I might do better, and went to sit as a model to photographers, at eighteen pence an hour, fastening my boot, or lolling on a sofa, showing my ankles. When I had a little more courage, I used to make a little more money. Indeed, the less clothes you have on, the larger price you get. I got up to three shillings; and I dare say you've seen me in lots of stereoscopic slides. They seized several thousands of me in Holywell Street, when Lord Campbell's Act was passed the other day. After a time I gave up that trade, and took to the music halls [...] Then I picked up a swell who introduced me to the duke; and now I'm with you.[15]

The firm of Vickers also supplied sensational material in their non-fiction productions. Transcripts of trials, including that of Boulton and Park, were popular and a best-seller of 1860 was the autobiography of one of the Strand's most scandalous characters the 'Lord High Baron' Renton Nicholson. The autobiography was, to some extent, revisionist, acknowledging Nicholson's numerous terms of imprisonment and friendships with prostitutes, but almost entirely ignoring excursions into bawdiness and semi-pornography. For most of his adult life 'Nick' had been a happy hypocrite, during the late 1830s jointly editing *The Crown*, 'a highly respectable, high-church paper' and *The Town* which recorded 'the Doings of Courtesans and Demireps of Quality'. In the prospectus for the latter – not the former – he announced his intention to 'expose all those evils which our publication will admit of', adding that he would employ his 'editorial whip over the raw of the thorough-bred leaders of real life in the West'.[16] Although *The Town* did carry sporadic attacks against the police and courts, its editor was more interested in 'puffing' courtesans and night houses. There were also adverts for books of which an avowed moral reformer might have disapproved. Titles such as *Julia; or, I Have Saved My Rose; Onanism Unveiled; Nymphomania;* and *Memoirs of the Celebrated Fanny Hill* were published by 'H. Smith' whose address, 37 Holywell Street, indicates that he was none other than William Dugdale operating under one of several pseudonyms.

During the 1840s Nicholson and 'H. Smith' also seem to have co-operated in the production of several editions of *The Swell's Night Guide*, comprehensively subtitled:

> A Peep Through the Great Metropolis, Under the Dominion of Nox: Displaying the Various Attractive Places of Amusement by Night: the Saloons; the Paphian Beauties; the Chaffing Cribs; the Introducing Houses; the Singing and Lushing Cribs; the Comical Clubs, Fancy Ladies and their Penchants, etc. etc. Carefully corrected by the Lord Chief Baron, the Arbiter Elegantiarum of Fashion and Folly.

Just as *The Town* and *The Swell's Night Guide* presented an incandescent picture of the capital's night haunts, a series of low-priced booklets claimed to supply the words to the outrageous songs that were performed in them. Under his 'H. Smith' pseudonym, Dugdale published *The Cider Cellars Songster* and *The Coal Hole Companion*. In *The Sam Hall Songster* additional verses that were given for Ross's famous song contained mildly indecent language:

> Can't they stop that bloody bell,
> Bloody bell;
> Can't they stop that bloody bell
> What it means I know too well,
> Kick the ringer's soul to hell
> Bla-st his eyes!

But other songsters claimed that overtly pornographic lyrics were sung at major tavern concerts. It was a link that was also taken up by *Lloyd's Weekly London Newspaper* in an imagined address to the Home Secretary on the first day of 1853:

> In the *Morning Chronicle* it was stated that the great singing-houses – as Evans's, the Cyder-cellars, and the Coal Hole – had undermined the occupation of the poor street ballad-writers. The publisher of low songs will not employ original writers, because he knows he can get first-rate effusions from these fashionable resorts. Here are to be found songs in which the basest things are expressed with a point and cleverness which give a strength to the poison – from these taverns, where most fashionable men will be found listening, in comfort, to sentiments and words that should shock every human ear, are issued writings that spread their poison over the country. From Holywell Street to the Coal Hole is a short distance. Very convenient to the patrons of both places must this proximity be![17]

It is not possible to establish how 'low' songs actually were. When the Wych Street publisher William West stated that the 'Famous Amatory Parody on "The Sea!"' was 'sung at the Cider Cellars', was he merely fulfilling a public expectation of the type of material that might be heard in such a resort? Or had he dropped in at his local concert room and taken down the words of an actual performance? 'The Bride' was certainly more explicit than any songs known to have been performed at early music halls:

> My bride! My bride! My luscious bride,
> No other one I'll kiss beside!
> With belly plump – and round and fair,
> And your little spot all clad with hair!
> You make me queer – when I feast my eyes,
> On your private charms – your ivory thighs!

*The Rakish Rhymer; or, Fancy Man's Own Songster and Reciter* (known only from a 1917 reprint) preserves several songs whose qualified indecency make them more likely to have been presented before an audience. Appearing as a woman in 'The Randy Wife's Dream' a popular Cyder Cellars' comedian, J. W. Sharp, gave a vision of marriage that was in stark contrast to the rampant enthusiasm of 'The Bride':

> I'll daily put my trust in gin, may it give me strength to bear
> The trials sent us, female souls, when men go you know where.

So if with gals he should get a bit, and get it burnt for life,
I hope he'll keep away from home nor give it to his wife.

Songs about prostitution frequently featured in the bawdy songsters, although 'The Blowen's Ball' was unusual in providing comic rather than sexual content:

Come, listen awhile unto me,
You Sheena's of ev'ry degree;
I sing of a bit of a rout,
To which all the motts were asked out;
Togg'd in their best clothes so grand,
At a bawdy-ken just by the Strand.,
The bawd had just come to some cash;
So determined she was to be flash;
She invited the blowens so free,
To dinner and also to tea;
She searched all the streets for the gals,
And invited the whole of their pals;
And at night, what was better than all,
She gave all the blowens a ball,
All the blowens together
Where met at the bawdy-house ball![18]

Although the single-page broadsheets that had flourished from the seventeenth century still continued to present heavily stylised accounts of murders and executions, songster booklets largely replaced the earlier publications as transcripts of popular and traditional songs. Differing from their earlier counterparts in tone as well as format, songsters approached similar subjects with studied irony rather than dogged narrative. Old ballads and the ballad format were provided with a modern gloss, an injection of humour intended to appeal to the supposed sophistication of their audience. Where the criminal career of that infamous inhabitant of Wych Street, Jack Sheppard, had been described in numerous ballads, each with a conventional 'moral' added to absolve the motives of the chronicler, by the 1840s the subject was more likely to receive a tongue-in-cheek, semi-comic treatment:

They took him three times more to prison,
'Cause three times more he got away;

Till he was tired of escaping,
And let them hang him up one day.
Ri tol, &c.

Now he lives renowned in story,
In three volumes is his life;
Ainsworth shares Jack Sheppard's glory,
Who murder makes with morals rife.
Ri tol, &c.

MORAL
Know all ye youths, who would be famous,
Don't be left here in the lurch,
But take a lesson from my ditty,
Your master stab, or rob your church.[19]

\*     \*     \*

For much of the century Holywell Street was doubly condemned: physically as a dirty and decaying obstruction to the efficient running of the Strand and morally as a source of pollution poisoning impressionable minds. The street's very setting − hidden but occupying a situation close to the heart of society − was analogous to pornography, while its easily monitored access points and convenient escape route down Pissing Alley were expressive of the evasion of justice. Despite the death of William Dugdale and the suppression of much overtly displayed indecent material, the street's history and appearance ensured that it would always possess an evil reputation. Writing an apparently factual account of one of his own police investigations, Maurice Moser chose to portray the Holywell Street of 1881 as it was in Dugdale's heyday in the 1840 and 1850s:

> There is a certain almost too well-known portion of the Strand which has for a large number of years held a very unenviable notoriety, and it is the earnest wish and hope of all those who are interested in the welfare of youths in particular and morality in general that the contemplated improvements of that district will be of such a radical character as to sweep away altogether that foul sink of iniquity to which I allude, and which is known by the name of Holywell Street.[20]

Not only did Moser present a stereotyped version of Holywell Street, but he appears to have changed the location of the pornographer's residence from Drury Lane for the sake of dramatic effect (see

Chapter 11). The purchase of indecent images was said to have taken place in a room whose surroundings evoked the seedy nature of the transaction:

> At last, after considerable conversation, I prevailed upon the man to let me have some of his more valuable wares, and followed him upstairs into a dirty little place, which was part bed-room, part workshop, part store-room, part anything – as filthy a hole as I have ever been into. I sat on a rickety chair before an equally rickety table, my face looking towards the window, whilst the man was picking out the photographs from a tin box he had pulled from under the bed, and placing them on the table, his wife watching the proceedings over my shoulder.

Although indecent and risqué photographs appear to have been widely available, the sale of much pornographic literature had undergone a transformation, driven deeper underground by the constant threat of prosecution. Books were produced in smaller numbers and sold to a 'connoisseur' market for higher prices. Leonard Smithers, who at one time operated from Effingham House, issued works by leading 1890s authors alongside select pornography – including a four guinea edition of the homosexual epic, Teleny (1893). One of the most notorious works of the genre, The Sins of the Cities of the Plains (1881), was published by William Lazenby in an edition of 250, also priced at four guineas. Allegedly narrated by the Peter Pan of rent boys, Jack Saul, 'the recollections of a Mary-Ann' included a highly coloured account of Amos 'Charlotte' Gibbings' ball at Haxell's Hotel attended by Ernest Boulton and Frederick Park. Like Moser's description of the Holywell Street sting, the passage in The Sins of the Cities of the Plain fictionalised reality to provoke a strong response from the reader. In classic pornographic tradition both pieces of writing represent a couple involved in an illicit act, watched by a third party:

> Boulton was superbly got up as a beautiful lady, and I observed Lord Arthur was very spooney upon her.
>
> During the evening I noticed them slip away together, and made up my mind to try to get a peep at their little game. So I followed them as quietly as possible, and saw them pass down a corridor to another apartment, not one of the dressing-rooms which I knew had been provided for the use of the party, but one which I assume his lordship had secured for his own personal use [...]

Quietly kneeling down I put my eye to the [key] hole, and found I had a famous view of all that was going on in the next room. It put me in mind of the scene between two youths that the notorious Fanny Hill had once related to have seen through a peephole at a roadside inn. I could see and hear everything that was passing.[21]

The changes in the format and, to some extent, the content of pornography created by the Obscene Publications Act were systematic of the ways in which the bawdy, anti-authoritarian 'flash' lifestyle of the first half of the century was steadily repressed and discouraged. Increasingly conscious of London's position as the capital of a great empire, lawmakers and enforcers laboured to impose dignity and order to its streets. By the mid-1880s the culture of round the clock drinking had been largely eradicated; prostitution, although still prevalent, was under stricter control; the age of consent had been raised to 16 years; all sexual acts between men were illegal; the cancan had been prohibited in theatres; and Jack Sheppard had not been seen on the London stage for a quarter of a century. Crime was less likely to be romanticised. 'Penny Dreadfuls' had shifted their emphasis from juvenile lawbreakers to young heroes like Jack Harkaway who combated the criminals at home and brigands, pirates and unruly natives abroad. The noble Harkaway first appeared in 1871 in the *Boys of England*, a periodical whose creation in 1866 emphasised the widening split between a juvenile and adult readership.

Older readers were now likely to consume tales of real crime. In the late 1860s, George Purkess, whose father had published *The Life and Surprising Adventures of Jack Sheppard* in the 1840s, took over *The Illustrated Police News*, a mass-circulation periodical devoted to the 'leading murders, suicides, offences, and casualties of the week'. Outside the offices at 286 the Strand, a small crowd were usually in attendance gawping at enlarged illustrations depicting scenes of bloodshed and violence. Despite its sensational nature, Purkess felt that his publication acted as a deterrent 'because it warns people of the horrors of crime, and the results following upon the commission thereof'.[22] The crimes that possessed the greatest horrors were reported in greater detail in special supplements, one of the best-selling being *The Life and Examination of Boulton and Park: the Men in Women's Clothes*.

In 1877 the police intervened to suppress a long-running penny-issue serial about a sewer-dwelling gang of young roughs called *The Wild Boys of London; or, The Children of Night*. While Charley Wag and the Wild Boys had been banished, the most famous youthful miscreant was about to stage a remarkable comeback. Just as it had been difficult to keep Jack Sheppard in prison, it was to prove impossible to keep him out of the theatre. The Lord Chamberlain finally rescinded the 1859 embargo to allow the Gaiety to produce the musical burlesque *Little Jack Sheppard* at Christmas 1885. To facilitate Jack's dramatic return his character had to be drastically reconstructed and the details of his career completely disregarded. In keeping with theatrical tradition, the hero was played by a woman, the perennial Gaiety favourite and 'best "principal boy" ever seen upon the stage', Nellie Farren. Jack was portrayed as a 'gallant and picturesque young gentleman'[23] with little reference to his criminal exploits. The plot, barely discernable between the songs, dances and elaborate scenery, was confined to a fairy tale battle between good and evil as represented by the boyish-girlish Jack and the 'Thief Taker General', Jonathan Oscar Wilde (played by Fred Leslie). Above all, *Little Jack Sheppard* was a caricature of theatrical melodrama, a gentle put-down of a form of entertainment that was rapidly becoming laughably archaic.

It was to be the final production for 'Honest' John Hollingshead, the theatre's owner and guiding hand since its opening in 1868. Although *Little Jack Sheppard* was among the Gaiety's most popular productions, Hollingshead was acutely aware that there was a section of society that viewed his theatre with hostility. In *Gaiety Chronicles* he complained:

> Its festive title, which, unfortunately, was not always justified by its productions, gave it a character amongst that very well-meaning, commonplace, highly respectable, and generally very stupid class, who are too often to be found amongst the supporters of the Nonconformist conscience. Amongst these people the theatre generally was not much beloved, while that particular playhouse was honestly looked upon as a perfect sink of iniquity. 'Ichabod' was plainly written on its brazen front, illuminated by the best gas or electric device that the Messrs. Defries and Sons could supply. The sins of ancient Babylon were revived within its gilded walls, but the

destruction which ought to follow such sins, in various forms of volcanic disturbance was evidently a long time coming.[24]

It was not only a dedication to fun, frivolity and actresses showing their legs that troubled the supporters of the Nonconformist conscience. As demonstrated by Florence St John and Claude Marius, theatrical performers led irregular and immoderate private lives. If not openly promiscuous, they were frequently permissive, sharing an ill-regulated and dissolute existence commonly labelled 'bohemian'. During the run of Little Jack Sheppard one of the cast was about to undergo an apotheosis that transformed him from a comedy actor of long experience into the uncrowned king of 'bohemia', a position he occupied with unswerving determination for the next 40 years.

Making his debut in 1855 at the age of 22, Edwin 'E. J.' Odell had a 30-year career in drama, comic opera and burlesque. His idiosyncratic acting style was often eccentric and over histrionic, but he was sufficiently well regarded to obtain engagements with many leadings actors, including the Bancrofts and Henry Irving (whom he sometimes imitated). By the late 1870s he was spending more time in cultivating his offstage than onstage persona, his unkempt appearance being 'more familiar to the public in the Strand than in the pit, gallery, or stalls'.[25] Little Jack Sheppard was to prove Odell's penultimate engagement after which his late nights and idle days appear to have been largely funded by handouts from fellow actors and the income from the occasional benefit performances. Described by Bernard Ince as 'a supreme self-publicist who excelled at imitating himself',[26] Odell became a permanent fixture at the Savage Club, a society whose membership was only slightly less bohemian than he was. From the club's headquarters in Adelphi Terrace he would wander into the Strand, conspicuous by a wide-brimmed sombrero, white beard and a complete disregard for passing traffic. Noted for possessing a mordant wit, a fund of anecdotes and, more than anything, for just being 'Old Odell', his cultivation of shabbiness extended to distressing nearly new clothes that were presented to him. He died at the age of 93, a disruptive resident of the Charterhouse almshouses where he was said to have broken every rule.

Odell's anecdotes about his own life have been largely lost along with an autobiography that was never published. Other bohemians, however, chronicled their times in some detail. A network of different coteries (theatrical, music hall, literary, sporting), each with their own favoured clubs, pubs and restaurants, were interlaced with writers and journalists who recorded the more interesting developments that occurred in their milieu. Some, like George R. Sims, 'Doss Chideross' (A. R. Marshall) and Henry S. Leigh, wrote both comic and serious verse about the more unconventional side of London life. Sometimes a sentimental or romantic treatment was in evidence, as in Jeff Prowse's anthem to bohemia, 'The City of Prague' (for Prague read London):

> How we laughed as we laboured together!
> How well I remember to-day
> Our 'outings' in midsummer weather,
> Our winter delights at the play!
> We were not over-nice in our dinners,
> Our 'rooms' were up rickety stairs;
> But if hope be the wealth of beginners,
> By Jove! We were all millionaires,
> Our incomes were very uncertain,
> Our prospects were equally vague;
> Yet the person I pity, who knows not the City,
> The Beautiful City of Prague!

Prowse had not much past to look back on, dying of consumption at the age of 29, but others lived long enough to pen extended accounts of their happy hardships and fallen friends. If the lives of London bohemians were, in the main part, less harrowing than those of the characters portrayed in Henri Murger's *Scènes de la vie Bohême*, in later biographies they became positively cosy. During the 1890s urban life became a favoured subject of a group of self-conscious 'decadent' poets who sought to extract beauty from the prosaic and unattractive world around them. Richard Le Galienne, a would-be bohemian who commuted into town from the comfortable suburb of Bedford Park, found the streets of London suffused with romance:

> Lamp after lamp against the sky,
> Opens a sudden beaming eye,
> Keeping alight on either hand,

The iron lilies of the Strand.

Like dragon flies, the hansoms hover,
With jewelled eyes to catch the lover;
The streets are full of lights and loves,
Soft gowns, and flutter of soiled doves.

Conversely, another major producer of poetry, the music hall,
preferred the prosaic and unattractive to the beautiful and romantic.
Most of the songwriters to be found in clubs, bars and taverns
along the Strand were able to compose a song on any subject in a
matter of minutes. Stereotypes, embroidered to a lesser or greater
extent, were their stock in trade – a predictable array of convivial
drunks, upstart clerks, henpecked husbands, knowing schoolgirls,
frustrated spinsters and fast, sometimes breathtakingly fast, young
women. Although references to prostitution were never as overt
as in 'The Blowen's Ball', the profession was strongly suggested in
many numbers. The relationship between Nancy and her suitor in
a song performed by blackface comedian E. W. Mackney may have
been perfectly innocent:

I wish I was with Nancy, I do, I do.
In a second floor, for evermore,
I'd live and die with Nancy.
In the Strand, in the Strand,
I wish I was with Nancy.[27]

But other ladies described by comic singers were clearly looking
for relationships that lasted minutes rather than years. In the early
1880s Fred Coyne presented a series of situations and conversations
which were 'Unfit For Publication':

I met a lady t'other day while walking down the Strand, sirs,
She'd a lovely colour to her cheek and a latchkey in her hand,
sirs,
Said she 'Now ducky, stand a drink!' I declined in consternation,
And the language of that lady was unfit for publication.[28]

During the 1890s Walter Kino's 'Strolling Down the Strandity'
described the problems inherent in accepting such a proposition:

Evr'y nation's celebrated for the beauty of its girls –

They have ways and smiles bewitching,
Some with dark and golden curls:
See them with their baby faces
Partial to the puff and paint –
Meet them when they've miss'd the last bus,
Each one talks just like a saint.
And we meet them –

CHORUS
Strolling down the Strandity,
That's where the girls do the grandity –
Lovely dresses, golden locks,
Curls at three and six per box:
Strolling down the Strandity.
See them doing the grand,
Pretty, but naughty, from fourteen to forty,
Strolling down the Strand...

John the Masher hails a cabby
When it's far too late to roam –
Couldn't think of acting shabby,
So he sees the lady home.
How he smiles – it's awf'lly jolly –
See him spooning with his Flo;
But next morn he sees his folly –
Stony-broke in Pimlico.[29]

Male frequenters of the Strand were usually portrayed as dudes or
derelicts, sometimes both at the same time. In 1880 T. S. Lonsdale
and W. G. Eaton wrote a song for 'The Great Vance' linking a recently
demolished architectural landmark with enslavement to close-
fitting masculine fashion:

How do you like London? How d'you like the town?
How d'you like the Strand, now Temple Bar's pulled down?
How d'you like the 'La-di-da', the toothpick, and the crutch?
How did you get those trousers on, and did they hurt you much?

Four years later another Lion Comique, Charles Godfrey, introduced
a song featuring a man about town which indirectly inspired one
of music hall's greatest hits. Although sometimes strapped for cash,
'The Masher King' was imperious in his swaggering progress along
the Strand

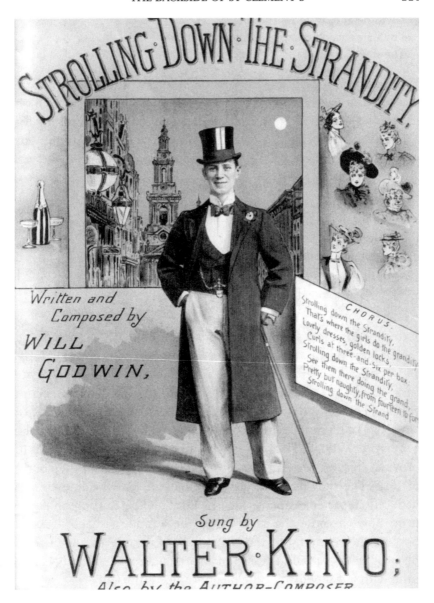

**ILLUSTRATION 28.** 'Strolling Down the Strandity', a popular music-hall song from the 1890s (courtesy of Tony Barker).

I'm a strut up the Strand-ity, cane in my hand-ity,
Doing the grand-ity swellah,
Very much baron-ly, see Nellie Farren-ly,
Row with the cab-ity fellah.
Smoke a cigar-ity, with the Majah-ity,

Dwiddle and dwaddle and drawl,
I'm a rick-ity, rack-ity, trick-ity, track-ity
The finest mashah of all.[30]

The song's popularity caused George Byford to adopt a threadbare
frockcoat and seedy top hat to present the same character fallen on
hard times, a reduction in circumstance that led to him cadging for
coppers and carrying an advertising board along the Strand. His
parody of 'The Masher King' was set to the same music:

I'm a gone to the deuce-ity, not any use-ity,
How flag of truce-ity fellah,
Crawl up the Strand-ity, matches in hand-ity,
Pipe lights, Sir? Loudly I call.
Wear shabby clothes-ity, boots without toes-ity,
Cold in my does-ty Swellah,
Wash at a pump-ity, doss in the lump-ity,
Bottles up Masher of all.[31]

Sixteen years later the male impersonator Vesta Tilley introduced
'Burlington Bertie' into her gallery of impeccably dressed 'Toffs'
and 'Johnnies'. Her creation was a womanising fop with a 'Hyde
Park drawl and a Bond Street crawl' who made up for a feckless
existence by volunteering to fight in the Boer War. It was not one of
Vesta's most memorable songs, but it was picked up in 1915 by the
songwriter William Hargreaves who, like George Byford, used it to
provide a vision of what Bertie might have become in the course
of time. The drawl and the crawl remained, but the fine clothes
had long departed. As performed by Ella Shields, 'Burlington Bertie
from Bow' became the *genius loci* of the Strand, a shabby-genteel
boulevardier clinging to the last shreds of dignity by the ends of
his grubby fingernails. Dressed in an archaic frock coat and beating
time with a clapped-out cane he announced himself:

I'm Bert, p'raps you've heard of me.
Bert, you've had word of me,
Jugging along, hearty and strong,
Living on plates of fresh air,
I dress up in fashion, and, when I am feeling depress'd,
I shave from my cuff all the whiskers and fluff,
Stick my hat on and toddle up West.

CHORUS
I'm Burlington Bertie,
I rise at ten thirty and saunter along like a toff,
I walk down the Strand with my gloves on my hand, then I walk
down again with them off,
I'm all airs and graces, correct easy paces, without food so long I've
forget where my faces is —
I'm Bert, Bert, I haven't a shirt, but my people are well off, you
know!
Nearly ev'ry one knows me, from Smith to Lord Roseb'ry
I'm Burlington Bertie from Bow.

Bertie usually acquired his cigars in the Strand, not from any of
its numerous tobacconists, but from the pavements where they
had been discarded. With a cravat carefully arranged to disguise a
major wardrobe deficiency he bore a close resemblance to George
Byford's 'Broken Down Masher' who lamented 'Gussy and Bertie-
ity, treat me like dirt-ity, / Minus a shirt-ity swellah'. Burlington
Bertie was deliberately anachronistic in costume, language and
manner, an echo of Victorian times set against a Strand that had
changed radically since the beginning of the twentieth century. The
ancient houses of Wych Street and Holywell Street had been swept
away, the old Gaiety demolished and the Tivoli recently shut down.
With the outbreak of war in Europe many familiar faces were also
conspicuous by their absence, glimpsed again only if they survived
long enough to obtain leave from the front line. One of the earliest
air raids on London had resulted in the death of a soldier and an
old woman by the pit entrance of the Strand Theatre. An uncertain
present and a forbidding future meant that the past had become an
attractive source of comfort and distraction.

Following World War I, the Strand drew a line under its own
chronicle. With the wholesale removal of crowded, multi-tenanted
buildings and their replacement with large-scale commercial premises
there were no places left to harbour the composers of the saga, or those
upon whom it was based. A reduction in the number of theatres in and
around the Strand had resulted in London's live entertainment centre
shifting westward, causing actors and variety performers to regroup
in the vicinity of Shaftesbury Avenue and Piccadilly Circus. Bohemians
of the old school had virtually ceased to exist, leaving Odell, the
'Ancient Mariner of the Strand',[32] to seek his nocturnal amusements

in a dwindling number of resorts. Fewer taverns, clubs and restaurants resulted in fewer revellers and fewer cases of public disorder. Although numerous, the clients of the huge Lyons' Corner House were seldom as troublesome as the Jolly Dogs. Crime, of course, was still widespread, but the 'Lord Chief Baron' might have adjudged that the 'flats' now held the whip hand over the 'sharps'. In November 1921 The Strand magazine published Tracey Almoner's short 'Where was Wych Street?' The customers portrayed in a smoky London bar attempting to locate the lost street in their collective memory might also have struggled to decide who were PC Cooke and Inspector Moser, what was the Judge and Jury Society and why Lottie Collins was reputed to have had no drawers. Fact, fiction and fantasy were becoming inseparable as urban folklore and nostalgia became the order of the day.

Visitors to the Strand had always looked upwards at its tall buildings. By the 1930s necks were craned to their limit as a series of giant office blocks began to dominate the skyline. The Hotel Cecil, one-time wonder of modern architecture, was demolished within four months to make way for a 190-foot-high Shell-Mex House. Despite a public outcry Adelphi Terrace also succumbed to developers, with the erection of an 11-storey Modernist monolith inheriting the name of its Georgian predecessor. At 51–55 Strand the Halifax Building Society erected a towering London headquarters notable for its severity and lack of ornament. Across the road the Adelphi Theatre did not grow taller, but was reconstructed in the Art Deco style with a shining black façade that reflected the changing face of the Strand. Although its ancient neighbour, the Cyder Cellars, had been closed for many years, the building at 21 Maiden Lane continued its remarkably varied existence, serving in the twentieth century as a rehearsal room for Diaghilev's Ballets Russes and as the first offices of the British Communist Party. Another rare survival, the notorious 164 Strand, stood for 300 years until 1966 when King's College decided to extend its university campus. The new Gaiety Theatre served only 35 years as a place of entertainment, closing in 1938 and standing for half as long again as a derelict shell.

*    *    *

The modern Strand is not a place for ghost-hunting or time-shifting revelations. Only a few locations survive to give some faint idea of its Victorian past. Through a small arch situated between the Adelphi and

Vaudeville Theatres is Bull Inn Court, a narrow, gloomy alley partly illuminated by the lights of the Nell Gwynne Tavern. Close to the court's exit in Maiden Lane is the Royal Entrance to the Adelphi where 'Breezy Bill' Terriss was assassinated by 'Mad' Archer. On the south side of the Strand, at Lower Robert Street, just one of the 'Dark Arches' remains open, although it is now used mainly by cab-drivers taking a short cut to the Embankment. The Strand's bulwark against criminality – Bow Street Police Station – closed in 1992 with the adjoining Magistrate's Court hearing its final case 14 years later. In 2013 it was announced that the cells that once strained to accommodate a relentless flood of offenders were to be transformed into the comfortable bedrooms of a law and order-themed boutique hotel.

**ILLUSTRATION 29.** Eastern end of the Strand at Temple Bar, photographed by Valentine Blanchard during the early 1860s.

# Notes

## 1  WHERE'S TROY?

1. [Robert Blatchford], *Dismal England*. London, 1899, p. 78.
2. This establishment was referred to as both the 'Cyder Cellars' and 'Cider Cellars' throughout the period.
3. The Opera Comique was actually situated in Holywell Street, but had its main entrance at 299 Strand.
4. Renton Nicholson, *The Lord Chief Baron Nicholson. An Autobiography*. London, [1860], p. 84.
5. Max O'Rell, *John Bull and His Island*. London, [1883] p. 75.
6. 'Let's All Go Down the Strand', written and composed by Harry Castling and C. W. Murphy, 1908.
7. John Hollingshead, *Gaiety Chronicles*. London, 1898, p. 7.
8. 'One of the Old Brigade', *London in the Sixties (With a Few Digressions)*. London, [1906], p. 1.

## 2  THE DISAPPEARANCE OF LOVE

1. John Hollingshead, *Gaiety Chronicles*. London, 1898, p. 6.
2. *Mr and Mrs Bancroft: On and Off the Stage*. London, 1889, p. 2.
3. Emily Soldene, *My Theatrical and Musical Recollections*. London, 1898, p. 64.
4. *Ibid.*, p. 63.
5. *The Era*, 13 July 1889.
6. *Ibid.*
7. *The Penny Illustrated Paper*, 7 January 1888.
8. Although Mabel is not usually listed as one of the quartet, her name features in early descriptions of the dance, e.g., 'One of the principal successes of the evening was the Pas de Quatre danced in the second act by the Misses Lillian Price, Mabel Love, Florence Levey and Sprague.' *The London Standard*, 31 October 1888.
9. *The Illustrated Police News*, 30 March 1888.
10. *The Entr'acte*, May 1889.
11. *The Era*, 29 June 1889.
12. *The Pall Mall Gazette*, 16 July 1889.
13. Quoted in *Trewman's Exeter Flying Post*, 19 July 1889.
14. George R. Sims, *My Life*. London, 1917, p. 196.
15. *Birmingham Daily Post*, 17 July 1889.

## 3  THE DARK ARCHES

1. Henry Mayhew, *London Labour and the London Poor*. Vol. IV. 1862, p. 221.
2. *Lloyd's Weekly Newspaper*, 9 May 1859.
3. Old Bailey Proceedings Online (www.oldbaileyonline.org, version 7.0), accessed 29 June 2014.
4. *Paul Pry*, Number 37 [1849?].
5. In the context of the song, 'Flam' might mean either trickery or very little.
6. 'Bam' probably means a hoax.
7. www.horntip.com, accessed 2 July 2014.
8. *Reynolds's Newspaper*, 3 October 1852.
9. 'One of the Old Brigade', *London in the Sixties (With a Few Digressions)*. London, [1906], pp: 64–5.
10. *The Morning Chronicle*, 18 September 1852.
11. *The Era*, 19 November 1865.
12. *The Daily News*, 14 September 1858.
13. *Reynolds's Newspaper*, 21 January 1883.
14. Ibid., 11 September 1887.
15. Max O'Rell, *John Bull's Womankind*. London, [1884], pp. 52–3.
16. 'Slap Bang, Here We Are Again, or the School of Jolly Dogs.' Written by Harry Copeland, published c. 1865.
17. Thomas Burke, *English Night-Life*. London, 1941, p. 129.
18. *The Morning Post*, quoted in *The Penny Illustrated Paper*, 25 November 1865.
19. *Reynolds's Newspaper*, 1 September 1889.
20. *Portsmouth Evening News*, 19 September 1889.

## 4  THE LORD CHIEF BARON OF THE COAL HOLE

1. Renton Nicholson, *The Lord Chief Baron Nicholson. An Autobiography*. London, [1860], p. 5.
2. Ibid., pp. 7–8.
3. Ibid., p. 12.
4. Ibid., p. 97.
5. 'Gay' was the principal Victorian term denoting prostitute.
6. Nicholson, *The Lord Chief Baron Nicholson*, p. 139.
7. Ibid., p. 156.
8. 'A Sigh for the Sorrowful', *The Era*, 24 December 1842.
9. Eclipse (1764–89) was the most famous racehorse of the eighteenth century.
10. Nicholson, *The Lord Chief Baron Nicholson*, p. 227.
11. *The Town*, published by W. Wynn, 34 Holywell Street, 1849.
12. *The Era*, 28 August 1842.
13. J. Ewing Ritchie, *The Night Side of London*. London, 2nd revised edn., 1858, pp. 90–1.

14. Nicholson, The Lord Chief Baron Nicholson, pp. 291–2.
15. Edmund Yates, Edmund Yates: His Recollections and Experiences. London, 1885, pp. 95–6.
16. Nicholson, The Lord Chief Baron Nicholson, pp. 352–3.
17. Reynolds's Newspaper, 14 December 1862.
18. The Era, 10 January 1869.
19. East London Observer, 30 January 1869.
20. The Saturday Review, 16 January 1869.
21. E. L. Blanchard, The Life and Reminiscences of E. L. Blanchard, Compiled by Clement Scott and Cecil Howard. London, 1891, p. 258.
22. The Era, 26 May 1861.

## 5  OLD STOCK AND FANCY GOODS

1. Henry Mayhew, London Labour and the London Poor. Vol. IV. 1862, p. 248.
2. Max O'Rell, John Bull and His Island. London [1883], p. 74.
3. Mayhew, London Labour and the London Poor, p. 217.
4. William Acton, Prostitution, Considered in its moral, social and sanitary aspects in London, and other large cities. London, 1857, p. 73.
5. Renton Nicholson, The Town [1838] quoted by Pearl, Cyril, The Girl with the Swansdown Seat. London, 1955, p. 20.
6. Lloyd's Weekly Newspaper, 19 October 1856.
7. The Morning Chronicle, 25 October 1856.
8. Old and New London. A Narrative of its History, its People and its Places. London [1878], p. 70.
9. Lloyd's Weekly Newspaper, 28 September 1851.
10. John Diprose, Some Account of the Parish of Saint Clement Danes (Westminster) Past and Present. London, 1868, p. 100.
11. Parliamentary Papers, 1865. Quoted in Michael Fort, 'From Carey Street to the Embankment and Back Again' in London Topographical Record. Vol. XXIV. London, 1980, p. 169. The now-offensive phrase 'Nigger Minstrel' was widely used in Victorian England to denote performers who adopted blackface make-up to provide a romanticised, but often patronising portrayal of the American Negro.
12. Morning Post, 31 October 1872; Illustrated Police News, 14 December 1872.
13. Renton Nicholson, The Lord Chief Baron Nicholson. An Autobiography. London, [1860], pp. 32–3.
14. The Town, number 2 [1849].
15. Quoted in W. H. Holden, They Startled Grandfather. London, 1950, p. 84.
16. 'A man of colour' was one of several terms indicative of how a black person would have been described in Victorian London.
17. London Daily News, 24 July 1854.
18. J. Ewing Ritchie, The Night Side of London. London, 2nd revised edn., 1858, pp. 48–9.
19. Ibid., p. 46
20. Mayhew, London Labour and the London Poor, p. 248.

21. Old Bailey Proceedings Online (www.oldbaileyonline.org, version 7.0), accessed 29 June 2014.

22. Ibid.

23. The Times, 26 January 1870.

24. London Daily News, 26 January 1870.

25. Morning Post, 9 October 1872.

26. Joseph Hatton, 'On Music with a "k."', The Idler, April 1892.

27. [Robert Blatchford], Dismal England. London, 1899, pp. 81–3.

## 6 THE IMPORTANCE OF BEING ERNEST ... AND FREDERICK

1. The Trial of Boulton and Park with Hurt and Fiske. London, 1871, p. 6.

2. Saturday Review quoted by Cyril Pearl, The Girl with the Swansdown Seat. London, 1955, p. 23.

3. The Era, 7 April 1861.

4. Ibid. 6 September 1868.

5. Ibid., 17 April 1870.

6. The Days' Doings, 13 May 1871.

7. The Argus (Melbourne), 19 April 1873.

8. Reynolds's Newspaper, 10 April 1870.

9. The Examiner, 9 April 1870.

10. John Hollingshead, Gaiety Chronicles. London, 1898, p. 4.

11. Quoted in Neil McKenna, Fanny and Stella. The Young Men who Shocked Victorian England. London, 2013, p. 35.

12. Ibid.

13. Ibid., p.90.

14. The Pearl, November 1879.

15. The Trial of Boulton and Park with Hurt and Fiske. p. 5.

16. McKenna, Fanny and Stella, p. 315.

17. Ibid., p. 36.

18. Ibid., p. 59.

19. Charles Hirsch, a French bookseller, with a bookshop in Coventry Street, London, recalled supplying Wilde with a copy of The Sins of the Cities of the Plains.

20. Oscar Wilde, The Importance of Being Earnest. London, 1909, p. 34.

21. Ibid.

## 7 SAM AND MAUD

1. The claim was emphatically denied by the manager of The Peacock who claimed that no-one of Maud's description had been employed in the pub.

2. Old Bailey Proceedings Online (www.oldbaileyonline.org, version 7.0), accessed 29 June 2014.

3. Ibid.

4. Ibid.
5. Lloyd's Weekly Newspaper, 16 July 1893.
6. The London Standard, 25 July 1893.

## 8 KICKING OVER THE TRACES

1. Henry Mayhew, London Labour and the London Poor. Vol. I. 1851, p. 12.
2. Max O'Rell, John Bull and His Island. London [1883], pp. 113–14.
3. William Acton, Prostitution, considered in its moral, social and sanitary aspects in London, and other large cities. London, 1857, p. 103.
4. Ibid., p. 105.
5. Victorian slang: 'tart' means attractive young woman; 'bun' means the vagina.
6. Quoted by Cyril Pearl, The Girl with the Swansdown Seat. London, 1955, p. 221.
7. Reynolds's Newspaper, 29 March 1868.
8. The Times, 14 October 1870.
9. The Morning Post, 8 December 1874.
10. Gaiety Theatre programme.
11. Pall Mall Gazette, 12 March 1892.
12. The Era, 5 March 1892.
13. Quoted in J. E. Crawford Flitch, Modern Dancing and Dancers. London, 1912, p. 97.
14. Black and White, 28 May 1892.
15. Edward Carpenter, Love's Coming-of-age. London, 1896, p. 57.
16. Harry Randall, Harry Randall Old Time Comedian. London, [1931], p. 104.
17. W. R. Titterton, From Theatre to Music Hall. London, 1912, p. 120.
18. Quoted in D. F. Cheshire, Music Hall in Britain. Newton Abbot, 1974, p. 69.
19. Flitch, Modern Dancing and Dancers. p. 91.
20. Holbrook Jackson, The Eighteen Nineties. London, 1913, p. 35.
21. Punch, 5 March 1892.
22. Lloyd's Weekly Newspaper, 3 July 1892.
23. Birmingham Daily Post, 19 July 1892.
24. Quoted in The Bristol Mercury and Daily Post, 11 February 1892.
25. Pall Mall Gazette, 12 April 1892.
26. Shaw Desmond, London Nights of Long Ago. London, 1927, pp. 112–13.
27. Sir Malcolm Morris, The Nation's Health. The Stamping Out of Venereal Disease. London, 1917, p. 19.
28. Pall Mall Gazette, 16 July 1897.
29. The Penny Illustrated Paper, 10 September 1892.

## 9 A PEEP INTO THE UNKNOWN

1. Mervyn Heard, Phantasmagoria: the Secret Life of the Magic Lantern. London, 2006, p. 131.

2. Terry Ramsaye, *A Million and One Nights*. New York, 1926, p. 119.

3. Ibid., p. 148.

4. *The Westminster Budget*, 17 November 1893.

5. Fun, 22 January 1895.

6. Quoted in Paul C. Spehr, *The Man who Made Movies: W. K. L. Dickson*. New Barnet, 2008, p. 14.

7. J. C. Woollan, 'Hotel London', in *Living London*. London [1903], p. 238.

8. *The Daily News*, 13 September 1899.

9. Richard Brown and Barry Anthony, *A Victorian Film Enterprise, The History of the British Mutoscope and Biograph Company, 1897–1915*. Trowbridge, 1999, pp. 321–4.

10. *Sheffield Evening News*, 5 August 1901.

## 10  LOOKING FOR MUGS IN THE STRAND

1. Arthur Roberts, *Fifty Years of Spoof*. London, 1927, pp. 93–4.

2. *Whitstable and Herne Bay Herald*, 18 April 1891.

3. *The London Standard*, 20 April 1894.

4. *Lloyd's Weekly Newspaper*, 12 April 1891.

5. Old Bailey Proceedings Online (www.oldbaileyonline.org, version 7.0), accessed 29 June 2014.

6. Ibid.

7. *Lloyd's Weekly Newspaper*, 3 November 1895.

8. *Aukland Star*, 4 January 1896.

9. Maurice Moser and Charles F. Rideal, *Stories From Scotland Yard*. London, 1890, p. 39.

10. *Ibid., p. 108.*

11. *Preston Chronicle*, 6 August 1892.

12. *Old Bailey Proceedings Online (www.oldbaileyonline,org, version 7.0), accessed 29 June 2014.*

13. *Sheffield Daily Telegraph*, 17 June 1901.

## 11  THE CASE BOOK OF MAURICE MOSER

1. Maurice Moser and Charles F. Rideal, *True Detective Stories*. New York, 1891, p. 7.

2. Ibid., p. 8.

3. Maurice Moser and Charles F. Rideal, *Stories From Scotland Yard*. London, 1890, pp. 26–7.

4. Ibid., pp. 44–5

5. *Sheffield Daily Telegraph*, 18 September 1896.

6. 'The Irish Colony in Paris. By an Old Colonist', *St James's Gazette*, quoted in the *Brisbane Courier*, 11 June 1884.

7.  *The Era*, 26 January 1884.

8.  *The Times*, 7 March 1887.

9.  Moser and Rideal, *True Detective Stories*. p. 41.

10. *St James's Gazette*, 8 August 1889.

11. *Bruce Herald*, 18 October 1901.

12. *Lloyd's Weekly Newspaper*, 27 July 1890; *National Archives* J 77/433/3201.

13. *National Archives*, J 77/447/3639.

14. *The London Standard*, 2 January 1893.

## 12  ALIAS JACK THE RIPPER

1.  *The London Standard*, 22 March 1887.

2.  Ibid.

3.  The Old Bailey Proceedings Online, 1674–1913 (www.oldbaileyonline.org, version 7.0), accessed 29 June 2014.

4.  *The Evening News*, 1 October 1888.

5.  Ibid., 4 October 1888.

6.  Old Bailey Proceedings Online (www.oldbaileyonline.org, version 7.0), accessed 29 June 2014.

7.  *Nottingham Evening Post*, 1 June 1889.

8.  Old Bailey Proceedings Online (www.oldbaileyonline.org, version 7.0), accessed 29 June 2014.

9.  Ibid.

10. *The London Standard*, 7 October 1891.

11. *Edinburgh Evening Penny Post*, 24 November 1891.

12. *Old Bailey Proceedings Online (www.oldbaileyonline.org, version 7.0), accessed 29 June 2014.*

13. Ibid.

14. Ibid.

15. *Internet speculation that Le Grand was 'Jack the Ripper' has been led by Tim Wescott. My research for this chapter has been drawn mainly from contemporary newspaper reports and has not made use of material posted on the internet.*

## 13  CRYSTALS OF MORPHINE

1.  *Glasgow Herald*, 2 March 1878.

2.  *The Bristol Mercury*, 1 October 1892.

3.  *Reynolds's Newspaper*, 2 October 1892.

4.  Ibid.

5.  Ibid., 25 September 1892.

6.  Ibid., 2 October 1892.

7.  *Pall Mall Gazette*, 27 September 1892.

## 14  AN ADELPHI DRAMA

1.  Erskine Reid and Herbert Compton, *The Dramatic Peerage*. London, 1892, p.3.
2.  Ibid., p. 201.
3.  Arthur J. Smythe, *Life of William Terriss*. London, 1898, p. 153.
4.  John M. East, *'Neath the Mask*. London, 1967, p. 55.
5.  Seymour Hicks, *Between Ourselves*. London, 1930, p. 37.
6.  Ibid., pp. 38–9.
7.  *Lloyd's Weekly Newspaper*, 2 January 1898.
8.  *Dundee Courier*, 23 December 1897.
9.  *The Chronicle* [Adelaide], 29 January 1898.
10. *Dundee Courier*, 23 December 1897.
11. Old Bailey Proceedings Online (www.oldbailey.org, version 7.0), accessed 29 June 2014.
12. Ibid.
13. East,*'Neath the Mask*, p. 56.
14. The Old Bailey Proceedings Online, 1674–1913 (www.oldbaileyonline.org, version 7.0), accessed 29 June 2014.
15. *Glasgow Herald*, 18 December 1897.
16. Ibid.
17. Hicks, *Between Ourselves*, p. 42.
18. *Dundee Courier*. 23 December 1897.
19. H. Chance Newton, *Cues and Curtain Calls*. London, 1927, p. 46.
20. George R. Sims, *My Life*. London, 1917, p. 271.

## 15  MADAME ST JOHN

1.  Boyle Lawrence, *Celebrities of the Stage*. London [1900], p. 45.
2.  W. T. Vincent, *Recollections of Fred Leslie*. London, 1894, pp. 96–7.
3.  *The Theatre*, 1 December 1884.
4.  Vincent, *Recollections of Fred Leslie*, p. 98.
5.  Jessie Millward, *Myself and Others*. London, 1923, p. 215.
6.  *The London Standard*, 11 December 1891.
7.  Ibid.
8.  *Hampshire Telegraph and Sussex Chronicle*, 12 December 1891.
9.  *The London Standard*, 10 December 1891.
10. *Lloyd's Weekly Newspaper*, 12 December 1891.
11. *The Bristol Mercury*, 11 December 1891.
12. *Lloyd's Weekly Newspaper*, 13 December 1891.
13. Ibid.
14. *Reynolds's Newspaper*, 13 December 1891.
15. Lawrence, *Celebrities of the Stage*, p. 45.

## 16 THE BACKSIDE OF ST CLEMENT'S

1. Steven Marcus, The Other Victorians. London, pp. 74–5.
2. Thomas Frost, Reminiscences of a Country Journalist. London, 1886, p. 54.
3. Lloyd's Weekly Newspaper, 7 September 1851.
4. Ibid.
5. Reynolds's Newspaper, 20 July 1856.
6. The Illustrated London News, 1 January 1853.
7. The Morning Chronicle, 11 May 1857.
8. Ibid.
9. North Wales Chronicle, 28 November 1857.
10. The Bookseller, 1868, quoted in Cyril Pearl, Victorian Patchwork. London, 1972, p. 81.
11. Advert on back board of Renton Nicholson, The Lord Chief Baron Nicholson. An Autobiography. London [1860].
12. [William Stephens Hayward] Skittles in Paris. A biography of a 'fascinating' woman. London, 1884 (reprint of 1864 edition), pp. 3–4.
13. [Charles H. Ross], Charley Wag, the New Jack Sheppard. London, 1861, reprinted British Library, Historical Print Editions, p. 2.
14. Ibid., p. 48.
15. Ibid., p. 285.
16. Renton Nicholson, The Lord Chief Baron. An Autobiography. London [1860], p. 242.
17. Lloyd's Weekly Newspaper, 1 January 1853.
18. George Speaight, Bawdy Songs of the Early Music Hall. London, 1975, p. 81.
19. The Lover's Harmony, No. 46. London, c. 1840, pp. 362–3.
20. Maurice Moser and Charles F. Rideal, Stories From Scotland Yard. London, 1890, p. 36.
21. Jack Saul, Sins of the Cities of the Plain. [ ? ] 2006, p. 57.
22. Pall Mall Gazette, 23 November 1886.
23. The Daily Telegraph, 28 December 1885.
24. John Hollingshead, Gaiety Chronicles. London, 1898, p. 453.
25. Newcastle Courant, 31 January 1879.
26. Bernard Ince, 'Redefining the Grotesque; E. J. Odell, Actor and Comedian', STR Theatre Notebook, Vol, 65, No. 2, (2011).
27. 'In the Strand'. Written by Frank Hall to the melody of Dan Emmett's 'I Wish I was in Dixie', published c. 1861.
28. 'Unfit For Publication'. Written and composed by E. V. Page.
29. 'Walking Down the Strandity', Written and composed by Will Godwin.
30. 'The Masher King'. Written and composed by Harry Adams and E. Jonghmans, published c. 1884.
31. 'The Broken Down Masher'. Written and composed by George Byford and E. Jonghmans, published c. 1884.
32. H. G. Hibbert, A Playgoer's Memories. London, 1920, p. 55.

# Bibliography

Acton, William, Prostitution, considered in its moral, social and sanitary aspects in London and other large cities. London, 1857.

Glover, James M., Jimmy Glover: His Book. London, 1911.

— Jimmy Glover and His Friends. London, 1913.

Hibbert, H. G., Fifty Years of a Londoner's Life. London, 1916.

—A Playgoer's Memories. London, 1920.

Hicks, Seymour, Between Ourselves. London, 1930.

Holden, W. H., They Startled Grandfather. Gay Ladies and Merry Mashers of Victorian Times. London, 1950.

Hollingshead, John, Gaiety Chronicles. London, 1898.

Jupp, James, The Gaiety Stage Door: Thirty Years' Reminiscences of the Theatre. London, 1923.

Macqueen-Pope, W., Gaiety: Theatre of Enchantment. London, 1949.

McKenna, Neil, Fanny and Stella: The Young Men Who Shocked Victorian England. London, 2013.

Marcus, Steven, The Other Victorians. London, 1966.

Mayhew, Henry, London Labour and the London Poor. London, Vols. I-III, 1851, Vol. IV, 1861.

Millward, Jessie, Myself and Others. London, 1923.

Moser, Maurice, and Charles F. Rideal, Stories From Scotland Yard. London, 1890.

—True Detective Stories. New York, 1891.

Nead, Lynda, Victorian Babylon. London, 2000.

Nicholson, Renton, The Lord Chief Baron Nicholson. An Autobiography. London, [1860].

Pearl, Cyril, The Girl with the Swansdown Seat. London, 1955.

—Victorian Patchwork. London, 1972.

Richie, J. Ewing, The Night Side of London. London, 2nd revised edn., 1858

Rowell, George, William Terriss and Richard Prince: Two Characters in an Adelphi Melodrama. London, 1985.

Scott, Clement, The Drama of Yesterday and To-day. London, 1899.

Sims, George R. My Life: Sixty Years' Recollections of Bohemian London. London, 1917.

Speaight, George, Bawdy Songs of the Early Music Hall. London, 1975.

Spehr, Paul, The Man Who Made Movies: W.K.L. Dickson. New Barnett, Herts., 2008.

Yates, Edmund, Edmund Yates: His Recollections and Experiences. London, 1885.

# Index